My Odyssey
through the
Underground Press

VOICES FROM THE UNDERGROUND SERIES, EDITED BY KEN WACHSBERGER

Insider Histories of the Vietnam Era Underground Press, Part 1

Insider Histories of the Vietnam Era Underground Press, Part 2

My Odyssey through the Underground Press, by Michael "Mica" Kindman

Stop the Presses, I Want to Get Off: A Brief History of the Penal
Digest International, by Joseph W. Grant

Voices
from the
Underground
✳

My Odyssey through the Underground Press

MICHAEL "MICA" KINDMAN

EDITED BY KEN WACHSBERGER

Michigan State University Press · East Lansing

⊛ The paper used in this publication meets the minimum requirements of ANSI/NISO Z39.48-1992 (R 1997) (Permanence of Paper).

 Michigan State University Press
East Lansing, Michigan 48823-5245

Printed and bound in the United States of America.

18 17 16 15 14 13 12 11   1 2 3 4 5 6 7 8 9 10

LIBRARY OF CONGRESS CATALOGING-IN-PUBLICATION DATA
Kindman, Michael "Mica," 1945–1991.
My odyssey through the underground press / Michael Kindman ; edited by Ken Wachsberger.
p. cm. — (Voices from the underground series)
Includes bibliographical references and index.
ISBN 978-1-61186-000-9 (pbk. : alk. paper) 1. Kindman, Michael, 1945–1991. 2. Newspaper editors—United States—Biography. 3. Journalists—United States—Biography. 4. Underground press publications—United States—History—20th century. I. Wachsberger, Ken. II. Title.
PN4874.K5457A3 2011
070.92—dc22
[B]
2011002588

Cover design by Erin Kirk New
Book design by Sharp Des!gns, Lansing, Michigan

g green
  press
  INITIATIVE Michigan State University Press is a member of the Green Press Initiative and is committed to developing and encouraging ecologically responsible publishing practices. For more information about the Green Press Initiative and the use of recycled paper in book publishing, please visit *www.greenpressinitiative.org*.

Visit Michigan State University Press on the World Wide Web at *www.msupress.msu.edu*

Dedication

I'm only sorry Mica isn't here to be writing his own dedication.
His story takes on three themes: independent media, cults, and AIDS.

With those in mind, I dedicate this book

- to a strong independent media, copyright law, and—America's greatest gift to the world—the First Amendment;
- to the end of mindlessness, which is both the cause and the result of cults; and
- to finding a cure for AIDS in all of its forms.

And to Mica.

Contents

Foreword

PAUL KRASSNER

People magazine once called me "father of the underground press," and I immediately demanded a blood test. However, having launched *The Realist* in 1958, I did have a certain paternal feeling toward the anti-establishment papers that began burgeoning around the country during the 1960s, filling the void between what was experienced on the streets and how it was reported in the mainstream media. Of course, "underground" was technically a misnomer, since it was well known who published those papers and where more copies could be obtained. A *true* underground paper was the *Outlaw*, secretly published and distributed inside San Quentin Prison by anonymous inmates and guards.

Those "underground" weeklies included the *Free Press* in Los Angeles, the *East Village Other* in New York, the *Barb* in Berkeley, the *Oracle* in San Francisco, the *Seed* in Chicago, the *Drummer* in Philadelphia, the *Helix* in Seattle, *Nola Express* in New Orleans, the *Door* in San Diego, the *Great Speckled Bird* in Atlanta, *Kaleidoscope* in Madison, *Space City!* in Houston, *Quicksilver Times* in Washington, the *Fifth Estate* in Detroit, and *The Paper* in East Lansing—one of several struggling publications for which I offered to do a benefit in my capacity as a stand-up satirist.

Meanwhile, John Francis Putnam, who was the art director of *Mad* magazine, also wrote a column for *The Realist* titled "Modest Proposals." When I got married in 1963, he wanted to give us a housewarming gift. He had designed the word FUCK in red-white-and-blue lettering emblazoned with stars and stripes. Now he needed a second word, a noun that would be an appropriate object of that verb. He suggested AMERICA, but that didn't seem right to me. It certainly wasn't an accurate representation of my feelings. I was well aware that I probably couldn't publish *The Realist* in any other country. Besides, a poster saying FUCK AMERICA lacked a certain sense of irony.

There was at that time a severe anti-Communist hysteria flourishing throughout the land. The attorney general of Arizona rejected the Communist Party's request for a place on the ballot because state law "prohibits official representation" for Communists and, in addition, "The subversive nature of your organization is even more clearly designated by the fact that you do not even include your Zip Code." Alvin Dark, manager of the Giants, announced that

"Any pitcher who throws at a batter and deliberately tries to hit him is a Communist." And singer Pat Boone declared at the Greater New York Anti-Communism Rally in Madison Square Garden, "I would rather see my four daughters shot before my eyes than have them grow up in a Communist United States. I would rather see those kids blown into Heaven than taught into Hell by the Communists."

I suggested COMMUNISM as the second word on Putnam's poster, since the usual correlation between conservatism and prudishness would provide the incongruity that was missing. He designed the word COMMUNISM in red lettering emblazoned with hammers and sickles. Then he presented us with a patriotic poster proudly proclaiming FUCK COMMUNISM! I wanted to share this sentiment with *Realist* readers, but our photo-engraver refused to make a plate, explaining, "We got strict orders from Washington not to do stuff like this." I went to another engraver, who said no because they had been visited by the FBI after making a plate of a woman with pubic hair. So instead of publishing a miniature black-and-white version of the poster in *The Realist*, I offered full-size color copies by mail. And if the Post Office interfered, I would have to accuse them of being soft on Communism.

In 1964, investigative journalist Robert Scheer was deep into research for a booklet, *How the United States Got Involved in Vietnam*, to be published by the Fund for the Republic. He was frustrated because he wanted to witness firsthand what was going on in Southeast Asia, and they wouldn't send him. Since *The Realist* had already sold a couple of thousand FUCK COMMUNISM! posters at a dollar each, I gave Scheer a check for $1,900, the price of a round-trip airline ticket. He traveled to Vietnam and Cambodia, then wrote his seminal report. He also wrote an article for *The Realist* titled "Academic Sin," documenting the role of Michigan State University professors in the Diem dictatorship. In 1966, *The Paper* published a pair of articles exposing that scandal, and provided invaluable aid to *Ramparts* magazine on their quest for the MSU story.

When I performed at the fundraiser for *The Paper*, I met its founder, Michael Kindman. I was impressed by his idealism, his passion, and his outspokenness. On stage, naturally I displayed the FUCK COMMUNISM! poster and talked about it. Naturally *The Paper* quoted from my performance—and naturally that report caused a stir. At one college, a graduating student held up a FUCK COMMUNISM! poster as his class was posing for the yearbook photograph. Campus officials found out and insisted that the word FUCK be airbrushed out. But then the poster would read: COMMUNISM! So that was airbrushed out, too, and the yearbook ended up publishing a class photo that showed this particular student holding up a blank poster.

Each underground paper had its own peculiar genetic and geographical makeup. Still, as a charter member of the Underground Press Syndicate, *The Paper* benefited from their policy of allowing members to freely reprint each other's material, which gave readers the sense of a national movement. UPS also helped papers defend themselves in an increasing number of legal assaults.

By 1969, there were some five hundred underground papers. Altogether, according to *Newsweek*'s estimate, they distributed two million copies, but according to UPS, they distributed 4.5 million copies—"to radicals, hippies, racial minorities, soldiers and curiosity seekers." At the Revolutionary Media Conference, held in Ann Arbor that year, it was predicted that there would eventually be "a daily underground paper in every city, and a weekly in every town." Now, four decades later, the Internet has transformed that optimistic fantasy into a virtual reality.

Michael Kindman's revealing memoir, *My Odyssey through the Underground Press*, will take you through his adventures and misadventures in the larger context of an evolutionary jump in consciousness, from hippie to the New Age; from a control freak's cult to individual freedom; from sex, drugs, and rock 'n' roll to a spiritual revolution. Ultimately, this book will serve as a multifaceted slice of countercultural history.

Foreword

TOMMI AVICOLLI MECCA

Michael "Mica" Kindman and I shared something very special: a love of the underground press. He started an underground newspaper at Michigan State University in 1965 that became one of the first five members of the Underground Press Syndicate (UPS).

I started the first underground newspaper at my high school in 1969. It never made it to the UPS. I don't even remember what my friends and I called it. We distributed the three or four stapled, 11 × 17 sheets with the unsigned articles among our fellow students at Bishop (now St. John) Neumann High School in working-class South Philadelphia. It wasn't very popular. Few students questioned the war in Vietnam or supported the counterculture. We were the "hippie" outsiders. In fact, several classmates wished me "luck in the SDS" in my student yearbook.

The underground paper was started in response to my being fired from *The Rocket*, the official school publication. I was told by the priest in charge that my services "would no longer be needed," after I submitted two articles that were rejected without explanation. One was against the war in Vietnam, the other, the school's ridiculous hair-length rule (it couldn't touch the back of your shirt collar or Father Cox would pull you into his office and give you a haircut you didn't want).

The administration never discovered who was behind the underground paper. They would've been surprised to learn that a clean-cut boy on the Student Council printed it for us on the school's Gestetner when no one was around. We only published two or three issues that semester, as it was the end of our senior year.

Three years later, I was writing for underground newspapers, both gay and straight. I cofounded *Radicalqueen*, a 'zine that explored transgender issues from a radical feminist perspective. Our small but very vocal collective believed that everyone had the right to define themselves as whatever gender they chose, even if it meant inventing new ones. It's something Mica might have appreciated had he ever come across our publication. But our circulation was small and mostly confined to Philadelphia. I also wrote for the *Distant Drummer*, Philadelphia's leading underground publication, and eventually got a full-time gig at the *Philadelphia Gay News*.

Beyond our love for the alternative press, Mica and I had something else in common: we were both queer. While I immersed myself in the Gay Liberation Front at Temple University, where I went to school to avoid the draft, Mica got himself a permanent deferment and ended up living with a Boston-based cult headed by a charismatic musician, Mel Lyman, who had stepped on stage at the 1965 Newport Folk Festival to play "Rock of Ages" on his harmonica and calm the crowds who were pissed off at Bob Dylan for playing an electric set.

Mica's love/hate relationship with the communal group would continue throughout his life. As much as he tried to free himself of it, he never succeeded in rejecting the ideals that it espoused, or the people he met there. In the end, he had to confess that it gave him something he needed—a sense of belonging.

"Much of what I was hoping to find and attach myself to in the Community—purpose, eternal purpose, I mean, and a place in the evolution of mankind, family, security and the productivity and creativity which they can inspire—" Mica writes, "somehow never came to me while I was there, even though I did and do believe they were there."

While Lyman's group wasn't the right fit, Mica eventually found his inner peace and purpose in life with the Radical Faeries in San Francisco in the late '80s, a few years before he died of AIDS.

It's important to look beyond the hard, cold facts of the history and development of the underground press to the lives of those who founded the newspapers and magazines, wrote for them, and helped them grow and prosper. The '60s and '70s were not just about political movements and institutions; they were also about how the people who "tuned in, turned on, and dropped out" lived their daily lives.

Mica's recapitulation, as he calls it, is a record of an era long past—a time when idealism wasn't a bad word, and questioning was a rite of passage for many of America's young people.

Recapitulations such as his can only help us better understand the strengths of the struggles of the past and how to avoid the mistakes that were made all too often.

Editor's Introduction

KEN WACHSBERGER

ichael "Mica" Kindman was a legend of the Vietnam era underground press, that media invention of the antiwar counterculture of the sixties and seventies that led the drive to end the U.S. disaster known as the Vietnam War. He was a founder of *The Paper*, the first underground paper in East Lansing, Michigan, as well as one of the first five members of the Underground Press Syndicate, which was the first nationwide network of underground papers in the country. But his story takes in way more than just the underground press. He was on other historical cutting edges as well—even when the cutting edge wasn't necessarily a place where one would want to be.

In September 1963, he began his college career as a freshman at Michigan State University, the nation's first land-grant college. Only eight years before that, MSU had been known as Michigan State College of Agriculture and Applied Science, and previous to that as Michigan Agricultural College because it had been founded—and in the sixties and seventies still was best known—as a college to train future farmers. (It was technically known as Michigan State University of Agriculture and Applied Science until 1964.)

By this time, image change was already under way, led by MSU president John Hannah. Hannah, the former secretary of the State Board of Agriculture, became president in 1941 and thus began the largest sustained growth spurt in the college's history. Only a few years before Michael arrived on campus, MSU had replaced the University of Chicago in the Midwestern Big Ten athletic conference. The university's building program, Michael writes, "had already doubled the size of the developed campus in recent years and would double it again in the next few years." The student population grew from 15,000 in 1950 to well over double that size by the time Michael came to town.

More significantly, MSU's public-relations department had decided to upgrade its academic reputation. It did this by attracting nearly two hundred National Merit Scholars from all over the country with scholarships that were good only on MSU's campus. The year Michael was a freshman, MSU laid claim to more National Merit Scholars than any campus in the country.

As Michael recalls in his story,

The promotional literature did not talk about the generally sterile, almost rural atmosphere of both MSU and East Lansing, a dry (no alcohol sales), conservative place that looked like a picture-postcard college town, but offered little in terms of cultural opportunities or intellectual community and the stimulation these could bring. And, of course, the state capital was just a few miles away in Lansing; certainly the university fathers would not want to do anything or allow anything to occur that might raise the eyebrows of the legislature. All in all, it was sort of a company-town situation, but the enthusiastic series of promotional mailings we received from Gordon Sabine, vice president for special projects, and Stanley Idzerda, director of the Honors College, did not emphasize this aspect. As a result, we showed up in droves, not only from the Midwest but from all over the country.

Michael found a job immediately on the copy desk of the official student newspaper, the *Michigan State News*, final-editing the articles and writing the headlines. Even though he found his journalism courses to be "unexciting, taught by traditionalist faculty with a heavy commitment to what we have since come to know as 'the myth of objectivity,'" he enjoyed his experience working on the *State News*, reviewing local performances by folk musicians, and writing articles on developing news events. He was confident he was on the track to becoming editor in chief.

The Free Speech Movement in Berkeley in 1964, and the arrests of students sitting in at the university administration building there, brought to the attention of Michael and his fellow National Merit friends

> our growing frustrations with the situation we were in. We all felt shortchanged to one degree or another. . . . The Honors College program that had been offered to us whiz-kid recruits had turned out to be more hype than opportunity, more the extension of Stanley Idzerda's personality and intellectual enthusiasm than a real chance to do outstanding work ahead of the ordinary academic schedule. . . . [T]hose of us in the humanities and social sciences were becoming increasingly aware that MSU was something of a cultural backwater, not the center of intellectual debate we had been led to believe it was. Many of us were growing increasingly stir-crazy. Our education was working, but not in the way the university might have hoped: The more educated we became, the more frustrated we felt.

An invitation from the local Socialist Club to discuss what was happening at Berkeley and how that related to life in East Lansing led Michael into "an alternate reality of some kind. Someone played the new album by folksinger Buffy Sainte-Marie, the one with the politically inspiring songs 'Universal Soldier' and 'Now That the Buffalo's Gone.' We talked frustrations and strategies and made plans; by the end of the evening my life had been changed forever."

As a charter member of the newly formed Committee for Student Rights (CSR), he actively supported the committee's campaign to tackle hot issues of the day on campus that they saw as able to both gain quick student support and piss off the administration at the same time, beginning with dormitory curfews for women and the requirement that students live in dormitories for their first two years, and rapidly expanding to include other issues as well. In his role as *State News* editor, he published a guest column from a CSR member. CSR sought further confrontations through open debates, articles in their newsletter, and sit-ins at various locations around campus.

"Our activism jumped across the street, too, as a large number of students tried to pressure the East Lansing city government into adopting an 'open housing' (anti-discrimination) ordinance. Fifty-nine were arrested in a sit-in at East Lansing city hall in May 1965." Later, he and a few political friends would join Martin Luther King in the Selma-to-Montgomery civil rights march. The march gave Michael his "first experience of what I have ever since felt to be the religious uplift and inspiration of masses of people calling out in unison for what they believed and needed." Before long he was learning "about the little-known war then in progress in Vietnam."

> As much as I could, I documented my changing views in the *State News*, to increasing criticism from the rest of the staff and the advisor. My grades and academic ambitions were suffering from the loss of my interest, but it was worth it for the experience. And, I was deeply enmeshed in a community of like-minded friends, an interesting, diverse, and tolerant gang; that was definitely worth it. I quickly became known among my activist friends as the "conscience" of our movement; I seemed to have an instinct for the ethics of the struggle, and for keeping our actions proportional to our demands.

The following fall semester, *State News* staffers returned to campus to learn that they were now required to sign a loyalty oath if they were to remain as staffers: "You shall have no loyalty above the *State News*. If another organization claims your sympathy and you feel your membership will express that sympathy, this is permissible; but you shall exercise no leadership in any organization other than the *State News.*"

Michael recalls: "It was hard for me not to take this personally, in view of the way the previous year had gone. By October, I decided . . . that it was time for me to quit the *State News*. The increasing pressure there to be either an 'objective' journalist or an activist, but not both, was more than I could take." The first issue of *The Paper*—3,000 copies of an eight-page tabloid—was dated December 3, 1965.

Our times in East Lansing overlapped slightly. I began college at Michigan State University in the fall of 1967; Michael left town in early 1968, though *The Paper* was still being published by his successor staff members. Soon other papers would take its place. Five issues of *Swill and Squeal* appeared between May 6 and May 22, 1970, during the height of the nationwide student strike that followed the murder of four students at Kent State University by members of the Ohio National Guard. *Generation* and *Bogue Street Bridge* both began publication in the fall of 1970; after two issues apiece, they merged staffs and resources to put out an experimental "joint issue." My first *Joint Issue* staff meeting was in December of that year, when merger discussions were still taking place. The first Lansing-based underground paper, *Red Apple News*, merged into *Joint Issue* two months later. Although I traveled to all corners of the mainland United States throughout the seventies, mostly via thumb, and during the Vietnam era worked on underground papers wherever I landed, *Joint Issue* was the paper where I contributed most of my writing and energy during the period.

By 1974, *Joint Issue* was still around, but staff turnover had found a totally new generation of activists—none of whom had been part of *Joint Issue*'s founding years—now guiding the paper in their own unique direction. To reflect this new energy and this new direction, they changed the name from *Joint Issue* to *Lansing Star*. Two years later, in 1976, as the lone *Joint Issue* veteran who was still in town (back in town, I should say), I was invited by *Lansing Star* editor John Snyder to write a history of the Lansing-area underground press, which was serialized in three issues.

Flash forward now to just over a decade. By now the war was long over. *Lansing Star* was no longer around, nor were its various successors. We were closer to the nineties than the seventies, the country had slid politically way to the right, and Vietnam was rapidly—and deliberately, I believed—being expunged from our national consciousness. Few public-school history classes dared to rationally explore the years after "the greatest generation" vanquished Hitler. Even college courses on Vietnam were rare.

It was no accident. The United States government had been soundly defeated in its quest to remake Southeast Asia in its image. There had been no parades to honor the conquering heroes in 1975 when Nixon pulled out the remaining soldiers from Vietnam because there were no conquering heroes, and right-wing veterans' organizations and politicians blamed the antiwar movement. So, no, society in the latter years of the eighties was not yet ready to recognize the role of the antiwar movement, or to acknowledge that the heroes of that period included not only the soldiers who fought—willingly and unwillingly—in Vietnam, but also the activists who supported the troops by fighting here at home against our own government that was sending the troops to die needlessly in Vietnam.

I was living in Ann Arbor by this time and was tracking down veterans of the underground press for the book that came out in 1993 as *Voices from the Underground: Insider Histories of the Vietnam Era Underground Press*. I was using the history I had written for the *Lansing Star*, now updated for the book, as a prototype, sending it to veterans of other underground papers that I had read and admired during my *Joint Issue* days, and saying, "This is what I did for my paper. Can you do the same for yours?" I had been fortunate to find Charley Shively, a veteran of Boston's *Fag Rag*, one of the many gay papers that were published by the informal network of Gay Liberation Front chapters that arose throughout the country following the Stonewall Rebellion of June 1969. He had agreed to contribute the history of *Fag Rag*, and in our continuing conversation, I asked him if he knew anyone from another Boston-area paper, *Avatar*.

Avatar was the newspaper put out by a charismatic cult led by a musician-turned-guru named Mel Lyman. Later it would be immortalized in the book edited by David Felton called *Mindfuckers: A Source Book on the Rise of Acid Fascism in America, Including Material on Charles Manson, Mel Lyman, Victor Baranco, and Their Followers by David Felton, Robin Green and David Dalton*, but I didn't know that at this initial stage of my research. What I knew was that it had been one of the many papers that exchanged issues with *Joint Issue*, so I had seen many issues and remembered them as being impressive in both content and style.

Charley said he wasn't really friends with anyone from the staff, but that he knew someone who had done some writing for them, Michael Kindman. He didn't know how much of an insider Michael was, but Michael was the only name Charley could provide. He was living in San Francisco now. Charley gave me his phone number.

I called Michael, planning to use the same strategy I had used so far in finding "key people" from the papers I was profiling. I would find any name—usually a name from the local phone book that matched a name on a staff box—and then ask if that person was the right person to write the piece I wanted. Sometimes I hit the jackpot the first time. But more often than not, the person on the phone said, "No, the person you're looking for is . . . ," and would give me someone else's name. In this case, based on Charley's assessment, I assumed Michael wasn't the right person—but, I hoped, maybe he could tell me who was.

Michael said to me, "It's true I wrote for *Avatar*, but I was really better known for my work on a paper from the Midwest."

And that was all he said. Suddenly the light bulb went off over my head.

"Oh, you're Michael Kindman!" I exclaimed.

It was one of those obvious statements—I had called him looking for Michael Kindman; he had said "I'm Michael Kindman"—that nevertheless contained discovery. I had never told him that my base during the Vietnam era had been East Lansing–Lansing, or that by virtue of my series of articles for the *Lansing Star* I was now the historian of the underground press from the area. But certainly, in that role, I had come to learn about the legendary *The Paper*. I knew that it had been founded by dropouts from the *State News*—Michigan State University's student-run, but board-of-directors-controlled student paper—and that the name most closely associated with the paper was that of the ex-*State News* staffer who had been in line to be the next editor in chief before he turned politically to the left: Michael Kindman.

When Charley had said his name, the connection wasn't there. Now it was. The life of most underground papers was short—two or three years, give or take—especially in those early days before activists started taking the economics of running a paper seriously. In East Lansing, first there had been *The Paper*, then *Swill and Squeal*, then *Generation/Bogue Street Bridge/Red Apple News/Joint Issue*, so the paper where I made my mark could be seen as two generations removed from Michael's. He was my spiritual grandfather! Even though he was only four years my senior, I drew that connection immediately.

But now suddenly I knew him in relation to two underground papers from different parts of the country. He asked me where he should focus his energy: *The Paper* or *Avatar*—or, he offered, papers he had written for subsequent to his years with *Avatar*.

In response, I made one of the best decisions of my literary life, because it led to this book. I said, "Just tell your story and take it where it leads you."

Michael—or Mica, as he was now known—dove into the challenge. He was a prolific writer, and intellectually brilliant. And so the result was the longest chapter in the first edition of *Voices from the Underground*. As I read it then, I realized it deserved to be its own book. And now, thanks to the commitment of Michigan State University Press, it is.

Mica's story is the story of Michigan State University in the fifties and sixties, when the campus was exploding in both size and population—thanks in large part to secret funds from the Central Intelligence Agency, which chose MSU as the cover for its "pacification" program in South Vietnam. Through that program, the CIA paid the salaries of "faculty members" who, in fact, never stepped foot on campus or taught classes, but rather directed the effort to relocate the South Vietnamese peasants from the countryside into the cities, and then distributed national identification cards to all South Vietnamese adults so our government could keep better track of them.

Mica's story is the story of cults. The seventies were, after all, the age of cults: Jim Jones,

Charles Manson, the Guru Maharaj Ji, the *Avatar* commune. When Michael left *The Paper* in 1968, he headed east to Boston and joined the *Avatar* commune for the same reason I asked Charley Shively for the name of a staff member, because the paper's content and appearance were attractive to young, impressionable minds looking for spiritual answers to a harsh, materialistic world. During his time with the *Avatar* commune, he had a love-hate relationship with Mel Lyman and the entire experience, as he endured their mind games and tried to find personal meaning in them. After five years of struggling within himself, he fled the commune's rural outpost in Kansas, moved to Palo Alto, California, came out definitively as a gay man, changed his name to Mica, and settled in San Francisco.

Finally, Mica's story is the story of gay life in the eighties. For what it's worth, it might be said that I knew Mica better than anyone else in the world who never met him personally. I had a wonderful, intimate friendship with him for two years, over the phone and through the mail. Sadly, he was dying of AIDS the entire time. Two months after he finished his story, his partner, Anthony, called me to announce that Mica had died.

I was fortunate to know him. We all are fortunate that he lived long enough to complete his story. Mica wrote his story in part so he could make sense out of what happened to him and why. I believe he lived as long as he did so he could finish his story.

My Odyssey
through the
Underground Press

Michael Kindman, National Merit Scholar at Michigan State University, circa 1965.
Courtesy Ken Wachsberger archives.

CHAPTER 1

Going to College — But Not for Long

September 1963. I'm off to East Lansing, Michigan—far from my hometown on Long Island—to start college at Michigan State University, bright-eyed and enthusiastic, excited about the possibilities that await me. I'm an honors freshman in the journalism department, and one of hundreds of honors students from all over the country recruited into the freshman class. Nearly two hundred of us have been awarded National Merit Scholarships underwritten by the university and usable only there; together we represent by far the largest group of Merit Scholars in any school's freshman class. At Michigan State?

Our purpose in being there—from the point of view of the university officials who created the program, and the alumni who funded it—is to help upgrade the reputation and academic atmosphere of the giant school, which is still struggling to transcend its origins as an agricultural and technical school, "the pioneer land-grant college." The Land-Grant Act of the 1850s offered federal land to the states for the establishment of state-sponsored schools to encourage and promote agriculture and technology. Many state universities grew from these origins. The Agricultural College of the State of Michigan, founded in 1855, happened to be the first of them. It graduated to "university" status on its hundredth birthday.

Only a few years before, MSU had begun building a national reputation by becoming a major football power in the Midwestern Big Ten, replacing the University of Chicago in that athletic conference. Now it was striving to increase its academic reputation, particularly in the humanities and social sciences, as well as to justify its exponential growth in terms of services it could provide to the state. Competition with the University of Michigan (UM) in Ann Arbor was in full swing, and "State" was more than a little defensive about its standing.

Attracting huge numbers of top-ranked freshmen was just one tactic in the university administration's overall strategy of challenging UM's preeminence—a strategy that also included an enormously ambitious building program that had already doubled the size of the developed campus in recent years and would double it again in the next few years, as well as an aggressive lobbying campaign aimed at persuading the state to open a new medical school at State rather than expand the existing ones at UM and Wayne State in Detroit. The tactic of attracting high-ranking high school graduates into the freshman class included, in addition to the scholarship program, grouping us together on certain floors of the gigantic new dormitories, brick monoliths along the outer edge of the campus, far from town, and offering us accelerated participation in the "Honors College," a special program that sounded real good in the promotional material: special library privileges, the chance to do original research work under close faculty supervision, extra recognition for our academic success, et cetera—if we kept to a certain grade-point average.

The promotional literature did not talk about the generally sterile, almost rural atmosphere of both MSU and East Lansing—a dry (no alcohol sales), conservative place that looked like a picture-postcard college town but offered little in terms of cultural opportunities or intellectual community and the stimulation these could bring. And, of course, the state capital was just a few miles away in Lansing; certainly the university fathers would not want to do anything or allow anything to occur that might raise the eyebrows of the legislature. All in all, it was sort of a company-town situation, but the enthusiastic series of promotional mailings we received from Gordon Sabine, vice president for special projects, and Stanley Idzerda, director of the Honors College, did not emphasize this aspect. As a result, we showed up in droves, not only from the Midwest but from all over the country.

We honors freshmen may have suspected something was amiss, as we settled into our dormitory rooms in the farthest corners of the built-up campus, checked out the bland surroundings, and anticipated our courses, including the required freshman survey courses, American Thought and Language (ATL) and Natural Science—but if we did, it was only a dim awareness at first. We were concentrating on seeking each other out for intellectual companionship and emotional support among the much larger number of more typical midwestern types surrounding us.

Most of us lacked the sophistication to really evaluate the quality of the academic programs and were simply hoping for the best. I didn't really know what to expect from college, having had very little counseling and little else in my background to prepare me for it, other than the assumption that I would do something intellectually based with my life. I didn't understand the extent to which my growing up in the New York suburbs had already colored my expectations and experience, but I had known I didn't want to stay at home for college, and had passed up opportunities to go to Berkeley and other far-flung schools. I felt quite innocent, excited about what was being offered to us at MSU, and ready to develop a loyal connection to my future alma mater.

In addition to the academic opportunities, I was also looking forward to the option those of us in journalism had to work on the *Michigan State News*, the 30,000-circulation daily paper that was the official organ of the university, published by students under the close advisorship of a professional publisher employed by the university. I got a paying job right away on the copy desk of the *State News*, final-editing the articles and writing the headlines, and found it easy to keep up with my heavy course load despite the five afternoons a week I spent there.

One Saturday that fall, the university had all the freshman Merit Scholars pose for a picture for the alumni magazine, standing together to spell out "MS"—for Michigan State and for Merit Scholars; get it? The suspicion was starting to grow that we were being hoodwinked somehow. But I was making friends and gaining confidence.

The Beginning of the Beginning

One Friday in November, my ATL instructor came into class late, to announce he had just heard that President Kennedy had been shot and possibly killed. Class was dismissed; with it went much of our innocence and optimism. The ride was just beginning.

When first quarter ended just before Christmas, I took off for a visit to my sister's family in California. While I was there, my father had an accident at his job in New Jersey and died a few days later of his injuries. I flew home for his funeral and the obligatory mourning period. By the time I returned to East Lansing to move in with my new roommate, Larry Tate—one of my honors-program peers, who was also a budding writer—my world had been badly shaken, and I wanted deeply to be anchored in school and in my progress toward the future I was planning. I took heavy course loads through winter and spring and even summer quarters, and worked diligently on the *State News* as copy editor and reporter and occasional editorial writer.

The journalism courses were unexciting, taught by traditionalist faculty with a heavy commitment to what we have since come to know as "the myth of objectivity"; but it didn't matter much, because there was a real newspaper to play with. We got to work with wire-service news about world events, and to develop local angles when we could. I got to write reviews of local appearances by the folk musicians I admired. Little professional guidance was offered, but we were allowed a fair amount of room to maneuver. We had the chance to initiate coverage of issues we wanted to work on, within limits. I remember doing a series in the *State News* during the summer, when there was more freedom to experiment than during the rest of the year, on what I perceived to be the university's complicity in the pollution and degrading of the Red Cedar River that ran through campus—my first attempt at muckraking (so to speak).

By fall, I had achieved junior status and was named coeditor of the editorial page. My coeditor on the page, Sue Jacoby, was also double-timing through college (she did in fact graduate after two years and went on to a career with the *Washington Post* and the *New York Times*). Sue had grown up locally and had worked on the *State News* since high school; she had faith in the university and, by extension, the larger government and establishment it represented. I had the viewpoint of an outsider; I was rebellious and instinctively trusted what was new and spontaneous. She was conservative; I was liberal. We got to write our differing opinions about news events as they unfolded, and have thousands of people read and debate our ideas daily.

I was sure I was on a track leading eventually to the job of editor in chief, and then on to greater glory and success in the newspaper field. I took seriously the notions of freedom of speech and freedom of the press, and their correlate in the university context: "academic freedom," the hallowed right of instructors and students to examine any and all ideas freely and fearlessly, and to do so with the full encouragement and protection of the institution. I joined the local chapter of the American Civil Liberties Union.

It *Can* Happen Here

In October 1964, my friends and I all became transfixed by the drama that was unfolding in Berkeley, as students at the University of California began fighting for their right to freedom of political expression, over the opposition of their university's administration. The fight escalated for two months, and in December, hundreds were arrested for sitting in at the university administration building.

The Sproul Hall sit-in had almost immediate repercussions for those of us in East Lansing who had been nurturing our growing frustrations with the situation we were in. We all felt shortchanged to one degree or another for having been tricked into doing college at Michigan State University—"Moo U," as it was sometimes known (referring to the university's origins as an agricultural college)—in the conservative, teetotaling town of East Lansing, for God's sake, when we were all so brilliant and could have gone anywhere. The Honors College program that had been offered to us whiz-kid recruits had turned out to be more hype than opportunity, more the extension of Stanley Idzerda's personality and intellectual enthusiasm than a real chance to do outstanding work ahead of the ordinary academic schedule. In the sciences and technical fields, MSU generally had a legitimate claim to excellence and even leadership, but those of us in the humanities and social sciences were becoming increasingly aware that MSU was something of a cultural backwater, not the center of intellectual debate we had been led to believe it was. Many of us were growing increasingly stir-crazy. Our education was working, but not in the way the university might have hoped; the more educated we became, the more frustrated we felt.

The local Socialist Club had been discussing the Berkeley situation and its parallels in East Lansing, and the time seemed right to expand the discussion beyond the club itself. A first, secret planning meeting was called for a Committee for Student Rights (CSR). I believe it was at the suggestion of Mike Price, home-grown socialist and rebel, whose parents owned one of the local department stores, that I was invited to the meeting, despite my status as a bigwig at the *State News*, and despite the need for secrecy in organizing to challenge the university's authority. Nothing like that had been done before in East Lansing. After some negotiation, I showed up at a mysterious house off-campus for the meeting. I was aware of stepping into an alternate reality of some kind. Someone played the new album by folksinger Buffy Sainte-Marie, the one with the politically inspiring songs "Universal Soldier" and "Now That the Buffalo's Gone." We talked frustrations and strategies and made plans; by the end of the evening, my life had been changed forever.

CSR decided to start out by protesting the university's in loco parentis policies for governing students' behavior "in the place of the parents." Dormitory curfews for women and the requirement that all underclassmen live in dormitories for two years were the first targets—safe issues in terms of winning student support, and very explosive ones in the eyes of the university. I slipped a guest column into the *State News* in the name of the one member willing to go public, and we began publishing a single-sheet mimeographed newsletter for distribution in the dorms and campus buildings, along with a petition supporting our position. These publications stirred further controversy as the university stumbled over itself trying to prevent distribution. It became clear that the "rules" governing student behavior and activities were not a clearly defined set of principles and procedures, but rather were made up arbitrarily as the need arose, by administrators whose primary interest seemed to be to stifle the debate we were inciting, and to control the way students thought.

CSR sought opportunities to debate and negotiate with administrators on a wide range of university policies, and when these channels were insufficient, as was usually the case, challenged the university in our newsletters to open more channels for student participation in the governing process. When this failed, we demonstrated and sat in at various places around campus, gradually gaining support for our causes and for our right to engage in such activities. Many faculty members were happy to defend our right to express even unpopular opinions. Our protests were not just about political issues. On one occasion, we sat in at the main university library, calling attention to the low student-to-volumes ratio at MSU compared with other major universities.

That winter and spring, we demonstrated and leafleted under many banners, for many causes; a political community, an indigenous piece of the counterculture, was coming to be in East Lansing. We had a headquarters of sorts: Spiro's, a cafeteria and coffee shop across the street from campus on Grand River Avenue (everyone called the place "Kewpee's," for the "Kewpee-burgers" served there), where at any time of the day we could find some of our friends to hang out with. At last, an alternative to dorm life and bland, university-authorized activities.

Our activism jumped across the street, too, as a large number of students tried to pressure the East Lansing city government into adopting an "open housing" (anti-discrimination) ordinance. Fifty-nine were arrested at a sit-in at East Lansing City Hall in May 1965.

As each of these political actions occurred, I explained and defended them in columns in the *State News*, while in news articles, the university administrators and local politicians were making statements about "outside agitators" and "Communist sympathizers" infiltrating the otherwise calm environment of East Lansing. I found myself leading a double life, risking everything. All my own political, intellectual, and social assumptions were being challenged and reexamined. Whereas I formerly thought of myself as simply a liberal Democrat, now I was becoming a confirmed radical.

With a few of my political friends, I participated in the Selma-to-Montgomery civil rights march inspired by Martin Luther King in Alabama. The big march on the state capitol gave me my first experience of what I have ever since felt to be the religious uplift and inspiration of masses of people calling out in unison for what they believed and needed. My more informed friends were starting to encourage the rest of us to learn about the little-known war then in progress in Vietnam. As more of us figured out what was happening there, we sought ways to organize marches and teaching efforts to let more people know about this outrage. As much as I could, I documented my changing views in the *State News*, to increasing criticism from the rest of the staff and the advisor. My grades and academic ambitions were suffering from the loss of my interest, but it was worth it for the experience. And, I was deeply enmeshed in a community of like-minded friends—an interesting, diverse, and tolerant gang; that was definitely worth it. I quickly became known among my activist friends as the "conscience" of our movement; I seemed to have an instinct for the ethics of the struggle, and for keeping our actions proportional to our demands.

During the summer, a graduate student on temporary leave from school, Paul Schiff—president of the Socialist Club and editor of *Logos*, the CSR newsletter—was refused readmission to the university in what was widely seen as retribution for his political activism. One of the accusations held against him was that he had sought to "discredit" the university by speaking out against the mayor of East Lansing, Gordon Thomas, in the campaign for the open-housing ordinance; Thomas happened to be a professor of communications. Schiff decided to challenge the university in a lawsuit supported by the ACLU.

As for me, I took the summer of 1965 off from the process of school and politics and went home to Long Island to remodel my mother's house and deepen my relationship with my long-distance girlfriend, Carol Schneider. Carol and I had become friends working on our high school newspaper at a time when we were both quite inhibited and unhappy, but very successful in school affairs. We had both been offered journalism scholarships to Syracuse University in New York. A year younger than me, Carol had just finished her first year there, but she couldn't afford to return. By the end of the summer, we finally yielded our respective virginities to each other. In the fall, her college career having been stalled for the moment, Carol returned to East Lansing with me. She had come a long way from her repressive Catholic background. I wasn't sure what it meant to be living together, but I couldn't think of any reason not to.

Carol and I and my longtime roommate, Larry, rented a house off-campus. The landlady didn't protest or refuse as she signed the lease with all three of us, but then she turned right around and reported us to the university for "cohabiting." Larry and I found ourselves on "social probation," a nuisance and an insult and a threat to our scholarships. Carol rented a room in town as a cover, mainly for her parents' benefit, but never spent a night in it. It was expensive and stupid, one more radicalizing experience. I returned to the *State News* with full responsibility for the editorial page. Carol signed up for some courses at Lansing Community College and took a job as a waitress.

Conflicting Loyalties, Conflicting Oaths

Returning staff members at the *State News* were greeted with a handout called "The *State News* Commandments," a list of ten behaviors that would now be required of us. This list was the invention of the new editor in chief, Charles C. Wells, a follow-the-rules kind of guy, and the advisor, Louis J. Berman, who in his other life was the publisher of a small-town daily in western Michigan. In addition to emphasizing such admirable newspapering qualities as excellence, truth, honesty, compassion, and accuracy, these "commandments" demanded, "You shall have no loyalty above the *State News*. If another organization claims your sympathy and you feel your membership will express that sympathy, this is permissible; but you shall exercise no leadership in any organization other than the *State News*." This was "commandment" number one. It was hard for me not to take this personally, in view of the way the previous year had gone. By October I decided, in discussion with Carol and Larry, that it was time for me to quit the *State News*. The increasing pressure there to be either an "objective" journalist or an activist, but not both, was more than I could take. Larry had already stopped submitting the occasional reviews he had been writing.

We decided we would start our own weekly newspaper. The idea had been batted around among our circle of friends and fellow activists; it seemed clear that, with my combined experience of newspapering and activism, I was seen as the person most prepared to lead the way. I wrote a righteous letter of resignation, and we started networking for support for *L'Étranger*, as we planned to call our paper—after Camus's existentialist hero. Someone talked sense into us and we decided on *The Paper* instead; snobbery gave way to understatement. Support was readily available from the students and faculty members with whom we had worked in all the campaigns of the previous year. We easily raised enough money for our first couple of issues. The biggest obstacle we seemed to be facing was our lack of a telephone; the house we were renting was brand-new and several miles off-campus in a neighborhood that didn't have service yet.

The rest of the *State News* staff, with very few exceptions, scoffed at me, sure I had finally lost it. But a few weeks after my resignation, while we were still enlisting staff and support for our effort, four of the *State News*'s editors and the administration-beat reporter found it necessary to resign as well, in a controversy with the advisor and editor in chief over publication of some documents in Paul Schiff's readmission fight with the university. A number of other staff members in less responsible positions followed suit. Despite having been forced out by the party-line policies of the editor and advisor, they refused to join forces with us and issued public statements disavowing any connection with us or any other group. They were all immediately replaced, and the *State News* continued publishing without missing a beat, while both the old and the new staffs debated among themselves whether it was more important to keep publishing without missing a deadline, or to stop once in a while and review what the reasons were for publishing in the first place.

Meanwhile, we were making arrangements with a small print shop in Lansing to typeset and paste up our first issue, and with a newspaper publisher in Mason (the county seat ten miles out of Lansing) who also printed the *State News*, to do our printing on their big web press. We printed 3,000 copies of our first eight-page tabloid, dated December 3, 1965. It came back from the printer on the day our telephone finally arrived. I was listed as editor, and Larry was listed as arts editor. The masthead named two "inspirations": the *Michigan Daily*, the student-run paper from the University of Michigan down the road in Ann Arbor, and the *Promethean*, the off-campus paper founded at Syracuse University during the year Carol was there.

The issue included a front-page editorial, "As We Begin: A Loyalty Oath"—a response to item one of the "*State News* Commandments," the complete text of which we reprinted on page 2. "You shall have no loyalty above the *State News* . . . ," the first "commandment" said. I wrote:

I have a loyalty higher than that I once had to the *State News*. . . .

Our higher loyalty is to the practice of imaginative, creative, thoughtful journalism. We will not run a machine for processing copy which can run without people.

. . . We have a loyalty to the idealism on which the best journalism ever practiced has been based. We hope unabashedly to be a forum for ideas, a center for debate, a champion of the common man, a thorn in the side of the powerful. We hope to inspire thought, to attract good writing, to train newcomers in the ways of the press. . . .

We hope never to become so sure of our position and so unaware of our real job that we will concentrate merely on putting out a paper. . . .

And we intend to do all this in a spirit of editorial independence for which there is hardly a model on this campus. We may submit organizationally to the requirements of the university, but our editorial policies will be strictly our own. . . . We hope most sincerely that our attempt to prove the value of independence will be a satisfying one, and that we will keep alive the interest, enthusiasm and imagination of our readers.

It is for this hope that we reserve our highest loyalty.

On page 2, alongside the "*State News* Commandments," I offered an analysis of the censorship and resignation affair, "The *State News* Fiasco: A Cause without Rebels": "[T]hey had bigger issues they might have considered. . . . But they were afraid to shake it up . . . and so the establishment rushed in and proved to them they were expendable. Now, the *State News* is without a decent staff, the decent staff is without jobs, and the university is still without a good daily newspaper. They needn't have bothered to walk out."

The first issue also included articles on student government and the Committee for Student Rights; a reprint of a speech on world hunger by Georg Borgstromm, a professor of food science who was one of the first to warn of the dangers of uncontrolled population growth; film and theater and literary criticism; poetry and arty photographs; an impressionistic interview with Bob Dylan reprinted from the *Los Angeles Free Press*—and a marginal note on the back page: "Thanks . . . to Student Board for letting us sell this issue on campus." We had sought and received a special dispensation from student government to sell on campus under their aegis despite the lack of clear guidelines for how to obtain permission to do so; we wanted to avoid the trouble CSR had gotten into with *Logos* if we could find a way. We were off and running.

The second issue, a week later, included on the front page Larry's sardonic coverage of an early march on Washington against the Vietnam War; on page 2 a commentary from me on "MSU—The Closed Society," comparing Michigan State to segregationist Mississippi; and on page 3 a sympathetic interview with Paul Schiff, whose case for readmission to the university was heating up. Also included were more cultural coverage, a thought piece by a faculty member on "The Sick University: Is It Worth Curing?" and "Our First Letter to the Editor," a nasty piece by one of the resigned *State News* staffers, Linda Miller Rockey (briefly my successor as editorial-page editor), who wrote: "The first issue of *The Paper* has clearly convinced me that a competitive newspaper in this university community is an excellent endeavor, but that you are certainly not the person to edit it. . . ." She goes on at length to attribute complex motives of jealousy and arrogance to me in criticizing both the *State News* and the walkout, and remembers protesting an editorial I wrote for the *State News* the previous year, which proves I'm fallible, too. Et cetera, et cetera. "So in view of your inaccurate chastisement of myself and my colleagues, I can only wish you all the failure in the world with *The Paper.*"

Then it was time for finals and Christmas break, during which time Michigan State's highly touted football team went to the Rose Bowl for the first time in years, to compete with UCLA, which whomped them. *The Paper* returned on January 20, 1966, with Issue 3, our "first annual Rose Bowl issue"; its front-page article, "The Children's Crusade," was an anonymous report ("to protect the innocent") on the partying and touristing that accompanied the football pilgrimage undertaken by hundreds of Michigan Staters. An editorial cheered Paul Schiff's "routine" readmission to school in a move clearly intended by the university to avoid the embarrassment of a court trial, and decried the lack of clear policy change that accompanied it. We had switched to a different and somewhat less expensive method of typesetting, and began developing the habit of working closely with the person hired to do our paste-up.

A news article on an inside page covered the ludicrous trial of four antiwar protestors who had been arrested for leafleting in the Student Union, and whose trial in a tiny storefront courtroom in Lansing was characterized by the county prosecutor as just a routine case. The defense lawyer, Conrad Lynn, a well-known black civil libertarian imported from New York for the occasion, knew better, and called the president and one of the vice presidents of the university as witnesses, giving them their first chance to deny publicly that the university was coming down hard on antiwar protestors because it had had a role in helping create the Vietnam War. There would be more to say about that later.

By our fourth issue, we were settling into a routine. A humor piece about the competition between the *State News* and *The Paper* was on the front page; on the inside, the most interesting items were two treatments of the MSU-Vietnam connection. One, by one of our socialist friends, noted the deficiencies in the *State News*'s coverage of the subject; the other was excerpts of talks given at MSU by two spokesmen from Students for a Democratic Society, then still a small and fairly reputable Ann Arbor–based "New Left" organizing project with a national perspective. Both articles made reference to the role Michigan State had played in Vietnam in the 1950s, when its political-science department had sent a crew to Saigon to serve as advisors to the anti-Communist regime then being propped up by the United States, and questioned the freedom of thought and the larger political intentions of university personnel under such circumstances.

Is Anyone in Charge Here?

The fifth issue's front-page article, "Brave New MSU: University Planners Face the Future," was one of a long series of discussions we were to publish on the role of the modern university—or "multiversity," as University of California-Berkeley president Clark Kerr had called it. Long-time MSU president John Hannah was a staunch advocate of the social-service model of education who had reshaped the university to help meet the needs of technological society. We felt obliged at least to question this view. The writer, Char Jolles, was a compatriot of ours from our freshman days and was the only member of the *State News* staff who had quit in the mass resignations and then joined the regular staff of *The Paper*. She became a frequent commentator on educational policy and solicited articles from faculty members, which we were attempting to include in each issue.

Inside, my editorial explored the role of the Board of Student Publications, the mysterious university committee made up of administrators, faculty, and students, and chaired by the advertising professor who served as chair of the journalism department as well. The usual job of the "pub board" was to oversee the *State News* and the yearbook and a tame literary annual called *Red Cedar Review*. But the year before, it had been the official agency hauled out to harass *Logos*, and now it was finding itself in the unaccustomed position of having to think also about *The Paper* and *Zeitgeist*, an off-campus literary magazine that had come into being about the same time we started publishing. Would these upstarts be allowed to distribute on campus, or sell advertising, or even to exist at all, with or without "authorization" from the pub board? No one seemed to know, or to know how to find out. I wrote:

A much better system would be to have either no board at all or a board of publications which supervised the unrestricted distribution of publications, student or otherwise, around a campus increasingly difficult to reach by normal communications methods. For the moment we have merely a pub board that seems to content itself with simply making arbitrary rules which it plans neither to follow nor to follow through.

Issue 6 appears unremarkable in retrospect, further evidence that we were settling into a routine. On page 7 is a picture of one of our female volunteers staffing a card table in the Student Union, under the headline "Is there a place in America today for the small business-man?" The caption said *The Paper* could be found each week at four locations on campus and nine stores off campus.

The next week, however, no issue was published. Instead we put out a two-page mimeographed look-alike called Vol. 1, no. 6½, "Here We Stand: *The Paper* at the Crossroads." It turns out the student government, which had been sheltering us informally with permission to distribute on campus for "contributions" in the absence of any clear policy from the publications board to govern such circumstances, had taken offense at our decision to begin publishing advertising and "selling" copies on campus, which appeared to them to bring us within the purview of the pub board's regulation. They had responded by hauling us before the Student Judiciary to face charges. The emergency issue invited the public to attend our "trial" that evening. "We did not set out to defy authority; we set out to survive."

Our appearance before Student Judiciary received lots of coverage in the *State News* and elsewhere. We chose to refrain from publishing for a while to see if things would clarify. They didn't, so we went back to student government for permission to conduct another "fund drive." Two weeks later, we were back on the stands with Issue 7 of THE controversial PAPER. (The descriptive adjective, quoted from the *State News*, was pasted in, in tiny six-point type, between the words of the nearly two-inch-high flag; we never again published an issue without some wordplay in the title.) The headline and lead read, "You Won't Believe This, But . . . this issue is being sold on campus by permission of Student Board. Just like in the Good Old Days." The front-page editorial went on to give the complete history again of our continuing attempts to obtain some kind of legal status from someone that would guarantee us the right to do business in a normal fashion, our attempts by then being stonewalled by several different branches of the administration to which we had appealed. Student Board, the legislative branch of the student government, was choosing to step in again as a way of expressing its own disgust for the administration's delaying tactics.

What we expected to come of all this was a definition of our position by the time this issue was ready for sale. . . . [if this didn't occur] we would have exhausted the channels and were prepared to go on selling without any authorization, in protest against a set of rules which flatly refused to recognize our existence. . . . [W]e still need some definition of our status so we can either be legal once and for all or can be illegal and can start fighting, in total war, the obvious unconstitutionality of the whole business by which we've been held up thus far. . . . Meanwhile, here we are, "giving away" copies of our "free" publication in a "fund drive" which is not quite a campus-wide sale of a newspaper. But almost. Someday, maybe we'll know exactly what we're doing and whether it's allowed.

The drama continued in Issue 8, *THE guilty controversial PAPER*, which appeared on the day the Board of Student Publications was scheduled to hear our latest appeal for "authorization." An editorial entitled "The Merry-Go-Round" discusses our being found guilty (without penalty) by the Student Judiciary, which also criticized the Student Board's role in half-heartedly protecting us. For our part, we pledged not to obey the latest directive from Student Board, to avoid distributing in classroom buildings, where the *State News* was routinely distributed.

> Our defense derives from the unequal and unnecessarily intolerant treatment accorded any individual or group seeking to follow the university's various policies on distribution. [Soon], unless more roadblocks are thrown in our path, *The Paper* will have exhausted all possible channels in the university for authorization of a student publication. It is up to the Board of Student Publications to decide at its meeting March 10 whether or not the last remaining channel will make provision for *The Paper*. If it will not, we will be left to survive in the university on the basis simply of the mandate from students and faculty we feel we have to continue publishing.

The issue also contained a letter from Paul Krassner, editor of *The Realist*, the small left-anarchist magazine published in New York, congratulating us on our efforts and offering to come to East Lansing to do a benefit for us.

(An ironic note: I was registered for, and presumably made at least some attempt to complete, a course in "Newspaper Editorial Management" during winter quarter, the term that ended with the issue quoted above. The transcript shows I flunked the course, after first taking an "incomplete" grade, even as I was willing a functioning newspaper into existence, over the objections of the journalism school faculty, among others.)

Guilty and Controversial, and Legal, Too!

As spring quarter began, we appeared as *THE guilty controversial authorized PAPER*. The pub board had come through. It remained to be seen what benefits, if any, "authorization" would hold for us. Our editorial response, "Gratitude Will Get Us Nowhere," simply promised to keep doing the job we wanted to do all along.

On the same page, Larry had an article on Jim Thomas, a student poet we knew slightly, who had quit MSU to enlist in the Marines and go to Vietnam. He felt called there, unlike everyone else we knew, and we felt moved to publish the poetry and essays he had given us and promised to continue sending. Larry describes their only meeting and ponders the increasing effect of the war on all of us. "I saw him only once, but I find myself speculating about him. He will be alive when this is printed. He will probably be alive when out-of-town subscribers finally get their copies. He may even be alive when the war is over. On the other hand, he may not. I am afraid for Jim Thomas. And for all of us."

Issue 10, *THE just-plain PAPER*, headlined "The Rites/Rights of Spring," was filled with reports of ongoing activism: the appeal trial and brief jail terms of the protestors arrested the previous fall for leafleting in the Student Union, and the sit-in vigil outside President Hannah's house staged in response; the trial of one of the dozens of protestors arrested the previous spring for demonstrating in East Lansing in favor of the open-housing ordinance; the opening of the Free University of East Lansing; a campus conference between progressive Christians and New Leftists; the continuing good-natured rivalry between *The Paper* and *Zeitgeist*, the off-campus literary magazine; participation by East Lansing folk in the Detroit aspect of the International Days of Protest over Vietnam, considered at the time the largest peace demonstration ever; and, of all things, interviews with the candidates for Student Board elections, including several whose stated goal it was to reform the whole business.

The next issue we lightened up a bit, using the front page for a mock exposé, "Hannah Revealed to be Palindrome." (Do you know what a palindrome is? "Madam, I'm Adam," for example.) This provided brief comic relief for our readers while we prepared ourselves for the next barrage of rebelliousness.

Ramparts, a slick progressive magazine published in San Francisco whose role resembled that of the current *Mother Jones*, had just released its April 1966 cover article on Michigan State's role in Vietnam during the 1950s: "The University on the Make, or How MSU Helped Arm Madame Nhu." We had provided support for their researcher when he was in town, leading him to information sources and giving him background information. The charge documented by *Ramparts* was that, under cover of an academic and advisory project to the puppet regime in Saigon, MSU had actually worked with the CIA to arm the Vietnamese military and help it set up the "strategic hamlet" program in which thousands of peasants were displaced from their homes into what amounted to concentration camps, thus setting the stage for the larger war that was to come.

The next week, our front-page article, "*Ramparts* v. MSU v. The CIA: The University on the Run," was a compilation of excerpts from the *Ramparts* article, the media's response to it, the original university reports on the project, and earlier commentary on the project from a pamphlet by Robert Scheer, one of *Ramparts*' editors, "How the United States Got Involved in Vietnam." The effect was to support the *Ramparts* charges and refute the university's denials. We also printed a full-page ad for the *Ramparts* article—which the *State News* had refused—which was headlined "What the hell is a university doing buying guns, anyway?"

The next issue's front page covered a press conference by MSU President Hannah, his attempt at damage control over the controversy set off by the *Ramparts* article. His defense was the "land-grant philosophy" on which his view of the university as a public servant had always been based: "When our faculty members are engaged in providing service, either within Michigan, elsewhere in our country, or overseas, we do not consider their activities as a 'diversion of the University,' but instead a recognition of a significant and defensible function of the University. International service in this day and age is a recognition by this University and a great many others that our country is a part of the larger world community. To say that a University should never undertake to serve the national policy is to deny the right of the public university to exist."

We were pleased at having helped force the university into the open on the question of exactly how it was serving the public interest. Our issue included further documentation of the charges in the *Ramparts* article, making it clear that if university officials were not aware they were being used as a cover by the CIA, they *should* have been aware of it.

The next week we lightened up again, publishing humor articles and discussion of the university's fraternity system on the front page. We were getting ready for our next controversy; Paul Krassner's benefit appearance for *The Paper* was scheduled for May 7. The event was a success, the reception afterward was my twenty-first birthday party, and with our coverage of it in Issue 15, all hell broke loose.

Krassner had been his expected iconoclastic self. In attempting to cover his talk in a way we could get away with, we printed Larry's account of hosting him, alongside excerpts from his talk, including a discussion of alternative ways to say "Fuck Communism," a slogan he had popularized with a poster. We didn't actually print "the F word" at all, instead using a small picture of Krassner holding his red-white-and-blue poster, in which the word was barely readable. The caption read, "What substitutes could you have, anyway? Make love communism, sleep communism, ball communism, meaningful relationship communism. . . ." In an unfortunate bit of timing, in the same issue we also published a lengthy, polite, thoughtful piece by Richard Ogar, one of our regular writers, on the origins and entrenched psychological underpinnings of society's prohibitions on nudity, suggesting that we might all be better off if the taboo was lifted.

Easy Come, Easy Go

The surprising upshot of this was a huge uproar and controversy, just as if we had started publishing hard-core pornography. The Board of Student Publications, which had so recently granted us "authorization" after months of waffling, summarily withdrew its seal of approval at a meeting to which we were not invited. I remember receiving a one-sentence letter announcing this news, and publishing a photocopy of that letter somewhere, but it doesn't show up in any issue of *The Paper*. I guess we must have put out a flier in our defense, as the *State News* was reporting on our "de-authorization." In Issue 16, we published yet another lengthy discussion of the irrationality and arbitrariness of the university's position: "Here We Go Again!!" We reprinted a brief excerpt from a *State News* interview with Frank Senger, chair of both the journalism department and the publications board: "Did he think that some observers might say that the board's rapid action constituted a violation of *The Paper*'s rights of due process? 'I suppose,' Senger said." The possibility didn't seem to bother him much.

The same issue included coverage of a hearing before the Higher Education Subcommittee of the Michigan House of Representatives in which MSU officials and *Ramparts* writers faced off on the subject of the MSU-Vietnam charges, and several articles on the dissolution then in progress of the university's political-science department, which everyone concerned denied was related to the *Ramparts* affair; we didn't buy that explanation. After the publication of our "sensationalized and lewd material," as the *State News* called our Issue 15, the printer we had been using refused to do further business with us and published a nasty editorial about us in its own paper, the *Ingham County News*, a copy of which the publisher sent to us with an insulting cover letter. We reprinted both in Issue 17, after finding a printer elsewhere in Michigan willing to take our business—something we would have to do several more times over the next year, traveling as far afield as Chicago and Windsor, Ontario.

But Issue 17 included a couple of items more significant to us. My front-page editorial, "It's Been a Gas!" included a letter from Walter Bowart, publisher of the *East Village Other* in New York, inviting us to join him and others in forming the Underground Press Syndicate (UPS).

On the same page, we published the first installment of "LandGrantMan," a Marvel Comics–style strip produced by some of our friends, in which Dr. John Palindrome, president of Midwestern Multiversity, is visited by a spirit who grants him special powers in order to fight the "vicious personifications of evil" surrounding him, in the form of student protestors, hippies, and the like. He transforms into the bungling superhero LandGrantMan, who vows, "Now to show those students whose multiversity this really is!"

With that, *The Paper* closed out its first notorious year of publication. East Lansing was never going to be the same.

I spent the summer of 1966 in an SDS organizing project in San Francisco, where some of my colleagues were students from the University of Texas. Hearing my stories of publishing *The Paper* in East Lansing, they decided they could do it, too. They returned to Austin and immediately began publishing the *Rag*, but not until one of them had guided me on my first LSD trip. The same week, I sent off my application as a conscientious objector to my draft board in New York, and *Time* magazine appeared with an article on the founding of the Underground Press Syndicate, "Underground Alliance," featuring brief interviews and photographs of the five of us who had founded the "shoestring papers of the strident left" that *Time* saw "popping up like weeds across the U.S."

Reflecting on what we had accomplished during the previous year, I was more than ever committed to carrying on the journalistic revolution we had stumbled upon. I was excited about the formation of UPS and wrote a letter singing its praises, which I sent to the editors of every alternative paper I had come across. I found opportunities that summer to acquaint myself with the other founding editors of UPS.

CHAPTER 2

Ambassador from Somewhere Else

R eturning to East Lansing in the fall, I definitely felt like an ambassador from a developing national counterculture, bringing news of the future back to my provincial homeland. My lady friend Carol having resumed her schooling in Albany, New York, and my accomplice Larry having chosen to rent an apartment with another friend, I needed to find a home for both myself and *The Paper.* I took over a small house near campus in whose basement was located the mimeograph on which all our movement leaflets for the previous two years had been printed; the front room became our office. We finally decided to begin doing our own paste-up; a local union activist donated a huge sheet of frosted glass that I turned into a light table big enough for three or four people to work at.

Our first issue of the year (twelve pages, circulation increased to 4,000) had a modest collage on the front page made up of our most memorable headlines and graphics of the previous year, and a piece from me that began "An Editorial (!!) . . . in which the editor states his preference for fun and good newspapers rather than fighting and hassling, and explains how fun and good newspapers have been pursued since he last published an issue; also including a statement of his plans for the coming year." One of our friends took one look at it and said, "Wow, Kindman's been taking acid." True enough.

But we still intended to stick thorns in the side of the MSU administration whenever we could. The opening issue for the year included our version of orientation articles on life in the multiversity, by Char ("The university is well-suited for the task of conditioning . . . its inhabitants psychologically for the outside world, for MSU, like American society as a whole, can be characterized by, among other things, the condition of anonymity, the pressure of conformity, and the spirit of competition"), and "Culture at MSU," by Larry ("Luckily for everyone, it won't take long" to discuss).

I'm unable to remember exactly what became of the enormous controversy of the previous year concerning our distribution on campus. Reading through the issues published during that second year, I find no sign of it, although plenty of new controversy was generated, and more inflammatory material than ever filled our pages. I presume the university just backed down and let us be; the times were certainly changing in many ways. We did form an organization called Friends of *The Paper* to serve as our foil when we wanted to rent rooms on campus and do that sort of thing.

Membership in the Underground Press Syndicate brought immediate benefits for us, in the form of a wealth of interesting articles available for reprinting as all of the member papers began exchanging copies with one another, as well as advertising from previously unattainable sources all over the country. Later, as UPS became more established, we began receiving advance copies of books and records for review. In addition, former staff members of *The Paper* were starting to migrate to graduate schools and urban centers around the country, and they began generating original copy for us to publish on the political and social happenings occurring in their areas.

Finally, we were playing the role we had hoped for. People waited for our issues, which came out each week virtually without fail, each one looking different and more experimental than the one before. We had coverage of the antiwar movement from all over the country, of the expanding rock-music scene, of the changes under way in the university. We had consumer news, arts reviews, analysis of the financial involvement of Big Business in the university, original poetry and fiction (including more poetry and commentary from Jim Thomas in Vietnam), and a new edition of LandGrantMan each week, providing ludicrous counterpoint to our other coverage of whatever had been happening on campus. Pretty much whoever wanted to do so could comment on whatever he or she wanted to, in whatever verbal or visual form, and we would probably publish it. *The Paper* was a wide-open experimental forum, unlike anything we had seen or experienced before.

In Issue 3, I published an editorial, "The Newspaper As Art Form," each paragraph interspersed with a line from the Beatles' song "Tomorrow Never Knows" ("Turn off your mind, relax and float downstream—this is not dying," etc.). I wrote: "Being *The Paper* feels different this year. There's a spirit to it, a feeling of community and creativity and enlightened consensus about it that proves to those of us who think about these things the value of the 'underground press' as an instrument of communication. . . . [W]e all on the staff understand now that our function is as innovative artists of journalism and that journalism is itself the art of relating importantly and currently to the concerns of people." In a way we had not anticipated but had been living for months—and for which we had lacked concepts until we started reading our fellow UPS papers and Marshall McLuhan's book *Understanding Media: The Extensions of Man* (source of the soon-to-be-ubiquitous phrase "the medium is the message")—we ourselves had become the news, the event worth watching. What would *The Paper* do next? What pulse would we and the community for which we spoke put our fingers on next?

One answer was going on in my small living room almost every night, after the work on the newspaper was done. More and more of us were exploring taking drugs and being stoned together. I was finding myself skilled as a trip guide, and had plenty of work. The tripping was accompanied by the inevitable soundtrack of the day, the profound new music that was teaching us ever more about what we were experiencing. That season, our instructors included The Beatles' *Revolver*, The Rolling Stones' *Aftermath*, Bob Dylan's *Blonde on Blonde*, Donovan's *Sunshine Superman*, and Simon and Garfunkel's *Parsley, Sage, Rosemary and Thyme*. The music contained messages far more relevant to us than anything taught in school. In Donovan's phrase, we stood "both young and old," on the brink of a new world. I remember one evening that fall when I ran out of wisdom, and one of my friends, *Paper* staff writer

Gregg Hill, helped me through my first-ever confrontation with my own mortality. But most of the time, we just got off on all the fun we were having, exploring the corners of our minds and finding new meanings in everything we looked at.

Orange Power Days

Another hint of the new pulse of the community came in a more familiar form in October, when it was learned that the American Thought and Language department, responsible for dispensing to thousands of freshmen each year the required course in literature and writing, had decided not to renew the contracts of three of its most popular young instructors—two of whom, Gary Groat and Ken Lawless, were involved in publishing the off-campus magazine *Zeitgeist*, and the third of whom, Robert Fogarty, was a talented up-and-comer in the department ranks. About the same time, we published a poem by Lawless, "The Orange Horse," that described the fantasy of an unhappy instructor being given a magic can of spray paint and turning the entire campus orange as an expression of his frustration. As the department's decision came under increasing scrutiny over the next several weeks, in the *State News* and *The Paper* and endless discussions all over campus, the orange horse became the symbol of the dissatisfaction many students were feeling at seeing some of their favorite instructors treated so shabbily, in evident retribution for doing exactly what it seemed they should be doing.

Several articles by Char Jolles set the tone of our coverage by casting the controversy as a generational dispute within the huge and bureaucratic ATL department, in which the younger and more creative instructors were lobbying for such changes as essay rather than multiple-choice exams, and whole-book readings rather than anthology selections—over the opposition of a scared and unimaginative administration. *Zeitgeist*, the magazine that Groat especially had inspired, and of which he was the titular head, was as iconoclastic as *The Paper*, but a lot more self-consciously artsy and free-thinking, a clear challenge to entrenched authority. The popularity of the three instructors with the students did not seem to be a factor at all to the faculty committee that had made the decision to let them go.

The dissatisfaction erupted into a rally at the classroom building where the ATL department was headquartered. The rally, which was organized by one of our regular writers, Brad Lang, grew into a week-long vigil by hundreds of students, which in turn spawned an organization called United Students, of which W. C. Blanton (known as "Coon"), one of the creators of LandGrantMan, and more recently *The Paper*'s sports columnist, became chair. Everyone was talking "orange power," and we continued writing about the firings and the vigil and their aftermath for weeks. In one article, Brad refuted the overheard faculty comment that the vigilers were "smelly, long-haired people" by documenting just who was present one Thursday at 4 A.M. It turned out that of 140 people sitting in at that time, over half were National Merit Scholarship winners of one sort or another, with a proportionate scattering of other academic and campus honors among the group. Protesting was no longer limited to the off-campus fringe, and it was no longer considered chic to distance oneself from the protest by demanding that there be a specific focus and reasoned strategy to any given protest action; simple frustration was a sufficient excuse for participating. The "orange power" movement was primarily a gut reaction against relentless mediocrity. The students were restless.

Meanwhile, John Hannah celebrated twenty-five years as president of MSU. We congratulated him with a front-page article, "Happy Anniversity," in which we excerpted dozens of his comments over the years on the subject of education and the role of the university, "so that [our] readers may know the quality of the man and the ideas we face in our president." He was an easy mark: a Michigan farm boy made good, whose only doctorate was an honorary degree in poultry science, whose politics were rock-ribbed Republican, and whose ideas for building a great university seemed to come mainly from the world of corporate development. In addition to aggressively building Michigan State up from a medium-sized and medium-grade technical and teachers college into an enormous multicampus school, with a wild and unorthodox array of professional schools and academic programs as well as business-funded training programs designed to groom personnel for particular industries, Hannah had led MSU into founding a number of overseas campuses in far-flung areas of the globe, a program with the distinct flavor of post–World War II American hegemony. Not a very inspiring leader, but one with unmistakable political ambitions and connections. An example of his thinking, from January 1963: "The University does not belong to the students. It does not belong to the faculty. It does not belong to the administration, or even to the Trustees. MSU belongs to the people of Michigan, who established it, who have nurtured it through the long decades, and who continue to sustain it. In the final analysis, MSU belongs to the larger social organization that is the nation, and of which the State of Michigan is but a part." (A couple of years later, Hannah would finally leave Michigan State in order to accept the job of heading up the U.S. Agency for International Development in the Nixon administration.)

But stranger things than John Hannah were on our minds. On November 17, Tim Leary visited the MSU campus and spoke on the subject "LSD: Man, God and Law" to an audience of four thousand people, most of whom knew of Leary and LSD mainly from newspaper and magazine accounts. He characterized himself as a spiritual teacher. "We seek to reaffirm the divinity of the human being, we seek to get man out of the manacles of his mind," by promoting, of course, the use of the new sacraments of psychedelic drugs, a new "visible, tangible method of finding grace," because we know now that "consciousness is a biochemical phenomenon." The front-page article in our next issue, "Turn On/Tune In/Cop Out," included our critical response to these ideas: "No religion has ever grown exclusively by the beliefs of its prophets, and the new spiritual age promised by psychedelics will be meaningless to humanity at large unless its values—and practices, which are inseparable—can be translated into many different life styles for many different groups. Many followers of the psychedelic scene seem to be realizing this, but if Leary does, he kept it hidden in what he said at MSU." We also published the first of what would be many articles on marijuana legalization, and announced an upcoming anniversary benefit dance for *The Paper* featuring—Freak Out!—the Mothers of Invention.

Our anniversary issue on December 8, "Happy Universary to Us!" included my discussion of the changes we had all been through in the preceding year, starting with that old "loyalty oath" about journalistic principles from our first issue, and running through our now-active involvement in the Underground Press Syndicate and alternative culture in general. I discuss the relevance of Marshall McLuhan's ideas in making sense of this evolution and say, "What we do understand ourselves to be doing is writing living, personal subjective history—and in so doing, portraying a more accurate objective picture of the action of our time tha[n] can be given through the use of linear-oriented, formula journalism that assumes all the answers are to be had in reducing things to familiar patterns." More than 1,200 people helped us celebrate with the Mothers as, to the best of our ability, we turned the ballroom of the Student Union into a psychedelic dance palace.

We had spent fall term publishing ten consecutive twelve-page issues. Our circulation was up to 5,000 (still small; university enrollment exceeded 38,000), and we were feeling strong. Our staff and volunteer organization numbered in the dozens. We were distributing papers in open racks in a number of campus buildings, as well as hawking them around campus. Rip-offs of papers and, worse, of the coin boxes attached to the racks presented a problem, but despite that, we were growing financially stronger due to the increased advertising volume.

Strange Things Are Happening

The landlady of the little house had decided to evict me, so I rented instead a much bigger house closer to the center of town, with our office and the big light table on an enclosed porch overlooking Abbott Road, one of the main streets. Behind the door, a group of us—mostly, but not all, *Paper* staffers—created a loose, chaotic communal household and tripping center. Things were getting stranger and stranger. Schoolwork was a distant memory. I had long since given up on my journalism major. Now I was in my second year as a senior, trying life as a history major and later moving on to English. But it was hard to feel any relevance in any of my courses, and it was hard for my instructors and advisors to fault me on what I was doing. I was operating in unknown territory. Sometimes I was in school, sometimes I dropped out; it didn't seem to make any difference. What *was* happening was the ongoing exploration with psychedelic drugs, informed, as ever, by the new music that kept coming out and telling us what was real. The Mamas and Papas, *If You Can Believe Your Eyes and Ears*; Donovan, *Mellow Yellow*; Judy Collins, *In My Life*; The Beatles, "Strawberry Fields Forever." I was spending more and more of my time, money, and energy finding out just how spaced out I could get and still function in the world. I sort of functioned as the daddy of both *The Paper* and the big house, and these roles took up most of my time and energy, but I also was finding more opportunities to play and explore with my new friends. It was all a trip.

As winter quarter began, Vol. 2, no. 11, *THE sad-eyed PAPER of the lowlands*, featured a front-page obituary, "Jim Thomas, 1946–1966." That which Larry had feared had come to pass; Jim had been killed in battle just before Christmas. Larry wrote, "America has lost a soldier, and America can afford that. But it has also lost a poet, and no nation can afford such a loss."

The next issue criticized *State News* reporter Andy Mollison, a friend of ours and the boyfriend (later, the husband) of our staff writer Char Jolles, for jumping the gun on what might have been a reporting scoop: the East Lansing SDS was considering forming the first chapter of what national SDS anticipated would become an anti-draft union, large numbers of men willing to publicly denounce the Vietnam draft, a felony offense. Andy saw an advance copy of the plans at Char's house, in the possession of one of her roommates, an SDS officer. He ran it as a copyrighted banner story in the *State News*, even before the local SDS chapter had voted on it. We had fun embarrassing him by detailing how his "scoop" had been obtained ("Even the Best of Us Have Our Off Days"). Over the next weeks we followed the developments as the local SDS chapter did, indeed, take a public anti-draft stance, in which many *Paper* staffers of both genders (including myself) participated.

After another issue, we skipped a week due to a big snowstorm, then came back with a twenty-page issue of *THE white PAPER*, headlined "Urban Renewal or, How Twenty-Four Inches of Snow Made a Better Place of East Lansing." In addition to our celebrating the unexpected winter holiday and the surprising beauty of town and campus, the article by Dale Walker, an advertising graduate student who was in the process of rethinking his values as he got to know our scene better (he lived in the attic room of the big house), commented on the failure of three "modern gods": business, government, and science. "If we are to make a better world for ourselves, we must disclaim all belief in the inevitability of progress, and we must ask of those in power that they TRY. . . . Someone must begin to lobby for the people. Until our efforts are properly directed and humanitarian values find their place in the modern world, we will continue to be embarrassed for our failures. Pray for snow."

I don't remember for sure, but we must have changed printers again in time for that issue, because for the first time a disclaimer appeared in the corner of the front page: "NOTE: Contents of this paper do not reflect views of Printers." Inside, in the masthead, is a second note, "The opinions expressed in *THE PAPER* are solely the responsibility of *THE PAPER*."

The next issue included the first installment of "The *Paper* Forum," a chance to air our laundry in public. Trouble was brewing in paradise. Larry Tate, now listed as assistant editor but feeling increasingly alienated from the changes in our lifestyle and the content of *The Paper*, and still interested mainly in finding or writing the great American novel, had written an open letter to me. In it, he angrily tore apart one of my articles, the paean to the underground press from our anniversary issue (quoted above, in which I credit Marshall McLuhan with formulating ideas to explain how our generation was living). Larry decried what he saw as our inexorable slide toward some anti-intellectual hippie hell. "It makes me more unhappy than I can say that *The Paper* might become just another underground newspaper."

In my response, written quickly on the way to the printer just before deadline, I was unable to counter the charge of hasty and careless writing, but I did feel the need to repeat what I had said previously about the role we were playing in exploring and defining the new culture that was coming into being around us. "I think we can easily identify an enormous impact we have had on the MSU community since we began publishing, and that impact is largely based on the loose kind of evolution I have encouraged within *The Paper*, including the movement to 'the underground.' That Larry is as blind as he seems to be to this impact simply amazes me."

The debate went on for several issues. John Sinclair, the infamous poet, community organizer, and marijuana advocate from Detroit, some of whose recent writing we had published, wrote to support my side: "I mean these guys have got to stop being so SCARED about everything that's happening—their precious intellects will still carry them through, if that's what they need. . . . My own identity [used to be] bound up with the existence of the little magazines, but as far as I'm presently concerned the little magazine is DEAD—the papers are much more public, faster to get out, regular, get to more people, etc., etc. YES."

Running on Empty

Despite this testimonial to the vitality of the underground press, it was becoming clear that not all of us wanted the same thing from *The Paper* or from this phase of our lives. How would this tension resolve itself? I was slowly becoming aware that I was running down in my enthusiasm for the process. Or, at least, that something was changing, some shift in the historical moment.

In Issue 16, late in February, I started a lengthy two-part article analyzing a report by a faculty committee who had worked for a year on a proposal to rewrite all the regulations affecting student affairs in the university. This was the university's response to more than two years of student protests, and soon the faculty would vote on the proposal. I pointed out, in agonizing detail, all the report's inconsistencies and evasions, as well as the clear victories for our side, such as the proposed abolition of the ridiculous Board of Student Publications. I recommended against faculty acceptance of the proposal as offered (but acknowledged that it would likely pass anyway) and encouraged my readers to engage in the long process of lobbying to refine the new regulations into what was needed. Clearly, this was an editorial position that implied we would be there to check up on the outcome and follow-through. Not so; the faculty report and the new regulations were barely mentioned again in *The Paper* from then until June.

Our attention was elsewhere, but it's hard to say exactly where. Certainly the continuing experiment we were living with psychedelic drugs was taking its toll. I remember waking up and/or coming down in various friends' apartments and reading *The Paper* as though for the first time; it was a hoot to read and it made me proud, but the clarity of my direction of it was waning, and it was not clear whether anything or anyone was emerging to replace me.

Winter quarter ended, and with it the ambitious communal-living-and-working arrangement I had encouraged us to explore for several months. I had found the chaotic environment too costly for comfort, in terms of both dollars and psychic energy. I don't remember whether it was my idea or the landlord's, but I gave up the big house and found another small one to rent, in the unincorporated limbo zone between Lansing and East Lansing, in the shadow of a freeway ramp, with a late-night liquor store next door. Once again, the giant light table filled half the living room. My small bedroom was painted black, the better to encourage psychedelic chalk drawings on the walls. In that room, the Beatles' *Sgt. Pepper's Lonely Hearts Club Band* and the Jefferson Airplane's *Surrealistic Pillow* would come to life. More than ever, the university seemed far away.

Our April 4 issue, the first of spring quarter, spent its front page announcing an event we were sponsoring the next week, borrowing an idea from the *Rag* of Austin for "Gentle Thursday," a one-day impromptu Summer of Love–type happening all over campus. (The actual so-called Summer of Love had yet to occur, but the mood was building.) "We are asking that on this particular Thursday everybody do exactly what they want. On Gentle Thursday bring your dog to campus or a baby or a whole bunch of red balloons." Et cetera, et cetera. You get the idea.

A large ad in the same issue announced the formation of the SDS anti-draft union anticipated two months earlier. Some forty-two men announced we would not go to Vietnam, would encourage others to do the same, et cetera; some twenty women signed on as supporting us. (Many years later we learned that if it hadn't been accomplished already, signing that ad definitely opened a dossier on each of us in the secret intelligence files kept by the Michigan State Police.) Another change in that issue was in the staff listing: four of us—Larry Tate and I, Brad Lang, and Eric Peterson, a relative newcomer to the staff who had become one of my closer friends—were now listed as the editorial board. A few weeks later, we added a fifth person, Ron Diehl, who had been handling business affairs for *The Paper* for most of the year. This was a first step in the inevitable transition to new leadership, as Larry was getting ready to graduate, and I was burning out.

The next issue gave our real rationale for calling for "Gentle Thursday": "It's like this: Spring had arrived. *The Paper* seemed suddenly to be a minor drag to produce each week. Radical politics had become almost totally wrapped up in the [student government election] campaigns. . . . Serious cracks were becoming evident in the once-quasi-solid wall of the hippy community. Last term's happy college drop-outs were becoming bored with their new bohemian life. Something, in short, had to be done." Thus, Gentle Thursday.

But first, it was time for student government elections. I wrote "An Elections Handbook, or Don't Throw Out the Bath Water Just Because the Baby Is Still Dirty, or How to Survive on Brutal Wednesday." Several of our staff writers and other friends were running for positions in the student government, and the tenor of the campaigns was clearly toward incorporating some of the positions as well as the leaders of the protest organization, United Students, that had grown out of the fall sit-ins. We encouraged this trend while continuing to promote the usefulness of direct action techniques, "for getting people involved in bringing about immediate change, both in their own lives and in their political environment."

Both "Brutal Wednesday" and "Gentle Thursday" went the way we wanted them to. Brad Lang and Jim Friel, the writer of LandGrantMan, were now on Student Board. Gentle Thursday had been a campus-wide hit, supported even by the *State News*. We were no longer the out-group; suddenly our little revolution had gained some real acceptance and a measure of authority. We spent an issue celebrating the shift. A collage of Gentle Thursday photos included one of John Hannah walking across campus holding a flower someone had given him.

Our next issue covered the controversial appearance on campus of American Nazi leader George Lincoln Rockwell, and also included original coverage of the antiwar Spring Mobilization from our correspondents on both coasts. One of the articles on the New York Mobilization was from an MSU-SDS member named David Stockman, who much later would gain fame as the precocious hatchet man of Reaganomics when he headed the federal Office of Management and Budget. Still a 1967 innocent, he wrote, "It will take more than a leisurely stroll down Madison Avenue, or even revulsion toward war atrocities to put this ghastly thing to an end. The real determinats [sic] of the war are built into the structure of the corporate system. Concomitantly, political indifference and moral insentiency are interwoven in the fabric of middle-class culture. . . . Unless a significant process of radical humanization begins in the near future, the City will never again see giant parades, or Love-Ins or Gentle Thursdays. Neither will it see people waving balloons, nor wearing flowers in their hair, nor . . ." Nor what? He doesn't say.

Was there a revolution in the works? It was hard to tell, hard to know where to look. Our next issue was dedicated to reprinting pamphlets of the Diggers of San Francisco, anarchist street people who, by their way of being, challenged all the assumptions of materialism.

Then we stepped back to East Lansing and spent a long front-page article looking at the first crisis of the new student government as it flexed its muscles on—could this still be happening?—the controversial question of abolishing dormitory curfews for women. Was this the revolution we were waiting for? If so, it seemed to be spinning its wheels a bit, and I drew a parallel to the situation of *The Paper*. "I didn't feel like editing this week's issue of *The Paper*, either. There is a connection here. . . ." I noted that whereas we had started publishing in a desperate situation, which both stimulated and suppressed us, as publishing became easier and the atmosphere became more permissive, we found it more difficult in some ways to sustain interest and keep the quality of the product up. "When it looks as though we are having difficulty maintaining the spirit to exploit our uniqueness, I tend, not alone, to get bored with it. This week has been a particularly bad week in this way. . . ."

CHAPTER 3

And Now, Something Completely Different . . .

It was by now the middle of May 1967 in my fourth year in East Lansing; many of my contemporaries were getting ready to graduate, but I wasn't, because I had thrown standard college stuff overboard in order to have this revolution. And now things were sort of settling down in a funny way, or it was time to move on, or it was time to really take a stand for social change, not just pretend, or . . . what was it time for, anyway? I certainly wasn't sure, but something new was rumbling through my life, and I wasn't feeling like carrying *The Paper* alone. I had a new girlfriend, Candy Schoenherr, who had joined our staff a few months earlier after being brought around by Eric Peterson, and she and I were spending time with a few new friends who, in turn, were looking at their sexual identities; together we were discovering bisexuality, and it was quite a rush for all of us. I remember going to Larry Tate, who had long since acknowledged his own homosexuality, one morning after a night of discovery and saying to him, "Me, too." He responded with less than perfect enthusiasm, but I was thrilled. After so many years of mental and abstract principled activity, finally my body was beginning to speak, too.

How would we incorporate this latest craze into our newspapering, and who would see that we met the deadlines? I tried bringing these disparate elements together by devoting space in *The Paper* to activities of the various people with whom I was exploring (they were, after all, active as writers, in student government, in the various protest activities), but this did not satisfy the conflicting urges I was feeling. Despite the naming of an "editorial board," I was still feeling like the sole party responsible for meeting the deadlines, and sometimes it hurt too much. In a slightly later era, the answer to my dilemma would become obvious: explore the sexual conflicts and gender-role expectations explicitly in the newspaper. But at the time, such questions were still too new and too threatening to be examined clearly.

One week late in May, when I was particularly depressed and when the help I needed from others wasn't there, I simply didn't put an issue together at all. Instead, I put out another two-page mimeographed flier made up to look like *The Paper*, as we had done more than a year earlier when political pressure gave us no other choice. This time I raised the question, "What if there were no issue of *The Paper* this week?" It was a desperate move; I needed to know whether anyone cared. I found that they did. Andy Mollison of the *State News* paid me a visit to remind me of my responsibility to my readership. The next week, a sufficient number of staff people rallied around to put out the last issue for the school year: Issue 26, twenty pages.

One of the most consistently enthusiastic staffers, Ron Diehl, wrote an article, "*The Paper* Is Dead, Long Live *The Paper*!" in which he reassured our readers that the experiment would carry on. On the subject of my mutiny the week before, he wrote, "At this point, Mike just wishes to swim back to shore and if the boat continues to float, well fine." A fair enough assessment. Somehow, it seemed I had run out of things to say, or the confidence to say them. I was burned out, that's for sure; my academic career was in ruins, and I urgently wanted the whole world to become a psychedelic wonderland so I could get some rest. But *The Paper* would continue. It was time to turn it over to a group of successors and take a break, maybe a permanent one.

I went home to New York for a brief rest, to get ready for a summer of driving and camping around the country with Will Albert, one of my new gay friends, a would-be poet and adventurer who was just having his first coming-out experiences, and with whom I was hopelessly infatuated. While I was away, somehow, the county prosecutor decided the time had finally come to bust *The Paper* for drugs. His troops invaded my little house one night while my girlfriend Candy and nine others were partying there, and arrested everyone for possession of marijuana. Finally, the obvious had been confirmed: that we had been watched and listened to for months, and that our drug habits made us legally vulnerable. So sad for the prosecutor that I was out of the state.

Candy called me in New York to tell me about the bust. There didn't seem to be anything I needed to do. The lawyer who had been hired had sprung her after a couple of days in jail; others had done about as well. Will and I started our trip. Passing through East Lansing, we found the little *Paper* house near the freeway still functioning without me. Despite the bust, folks were putting out a summer issue of reprints from the previous year, an orientation special for the new freshmen who were starting out in summer quarter. One of the few new articles in the issue was a commentary by Ron Diehl on the bust at the *Paper* office, focusing on the admitted police surveillance that had preceded it, and the violation of civil liberties that the major media took for granted, even celebrated. "[A]s each of us proceeds in this bugged, wired, voyeured life, may we have patience with those whose lives are so barren as to derive excitement from ours."

Candy headed home to spend the summer working in a factory and waiting for her trial. Will and I headed west, he with his copy of the gay-bar directory to guide him, I hoping for some clarity about something, anything to emerge from the trip. In several cities along the way, he met people and had little affairs, while I pined and waited. I felt quite unable, even ineligible, to "cruise" the bars, an activity at which Will excelled. We camped out in national parks and along roadsides. We discussed poetry and revolution. When we could, we paid brief visits to underground newspapers we knew about: the *Seed* in Chicago, *Helix* in Seattle, the *Seer* in Portland, our namesake *The Illustrated Paper* in Mendocino, California.

When we hit San Francisco, our first stop was a visit to *Vanguard*, a small, gay-oriented UPS-member magazine published in the Haight-Ashbury. Will and the one-man staff, Keith St. Claire, immediately became stuck on each other, and we stayed. I had my own room in

Keith's collective household, the gayest place I had been yet. I used the time to finally have some preliminary gay adventures of my own, as well as psychedelic adventures in the Haight. I remember sitting anonymously in the offices of the *San Francisco Oracle* one day, tripping my brains out with the rest of the troops. That evening, I went home and tried to rest, but a voice in my brain kept reciting Candy's name to me; it seemed to be coming very powerfully from far away, but I didn't understand how or why.

One time, we picked up two hitchhikers in the Haight, "lent" them $10, and drove them to an adjoining neighborhood to see a friend for some kind of "business deal," which was supposed to get us our money back. An inordinately long time later, they reappeared at the car, shit-faced and incoherent, their eyes rolling in their heads. Loaded.

But this brief exposure to the world of hard drugs did not dissuade us from our belief in soft ones. We decided to take advantage of our proximity to Mexico, still the source of much of the available marijuana, and collected $1,000 in drug money among ourselves and from some friends in East Lansing. With that money, I went to Southern California, in the company of some teenage friends of Keith's, to purchase a suitcase full of kilo bricks. All that weekend, the teenagers kept me stoned, listened to my political stories, taunted me a bit about my bisexuality, and kept the money (I'm convinced) by staging a "bust" of their contact. I felt foolish and disgraced returning to San Francisco empty-handed, but I didn't know what else to do.

After a month in San Francisco, Will and I were planning to stay on, maybe to go to school at S.F. State. During a trip back to New York with Keith to collect our goods (Will was from upstate), we stopped in Michigan for another visit.

We visited Candy at her parents' house and wound up spiriting her away and back to East Lansing, where one of the most exciting changes we discovered was the increasing number of new underground papers that had been coming in the mail. Among them were the first half dozen issues of a new paper from Boston, *Avatar*, which looked as different from the typical underground paper as the *San Francisco Oracle* did, but in an opposite way. Where the *Oracle* was lavishly decorated and colorful, setting it apart from the cut-and-paste collage style of our paper and most of the others, *Avatar* was airy and wispy, filled with pen-and-ink drawings and cloudlike, handwritten headlines. The content was unusual, too: articles on the spirit of the American revolution, on personal transformation, on the morality of drugs and hippie culture; lots of personal and spiritual advice by some guy named Mel Lyman. But I'm getting ahead of my story.

More School in My Future

By the time Will and Keith and I got to New York, the bloom was off for the two of them. Will looked at me one morning and complained, "He's plastic!" That was about as bad a name as you could call anyone. Keith returned to San Francisco; his household remained a stop on all our friends' circuits for quite a while. Larry Tate even lived there for a time. Will decided to stay on in New York City and instantly got into another affair. I had my conscientious objector hearing, after a year of waiting, at a draft-board office in far-suburban eastern Long Island, and of course was rejected. My personal values were not a sufficient reason not to fight a war; I needed to, but couldn't, demonstrate religious reasons for refusing to be drafted. It was looking like there was more school in my future. I called Candy in East Lansing and arranged to return and live with her and try MSU again, this time joining her as a psych major, with a radical, activist professor as advisor to both of us. She found us a sublet apartment over a store on the main thoroughfare of Lansing, and we really tried hard to be a normal young couple concerned about school.

The Paper was in the hands of others, and I felt and acted like an elder statesman, as best I could. The year's publication output began on September 18, 1967, with Vol. 3, no. 1/2, a four-page effort (one page of which was a full-page ad for Bobbie Gentry's record "Ode to Billy Joe"). The front page featured a picture of a billboard that had appeared at several places on campus during the summer, encouraging students and others to use a special phone number to report each other's suspicious behavior to the campus police. A letter from psychology professor Lauren Harris commented, in part:

> We can smile at it and say, "That's the police mentality for you"; but the smile would be forced. Joke about it as we might, we FEEL less free than before, and the sense of lost freedom, the atmosphere of suspicions created by such a sign, is so very destructive of ourselves and of our community. . . . The question we should ask ourselves is, What is there about our society that produces and supports the insensitivity of the police to the people whom they are supposed to serve?

Vol. 3, no. 1, on October 3, had a front-page article by Ron Diehl, which continued his coverage of consumer issues begun the previous year. The subject was "SpartanTown U.S.A.," a promotional event on campus by the East Lansing Chamber of Commerce that coincided with fall registration and illegally benefited from student-government funding. An inside article by Bertram Garskof, the psych professor who was Candy's and my new advisor, described his experiences auditing a freshman ROTC class, complete with its hysterical anti-Communist propaganda. The issue had no staff listing, but a mix of familiar and new names appeared on articles.

The next issue, two weeks later, listed ten people as staff—in no particular order, but Ron Diehl's name is first, Eric Peterson's is eighth, mine is ninth. A box at the top of the front page entreated people to "Confront the Warmakers, Washington, October 21." The lead article was a reprinted *L.A. Free Press* interview with Mort Sahl. The back page contained the return of LandGrantMan, in which John Palindrome is feeling overwhelmed by the proliferation of his duties as both a multiversity president and LGM. Once again he is visited by the spirit who had granted him his superpowers, and who now helps him share those powers with his "most trusted stooges": the vice president for account juggling, the vice president for crowd control, the vice president for propaganda and recruiting, the chief of the occupying forces, and the head of the association of virgin females.

On page 3 was my "An Open Letter: On My Living-Learning Experiences," which I had addressed to the instructors of the four courses I was taking. Obviously, my attempt to just settle in and be a normal student was putting unfamiliar strains on me.

In the letter, I praise my professors and courses for giving me an uncharacteristically satisfying academic experience. "I find each day of classes, each week of studying, a unified experience relatively free from the isolation and fragmentation that plagues practically all formal education—and all of this seems unified with the other commitments and concerns that make up my life." I go on to discuss my pleasant living situation and my unusually satisfying work-study job as an undergraduate psychology assistant, helping counsel introductory psych students through their first exposure to their chosen field. "I wonder how many other students would appreciate such interaction if they could find it, how many have other types of jobs or similar obstacles that prevent them from doing so—and how many are too intimidated by their schedules or by the structure of their educations even to think of the possibility." I lament the heavy course work that makes most students, and for a rare change was also making me, sacrifice other important interests and opportunities in order to meet the deadlines imposed by school. "This term, for once and at last, I really want to do all my work, but I don't see that I'm capable of it. I've already fallen so far behind that I worry even about taking the time to write this letter. But, generally, I'm not wasting time." I discuss the cutbacks I'd made in my activism, but also my continued need to remain in touch with my friends, to inform my academic learning with real experiences, with real people. "When one knows what one wants and needs, and one's commitments are designed to comprise the life one wants to lead, it is very difficult to make the adjustments sometimes required by a simple lack of time." But this is just the start of the real plaint:

I behave the way I do now because I have endured several trying years of defining myself, my interests and my world. Very little that I do seems accidental or unconscious, and it would be difficult to convince me significantly that I am making mistakes. As I have said, I like and respect your courses and recognize perhaps more strongly than ever the value of academics. But I also have strong and well-formulated ideas about how I should live, and if school happens to interfere with this I have no doubt which of the two I will favor.

I don't think there is anything wrong with this: it will take me a long time to get over the grudge I hold against Michigan State for letting me waste all the time I have spent finding my own academic direction, for forcing me to arrive with such difficulty at a tolerable compromise with the social environment here, for taking the role of adversary rather than guide through so many crucial changes I have undergone. Rather than criticizing me if I occasionally fail to perform up to par academically, I would caution you with the utmost respect to consider first the feelings of ALL your students confronting this leviathan from within the privacy of their own concerns.

I've made a temporary separate peace with the society, and I'm profiting from it. I am sure it will be temporary, however, simply because I don't trust the society to maintain for very long the conditions I'm enjoying, and because I don't trust myself to remain contented for very long. I've seen too much of both me and the society for me to expect us to remain in permanent equilibrium. Already I'm feeling the pangs that will probably lead to new involvements to save our social order from further decline; already I'm feeling concern for things my period of rest does not provide time to worry about.

Confronting Machines, of War and Otherwise

Prophetic words. Four days after publication of this epistle, Candy and I and a bunch of our friends joined thousands of others in Washington, confronting the war makers at the Pentagon, where we tasted our first tear gas but managed to avoid getting clubbed or arrested. Others did not do as well. We also dropped in on one of the first meetings of the Underground Press Syndicate and its new offshoot, the Liberation News Service, but we felt like visitors, not full-scale participants. On the way back to Michigan, my formerly dependable "Papermobile," my shiny blue 1964 Corvair, blew a gut on the highway. We spent three days in a motel in Maryland, acid-tripping with two friends while waiting for an engine rebuild. I now believe the job was sabotaged by the mechanics, but we were too stoned to know the difference. The new engine got us only as far as rural Pennsylvania, where we consigned the car to a wrecker. Friends drove down to pick us up and bring us back to East Lansing. Life was beginning to change, all right.

In the next issue, *THE American PAPER for Americans*, dated November 7, one of the new staff members, Jeffrey Snoyer, led the coverage of the Washington march with an article headlined with a mock postmark, "Washington D.C. Oct. 21, 1967—Prey for Peace." He told the story of the eye-opening and radicalizing experiences he had had on the march, intending to stay out of the fray and remain detached as a journalist, but finding himself inadvertently in the middle of a police riot and unable to keep his cool as heads were getting bashed all around him. He describes the orderly reaction of the crowd as the police repeatedly went berserk and started hitting demonstrators: "[E]ach time, there was an instantaneous uproar, then, in a few seconds, everyone would quiet down, no resisting. I was speechless whenever it happened—this was a heterogeneous, totally random group from all over the country, and such remarkable control was shown—I had never before seen a gathering of people as responsible and intelligent as these marchers were." He managed to avoid being arrested, returned to East Lansing to the disappointing, minimizing press coverage of the march, including LBJ's promise to "Keep [His] Commitment in Viet Nam," then picked up his mail and actually found a letter postmarked "Pray for Peace."

In the same issue, a front-page note to readers offered "our sincere apologies for the slow start we have had this year. There have been several complications including disorganization and bad breaks. Beginning this issue we will strive to be weekly and to provide you with a great deal of interesting, challenging features." The staff box named an editorial board of Ron Diehl, James Ebert, and Jeffrey Snoyer, and six other "paper people," of whom I was one. The issue included a two-page reprint from *Georgia Straight, the Vancouver Free Press*, giving details of that paper's harassment and censorship at the hands of civic authorities.

Vol. 3, nos. 4 and 5, *Take Me Out to THE PAPER* and *THE PAPER of Sisyphus Gathers No Moss*, published on November 14 and November 30, respectively, contained a trio of remark-able articles by some of us longtime staffers whose lives were in flux. The lead article of no. 4 was Larry Tate's story of having joined the draft resistance in the San Francisco Bay Area, where he had moved in order to begin graduate school at Berkeley: "BEFORE THE REVOLUTION; What to Do Till the FBI Comes, or Before the FBI; What to Do Till the Revolution Comes."

SIDEBAR 1

BEFORE THE REVOLUTION; WHAT TO DO TILL THE FBI COMES, OR BEFORE THE FBI; WHAT TO DO TILL THE REVOLUTION COMES
(by Larry Tate)

My feelings are as mixed as everyone else's but what I feel most strongly most often is that the Great Tradition [of Responsible Dissent in America] has failed, period. The American system can HANDLE dissent by denouncing it or ignoring it or (most subtly) praising it. We get to say what we want, they get to do what they want. Since all we ever do is talk anyway, we're happy to have had our say and feel morally free to crawl home and wait for the apocalypse.

I am truly sorry if I sound offensively melodramatic. I will just, now, try to tell you what I think is happening in America. As the overt violence of the South came home to the ghettoes of the North, the overt violence of Vietnam and the various other places we are Containing something or other is coming home to America. The difference this time is that the great white middle-class will not find itself putting down an alien people, but its own sons and daughters. Young people, dissenters, are getting to find out how it feels to have American armed might turned loose on them. And very possibly the darkest time in all of American history will be upon us.

THAT sounds melodramatic, surely. . . . The News media out there have been trying to make a big deal out of the fact that we didn't shut down the Induction Center; that we didn't shut down the Pentagon. Protestors Fail, they say again and again. Do they realize what they're saying? If we HADN'T failed, if we HAD taken over the Induction Center or the Pentagon, that would have been the Revolution. It would never have occurred to us to stress that we failed, since we knew there was no chance of our "succeeding." But the papers have to rush to reassure their readers that we didn't take the Pentagon by force, after all. Whew! Close shave!

SOURCE: From *Take Me Out to THE PAPER* 3, no. 4 (November 14, 1967): 1, 5.

At a rally in Oakland on October 16, simultaneous with rallies all across the country on that day, Larry, who previously had of course sympathized with the antiwar movement but had stayed somewhat above its rough-and-tumble, had turned in his draft card. "I suppose I ought to feel different now, but I don't. The main problem has been what to show for identification." He recounted how the huge crowd, which had prepared itself for another police riot, had suddenly found itself in control of downtown Oakland, with the police in disarray and unsure how to respond. Nevertheless, he concludes, "What I feel most strongly most often is that the Great Tradition [of Responsible Dissent in America] has failed, period" (see sidebar 1).

Glimpses of the Future

The next issue's lead article, "Sitting on a Cornflake, Waiting for the Burn to Come" (misquoting the Beatles' then-current "I Am the Walrus"), was by Dale Walker, the former advertising student who had now returned to Vermont to work as a draft counselor and was waiting for a decision on his conscientious-objector application (which did come through a few months later). Reflecting on the speed of social and technological change in modern society, he wonders whether it all represents any improvement in the quality of life, but admits, "I'm frightened about other things. . . . My American Hell is 1984. . . . The military-industrial Complex makes me uneasy. But Ronald Reagan and Shirley Temple scare me out of my wits. It is the union of government with the new technology's still-crude psychology of communications which constitutes a real threat. The CIA and FBI and the electronic police are a scary supplement, but they may someday become an outdated form of control. I'm afraid that the Madison Avenue–Hollywood–Washington Complex can create a dictatorship from within the mind."

━━━━━━━━━━━━━━━━━━━━━━━ SIDEBAR 2 ━━━━━━━━━━━━━━━━━━━━━━━

FROM "SITTING ON A CORNFLAKE, WAITING FOR THE BURN TO COME"
(by Dale Walker)

They are trying to rewrite history. . . .

America, within the next decade, may well create its own form if dictatorship. It may not appear as such because its methods may not be the traditional uses of the police and military for the suppression of dissent. It will feed upon the illusion of freedom, the reduction of fact to a question of public relations, and the manipulation of appetites (both as diversion and as substitute satisfaction). The coup from within will be effective because it will cut off debate at its source—the individual consciousness. . . .

We as a nation are looking at the same time for a hero, for a religion and for a pleasant way out of the imposed responsibility of the Electronic Age. We have the INCLINATION to become fanatic new converts of some new cause. We would like the feeling of release, I'm sure. We have the EXCUSE: war, the race riots, the rebelling youth, the linking of dissent with "crime in the streets." And we finally have the MEANS: a new freedom from democratic restraints, the marriage of advertising and politics, the evolution of public opinion as a creative art form. . . .

Our foreign policy is neither right nor wrong; it is merely a question of better lighting, a different profile, more make-up, a better choice of words or more repetition. The question of truth is becoming academic. And so will the question of freedom if we don't learn quickly to resist the sell. Right now we can thank God that Johnson was no movie star and that his Texas accent finally grew to nauseate us. Maybe we can thank the War, because it proved that reality still has a bite. But Johnson wasn't that good an actor (or he would have stopped being Johnson when it stopped working). But Reagan is. And whoever Big Brother will be, he will have a lot in common with Ronnie.

SOURCE: From THE PAPER of Sisyphus Gathers No Moss 3, no. 5 (November 30, 1967): 1, 4–5.

He discusses the decline in popularity of the Vietnam War and LBJ for all the wrong reasons, and the futile attempts by New Orleans mayor Jim Garrison and others to establish the truth about the Kennedy assassination in the face of the Warren Commission's whitewash (see sidebar 2).

In 1967, the Right Wing Revolution of the 1980s was almost visible in the distance, just over the horizon. I had no way to know how relevant Dale's musings would soon become to my personal experience. For my part, I was dealing with some more current dilemmas. My contribution to the trio of life-change articles was "The Dove Has Torn Her Wing" (using the title of the Jacques Brel song popularized by Judy Collins): "This weekend has sealed it, friends. Drugs are not, repeat NOT, the Revolution." A friend of ours, a sometime *Paper* staffer and a popular musician and guitar instructor around town, Bill Kahl, had been arrested for dealing and had pleaded guilty. It looked like he was going to be in jail a long time. Not only that, but one of the people whose money I had left in Southern California in my aborted drug-purchasing attempt the previous summer had decided to get even with me in the best way he could, by breaking into *The Paper*'s office (still the little house near the freeway in Lansing) over the weekend and trashing the place. The office was a wreck; the size of the issue, which was in fact the second anniversary issue, had to be reduced because of the emergency situation, and in his destructive frenzy he had broken the huge light-table glass that had become almost the trademark of *The Paper* to everyone who knew it intimately. And for what?

SIDEBAR 3

FROM "THE DOVE HAS TORN HER WING"
(by Michael Kindman)

"It's hard to be just angry. WE DON'T NEED DRUGS. HEAR THAT? WE DON'T NEED THEM!"

They don't make everyone nicer and wiser. They make nice people nicer and wiser, and send some nice people to jail. They turn some people into junkies, even when it's not junk they deal in.

WE DON'T NEED THEM! We shouldn't fight all our fights just for the drugs. We shouldn't sacrifice our friends, and then act like it's their problem when they get busted. Or burned, I guess. It's a stupid fight. . . .

You know what? I don't like the way this article is going, and I feel like smoking some grass and sitting and thinking about it so maybe it'll come later.

WE DON'T NEED THEM!! We can't be slaves to them!

Why can't they be legal, so we wouldn't always be hiding?

Drugs are beautiful! We should have them! We should change or destroy the society that won't let us have them, but we don't need them! Not at the expense of our hopes for making it in this world, not when they split us apart from each other and get us involved in useless fights, not when we offer our friends up on the altar of a steady supply. . . .

Once we've learned something from the drugs, or from the drug culture, we don't need them anymore. Once we've learned how we can regulate our moods and our talents, we don't need to be always doing something to our consciousness, in the hopes that we'll happen on something even groovier than we are already. We're it, and now we know something about how to be it. How many people know what it is to recognize a high that comes on by itself, without smoking or dropping anything? . . .

Consciousness can make us a generation of sages, and can make us effective in changing the course of our history. Drugs can't, not as long as we let ourselves destroy and be destroyed in the disservice of a dead taboo.

SOURCE: From THE PAPER of Sisyphus Gathers No Moss 3, no. 5 (November 30, 1967): 3.

I wrote about my involvement in the drug-dealing experiences of both men, and exclaimed passionately, "It's hard to be just angry. WE DON'T NEED DRUGS. HEAR THAT? WE DON'T NEED THEM!" Then I explained why (see sidebar 3).

That angry and hurt declaration turned out to be my last article for *The Paper*. It was left to others to put the office back together and rebuild the spirit. Which they did; *The Paper* continued publishing for the next several years, finally achieving some recognition and assistance from the university, and eventually was supplanted by a series of successor papers. But I had no part in it after my anti-drug article.

I'm unable to say what became of the man who broke into our office; I'm unaware of any charges ever being filed against him. For that matter, I'm unable to say what became of the marijuana trials of the ten people, including my girlfriend Candy, who had been busted in that same little house the previous spring. I remember Candy negotiating with her lawyer for something or other, probably a reduced-sentence plea bargain that didn't require any more time served than her original couple of days, and I guess the others did something similar. Somehow it faded away. Bill Kahl did serve some time in jail, did also try to escape to Canada at least once (I helped him get to Toronto one time, but I don't remember if that was before or after the bust discussed in my article), and did have a generally hellish time with his drug habit. He finally died of alcoholism and drug abuse in the mid-seventies. I also learned, long after the fact, of two others of our group of friends who overdosed on hard drugs during the seventies, and of course there were lots of busts for drugs. Myself, I've never had a bit of legal trouble for all my drug use over the years. Lucky, I guess.

CHAPTER 4

Moving to the Future

C andy and I continued trying to be normal people, but to no avail. Both of us were restless and scattered, unable to concentrate very well on our school and job respon-sibilities; real live people kept being more interesting to us. My friend Will came visiting from New York during December and, in a pattern that was becoming uncomfortably familiar, met a man he wanted to remain with. Candy and I also got on well with his new lover, Larry Babcock; the four of us decided to rent an apartment together when Candy's and my sublet ran out at Christmastime. We found a place in a middle-class Lansing neighborhood, a large apartment with a big attic playroom, and moved in in time for me to pay a quick visit to New York at New Year's.

When I returned in January 1968, it was time to decorate and play house. What would this phase of the experiment bring? Will and Larry, who was an art student, were busily making light fixtures and wall hangings, candles and makeshift furniture. The attic room became our tripping center and the place where the four of us could explore together sexually. Candy and I had a new crop of freshman advisees in our psych-department job. We developed the habit of bringing them to the apartment for meetings and discussions. The more daring of them became part of our tripping circle, and our tripping and our activism grew increasingly to be about pushing the limits of our sexuality and inhibitions. For this, we were receiving independent study credits in psychology.

It was winter, and we were without a car. I remember long nighttime walks through Lansing to where most of our friends lived, closer to campus, to bring this person or that back to our little den for a night of space travel and discovery. During this time, Candy was going through a personal trauma, remembering and assimilating the deeply painful memory of having been forced by her family to bear an unwanted child and give it up for adoption, shortly before Eric and I had met her. She spent many hours in the attic tripping room, shouting and crying out her grief in paroxysms I barely understood and could not penetrate with my concern.

In this context, in an LSD-induced haze one night during February, Candy and I decided that the time had come; we were done with East Lansing and had to leave. Now. But where should we go? We considered Northern California, where the back-to-the-land movement was picking up momentum and we might find some commune to join. But someone (was it Will and Larry? or was it some of our young advisees?) was interested in taking that trip with us, but only after winter quarter was over. We decided to kill the few weeks until that would occur by traveling to Boston, where that interesting underground paper *Avatar* came from, and see who those folks were. We were gone the next morning, having made minimal apologies and arrangements. Will and Larry left, too, heading for New York. Candy and I found ourselves hitchhiking with suitcases through what turned out to be a substantial blizzard, across southern Ontario and upstate New York, finally to Boston, where we showed up at the *Avatar* office late one afternoon. It felt to us like a great, magical adventure.

In those days, people showing up unexpectedly from halfway across the country didn't raise a lot of eyebrows. But our tale of having published our own paper in Michigan did make us relatively interesting drop-ins. We quickly took in the scene around us and saw both that we could learn plenty about this urban version of our kind of newspapering, and that we could offer them plenty in terms of skills and enthusiasm. But who were these people? How did it happen that their paper looked so different from all the others and affected us so differently?

Did Anyone Write These Words?

I knew that, in reading issues of *Avatar* as they had arrived in East Lansing over the months, feelings had been stirred in me that no other underground papers and, Lord knew, nothing else either had stirred. Besides dealing with the usual range of underground paper subjects—the drug culture, the Vietnam War and domestic resistance to it, ongoing changes in sexual mores, organizing in the black community to fight racism, all presented in a cool, New Englandy kind of way that I liked—*Avatar* also possessed qualities that seemed absent from the other papers. There were introspective writings, private journals of people obviously struggling to improve themselves, excerpted and made into examples for all of us. There were homilies on how to live in this complex age we were experiencing. There were astrology lessons, both theory and practical applications. There was advice of the most sweeping and the most personal kind from this Mel Lyman person, who seemed to be everywhere in the paper, and lots of different kinds of reactions to his writing from others. Sometimes, reading *Avatar*, especially reading Mel Lyman, I felt that the words had always existed somewhere, that no person could have written them, or that I had written them myself and forgotten. It was eerie.

Mel's first column, "To All Who Would Know," gives a taste of his hypnotic style, and his way of stating his truths in language that allowed space for absolutely no compromise:

To those of you who are unfamiliar with me let me introduce myself by saying that I am not a man, not a personality, not a tormented struggling individual. I am all those things but much much more. I am the truth and I speak the truth. I do not express ideas, opinions, personal views. I speak truth. My understanding is tinged by no prejudice, no unconscious motivation, no confusion. I speak clearly, simply, openly and I speak only to reveal, to teach, to guide. I have no delusions about what I am, who I am, why I am. I have no pride to contend with, no hopes, no fears. In all humility I tell you that I am the greatest man in the world and it doesn't trouble me in the least. I write here because I know that somewhere out in the jungle of the world there will be a few ears that can hear. The rest of you might just as well pass right now and write me off as an egomaniac, a madman, a self centered schmuck because I am going to attack everything you believe in, everything you cling to, I am going to shed light on your dark truths, I'm going to show you things as they REALLY ARE and not how you would like them to be. . . .

Something about this drew me in and caused me to start reevaluating everything I believed. I could see that other people who wrote for *Avatar* were also going through their own changes and reevaluations; some of the articles attempted to convey the spirit and the feeling of these changes. Others appeared to be personal journal entries by Mel and others that illustrated a kind of sensitivity and open-heartedness I found fascinating.

Here and there in *Avatar* were short poems, mysterious and moving — otherworldly poems, unsigned and unexplained except for the line, "from the box poems."

Every issue included numerous letters to Mel and his answers. Clearly, he was having an active dialogue with his readers, whose reactions in many cases resembled mine. Above the heading of the "Letters to Mel" section in one issue was a short poem, presumably by Mel:

> *We are here to become compassionate creatures*
> *Father forgive them, for they know not what they do*
> *I am totally responsible for all the ills of mankind*
> *I understand, and I will do all I can to help forever*
>
> *I feel all the pain in the world in my heart* AS *my heart*
> *All this and much much more is contained in the word compassion*
> *We are here to become compassion*
> *How are* YOU *doing*

All in all, *Avatar* made different use of the newspaper medium than anything we had seen or experienced. The results were compelling. And now Candy and I had arrived on the scene of the creation, or so we believed. It looked pretty much like a newspaper office to us, filled with the kind of people we were used to hanging around with. Where was the mystery part?

The Magic Sweeps Us Up

We were invited by a young couple working at the office to spend our first night, or longer, in their apartment on "The Hill." Where? It seemed that many, but not all, of the people working on *Avatar* also lived together in a commune elsewhere in town, on a hill in the mostly black neighborhood of Roxbury, where some of them owned houses and others rented apartments, and all of them took a lot of their guidance from Mel Lyman, the person whose energy so dominated *Avatar*. If you wanted to understand what was happening with *Avatar*, we learned, you had to get to know Mel Lyman and Fort Hill. We were game. A few days later, after spending time hanging out at the office and checking out people's living spaces in the evening, we didn't feel we knew any more about what made *Avatar* and Fort Hill run, but we were intrigued by the thought of staying on and becoming part of it all. Wayne

Hansen, one of the two listed coeditors of *Avatar*, was offering me a position as his assistant and encouraging us to move to Boston.

Candy and I decided to consult the *I Ching*, the Chinese oracle we were learning about from our hosts: "Work on what has been spoiled / Has supreme success. / It furthers one to cross the great water. / Before the starting point, three days. / After the starting point, three days."

The translator's interpretive note was hard to ignore:

What has been spoiled through man's fault can be made good again through man's work. . . . Work toward improving conditions promises well, because it accords with the possibilities of the time. We must not recoil from work and danger—symbolized by crossing of the great water—but must take hold energetically. . . . Decisiveness and energy must take the place of the inertia and indifference that have led to decay, in order that the ending may be followed by a new beginning.

Something magical was afoot here; we felt like the decision was being made for us. We stayed three more days, as the *I Ching* seemed to be instructing us to do, getting to know more of the people involved in both *Avatar* and Fort Hill (some people seemed loyal to both, and others seemed loyal to just one or the other; very complicated) and learning the rudiments of astrology, which all of them seemed to use as their chosen language when talking about people or the unfolding of events.

We traveled by bus from Boston to New York, where I pulled some money out of the bank to buy a used station wagon and we visited Will and Larry, who were setting themselves up in a small crafts shop in Greenwich Village. Then we drove on to Michigan, where we collected our goods and our cats and, as it turned out, a young boyfriend of ours who had been one of our psychology advisees. We gave the apartment away to some friends, terminated our jobs, and, incredibly, registered for ten units of independent study in psychology and social science during spring quarter, intending to write papers about our experiences in Boston. We said our goodbyes. I put a big box in storage in the basement of a collective house occupied by several of our friends. In the box was the entire documentary record of my years in college (my *State News* clipping file, class notes, and term papers) as well as my high school yearbook and a treasured collection of several hundred 45- and 78-rpm records; I never saw it again. Then we were off to Fort Hill, Roxbury, Boston, for who knew what adventures? It was early March 1968.

A Little Piece of History in the Front Yard

Fort Hill is named for the Roxbury High Fort that stood there during the American Revolution (the "first American revolution," as the current residents called it, anticipating, as they were, an imminent second one). A significant battle had been fought there, a victory for the colonial army, with the colonists on Fort Hill and the British across a small valley that now contained several major thoroughfares, on Mission Hill in Jamaica Plain. In commemoration of this mostly forgotten event, there was now a tall and mysterious-looking memorial, a brick water-storage tower with a roof that looked like a witch's hat, built during the Civil War era and itself now an ancient and unused relic. Around this tower was a small and little-maintained city park, and around that were rows of ramshackle houses and small apartment buildings, facing the tower from several adjoining streets.

The most ramshackle of the houses were on the closest adjoining street, an unpaved public way called Fort Avenue Terrace, with the tower practically in the front yards of places known as Number 1, Number 2, and so on, up to Number 6 Fort Avenue Terrace. There was even a Number 4½, set back slightly and looking just a bit newer than Numbers 1 through 4. Numbers 5 and 6 were two halves of a "semi-attached" house that also was a bit newer than the others. These were the houses of the Fort Hill Community. Not all of them were community property just yet, but they would be; you could feel it. Manifest destiny. There was also a row of three-story apartment buildings, Numbers 27, 29, and 31 Fort Avenue, around the corner—actually a short walk diagonally across the park—from these houses, in which members of the community rented additional space. Candy and I had stayed in a basement apartment in one of these buildings on our visit.

We quickly made the acquaintance of Number 4, which had been the first house occupied by Mel Lyman and his friends when they had made their way to the Hill in 1966. It was rented from a disagreeable elderly woman neighbor with whom there was a continuing rivalry, and it served as a sort of community center, with a big homemade table and benches in the dining room at which twenty or so people could be served. These large gatherings in fact happened often enough, as it was to Number 4 that the many visitors drawn to the Hill by *Avatar* would be shown, to have their own experience of the strange magnetism of these latter-day pioneers. The house was the home of Eben Given—the prolific, otherworldly artist whose drawings, handmade headlines, and visionary writings graced every cover and many pages of every issue of *Avatar*, bringing to them some of the windswept quality of his Cape Cod upbringing—and his Mexican American wife Sofie, who, we learned, had been Mel's teenage bride some ten years earlier. Sofie had seven children who lived there with them: four of Mel's (one by adoption, with a different birth father) and three of Eben's. A couple of other adults lived in the house as well, including Wayne Hansen, the coeditor of *Avatar* who had invited us to move to the Hill.

The other houses then owned by the group were more private, but almost as busy. Number 1 was the home of Jim Kweskin, long-time leader of the nationally known folk-music revival act Jim Kweskin and the Jug Band; his wife Marilyn; their two children; Marilyn's sister Alison; her husband George Peper; and their son. The basement housed a darkroom in which George produced his work as photographer for the community. The living room was a party space big enough for the whole community, fitting Jim's longtime role as entertainer and showman. But these days something was changing. Once Jim had been Mel's boss, having hired him into the Jug Band at the height of its fame to be its banjoist and harmonica player, at a time when Mel needed a steady job in order to meet terms of probation for dealing drugs. But the tables had turned. Mel's charismatic personality and uncompromising insistence on doing things his way had given him the upper hand in the power dynamic; the Jug Band, including such talented musicians as blues guitarist Geoff Muldaur and his wife, singer Maria D'Amato Muldaur, had run aground in this shifting momentum and had recently called it quits. Now Jim was working for Mel, handling business affairs for the growing community, running errands to help produce *Avatar*, and performing music with Mel and other community members only on those rare occasions when the mood was perfect and there were no obstacles or interferences. This was all more than mysterious to me, as a newcomer to the Hill and a long-time fan of the Jug Band's records. I was a bit starstruck by the presence close at hand of a famous musician, and confused by his willingness to give up his fame and career to follow this man Mel.

Number 2 was the home of David Gude, who had come into the group by working as recording engineer for Vanguard Records, the label on which the Jug Band (and many other famous folk-music acts of the day) had recorded most of its work, and on which the Newport Folk Festivals, those seminal events of the folk and folk-rock scene, had been memorialized. Mel had startled the closing concert of the 1965 festival by taking the stage after the famous Bob Dylan appearance in which Dylan let loose on the world the new phenomenon of electric folk-rock music, and attempting to calm the agitated crowd by playing an unannounced harmonica solo of "Rock of Ages." David had memorialized this moment by including it in the Vanguard album of highlights from that festival.

About a year later, David had been fired from Vanguard in a dispute with its owner over the proper way to mix and master the tapes of an album on which—who else?—Mel Lyman had appeared as a member of the backup band for a singer named Lisa Kindred. At Mel's urging, David had destroyed the original tapes, leaving only the version mixed the way Mel wanted—with Mel's harmonica and Lisa's voice given equal prominence. This unorthodox version was never released by Vanguard, and Lisa Kindred had moved to the West Coast for a career as a blues singer in nightclubs. Leaving his job at Vanguard had left David Gude free to move to the Hill and work for Mel, bringing with him his wife, Faith Franckenstein (daughter of the famous novelist, teacher, and political activist Kay Boyle), and their two children. Faith was also foster-mothering a young daughter of Mel's by Rita W., an acid-casualty friend from his days as a wandering musician and spiritual seeker. Also living with David and Faith in Number 2 were Faith's brother Ian, an aspiring actor, and a dreamy, rather melancholy woman named Melinda Cohn, some of whose poetry and other writings on her experiences as a mental patient had appeared in *Avatar*. Melinda was pregnant with twin girls, children of community astrologer Joey Goldfarb, whose columns explaining astrological theory and its application in the understanding of current events appeared in nearly every issue of *Avatar*. Joey lived across the way in Number 27. Faith had the idea of turning her house into a private school for all the community children. Ads had appeared in *Avatar* seeking a teacher to take on the task.

Number 3 was not yet in the family and was still occupied by others. Within months of our arrival, however, it would be purchased for the community by a couple newly moved to the Hill from Cambridge, Kay and Charlie Rose. Kay was one of the office workers for *Avatar*. For now, we would just walk past Number 3, pretending it wasn't there.

Same with Numbers 5 and 6. They were still owned and occupied by a family and tenants not involved with the community. But slow and careful negotiations were under way for them to be purchased. This effort would be successful in about a year, about the time the community would finally succeed in purchasing Number 4.

And there was Number 4½, the little house with the magical-looking garden in front. This was home to Mel and his current wife Jessie Benton, daughter of world-famous painter Thomas Hart Benton, an important chronicler of American country life and a muralist well known for his representational works produced for Franklin Roosevelt's Works Progress

Administration (WPA). Jessie had once been David Gude's wife, and in fact had a son by David a mere two months older than David and Faith's son; now she was first lady of Mel's growing family, and dark-eyed Jessie with the dark curly hair, and blue-eyed Faith with the long blond hair were the best of friends. They wrote poems for *Avatar* about their glamorous but trying lives as keepers of the spirit and the babies of the community; they oversaw the activities of all the Hill's residents and visitors with a loving kind of disdain, sort of a noblesse oblige; and they were fiercely protective of the privacy and quiet that Mel needed to do his work. Number 4½ was his retreat, his sanctuary from the confusion of community life, where he wrote on a typewriter no one else touched; where he kept his musical instruments and his cameras and his recording equipment in special rooms, special places where the mood would not be broken; where he occasionally guided individual members of his flock on life-transforming high-dose acid trips. Here Mel made his plans to expand his influence on the world and appear fully as the "world savior" he had already announced himself to be, in a small, self-published book, *Autobiography of a World Saviour*, that he now advertised regularly in *Avatar* and quoted freely from in his responses to letters sent to him by readers and seekers of all types, published in large numbers in *Avatar*. This was the home of "The Lord," as some on the Hill would have him be known.

CHAPTER 5

Settling In

None of this made much sense to Candy and me as we settled in from the highway, with our carload of household goods, our two cats, our young boyfriend along for the ride (who stayed only a few weeks), and our high hopes. And none of it would be made available to us just yet, either. We didn't get to live in the houses on Fort Avenue Terrace, or even in the apartments on Fort Avenue. There were other satellite houses and apartments farther away in the neighborhood, and we got to live in one of those. Rachel Brause—a slightly older, frumpy, but creative woman from New York who had somehow become a follower, but not a close friend, of Mel's—had an apartment a short couple of blocks away, with several bedrooms and a small sleeping loft. This was where we three were installed, at least until a more suitable place could be found. Rachel had endless stories about the Hill and its people, but we soon could see that she was not really an insider. With her house as our base, we set to work on *Avatar*, to the best of our ability. It was not easy to figure out what our role was.

Despite the intensity of community activity on Fort Hill, *Avatar* was headquartered in an old newspaper office in the South End, a rundown neighborhood of brownstone houses and commercial buildings close to downtown Boston, a ghetto populated mostly by blacks and hippies. Some of the people working on the paper lived in the neighborhood, which made sense to us as it resembled the way we had lived and worked in East Lansing, and some lived in Cambridge, where *Avatar* had originally been published, operating out of the offices of a music magazine named *Broadside*, whose editor, Dave Wilson, used to be involved in *Avatar* as well, but no longer was. We knew from reading the early issues in Michigan that *Avatar* had been at the center of a huge censorship controversy in Cambridge, another in the now-familiar series of attempts by local authorities to suppress the underground press on the basis of "obscenity." That attempt had failed here, as elsewhere, but in the process it had made *Avatar* a cause célèbre, giving Mel the opportunity to vent his literary spleen in wonderfully obscene tirades, and Eben the chance to create a notorious centerfold with the words "fuck shit piss cunt" in giant hand lettering—all these published as challenges to the would-be censors. The notoriety of the fight had helped increase the size of the staff and the circulation; had embarrassed the city fathers of both Cambridge and Boston, as well as the governor of Massachusetts, who couldn't resist getting involved; and had caused the *Avatar* offices to be moved to Boston in order to avoid the wrathful oversight of Cambridge officials. Now the office in the South End served as a sort of meeting ground for the various communities of folks interested in *Avatar*.

This was an entirely satisfactory arrangement for us, or at least for me, as a newcomer. I felt stimulated by all the different kinds of people who came through the place, and I had fun being in an urban environment close to the center of a city I found very interesting. Wayne set me up in a small office, where I had a rather empty desk and not a lot of responsibility. *Avatar* was published every two weeks, and all I knew for sure I would be working on was layout. Candy joined the team of typists who split time on a single IBM Selectric, laboriously producing the columns of justified copy for the paper in a tiny typeface. (Ironically, there was a full-scale Linotype machine sitting in the office, sort of a museum piece that, naturally, we didn't use.) We had plenty of time to explore the geography of the area, and to get to know the people we were working with. One day soon after we arrived, a guy named Abbie Hoffman showed up at the office, full of the idea he was promoting for a Youth International Party that would storm the upcoming Democratic National Convention in Chicago that summer. Most days were quieter than that.

But troubles had by now been brewing among the several factions of the loose alliance that was *Avatar* for a long time. From the very beginning, staff members allied with Mel Lyman and Fort Hill had insisted on a very major role for Mel's writings and his perfectionist standards in the production of the paper. This role had been controversial from the start. (Mel's first column, "To All Who Would Know," excerpted above, took up a whole page in the first issue but had accidentally been printed with a line omitted, and Mel, through his lieutenants, had insisted on reprinting it complete in the second issue, over strong objections.) At the same time, these high expectations had established a standard of graphic excellence that had helped make the paper's reputation. It had certainly pulled us in. But now, nearly a year after the start of publication, the tension was intensifying. Mel's steadily increasing volume of writing—columns with such challenging names as "Contemplations," "To All Who Would Know," "Diary of a Young Artist," "Telling It Like It Is," and "Essay on the New Age," as well as a voluminous flow of letters to and from Mel and other miscellaneous writings—had set both a tone and a personality for the paper that attracted many of its readers, and had caused the rest of the staff, those who were there for reasons of political organizing or to establish a more general voice for the counterculture, to feel forced into a corner of their own creation. They increasingly had the sense that Mel and his supporters were just using them and the forum of the paper to give voice to Mel's words, and that, given the chance, Mel would soon crowd them out completely.

Splitting the Baby in Two

Shortly before Candy and I arrived on the scene for our first visit, starting with Issue no. 18 in February 1968, this tension had resulted in a novel compromise: *Avatar* would henceforth be published in two sections: a full, metropolitan-size news section, with political and cultural content resembling that of more typical underground papers (although its visual appearance had the airy grace for which *Avatar* had become known), and a tabloid-sized inner section that contained Mel's writing and the other output from the community, including Eben Given's rambling, meditative "Journals of John the Baptist" (sometimes known as "John the Painter," "John the Wasted," or "John the Waspegg"); astrology columns by Joey Goldfarb and others; and pictures and poems of the Fort Hill children—usually with a drawing of Mel by Eben on the cover and numerous photos of Mel inside. Only the outer news section was being produced in the South End office. The Fort Hill tabloid section was being produced by Fort Hill people at Fort Hill. Candy and I had not yet entered that company in any real way.

This was part of the reason I had little work to do in my empty new office adjoining the layout room. Another reason was that I was unclear whether anyone wanted me to do any reporting or writing. Wayne's longtime coeditor, Brian Keating, was in the process of relocating back to his hometown of New York to undertake publishing a separate edition of *Avatar* there, so logically I thought there would be lots of work to do—but I couldn't find it, and nobody told me. I was given little sense of direction, and as a newcomer in town, I didn't feel I had any grounding for directing others to do anything. I remember writing one piece of commentary (I don't remember the subject) that got as far as being typeset and pasted up, until David Gude, visiting the office one day, read it in its pasted-up form and simply tore it off the page, saying, "This is bullshit," or words to that effect. I didn't challenge him, didn't know how the rules worked or where the lines of authority lay, but I soon learned that this was very much the way events tended to unfold around *Avatar*. The Fort Hill behavioral model gave full authority in the moment to whoever was feeling something strongly enough to take a risk and act, no matter what action he or she took, independent of any prior system of morality. This rule was not usually put into words; only the behavior of the actors revealed what the rules were.

But both Candy and I were certainly captivated by what we saw and felt going on around us. We were both reduced emotionally to childlike conditions by the complexity of the life and subculture we had stumbled upon. We had both expressed this situation during our first visit in letters written to Mel that were published in consecutive issues, nos. 20 and 21, during March, about the time we arrived to stay. They give a good idea of our respective states of mind at the time. Mine, "Note from a Visitor," was laid out alone on a page with one of Mel's "Telling It Like It Is" columns:

What a waste it would have been, thinking how I came all this way and did not talk to Mel. But I sit here and I'm glad. Why am I glad? I am afraid to talk to him. I am afraid to go in and say, "Hello, I'm Mike and I came to talk to you," with big exuberant exclamation points.

But I sit here all nervous and glad to retreat unnoticed to a corner.

There is greatness in the next room . . . too much for me to touch without getting burned bad, burned good. I never in my life met anybody who I did not feel as if I could crush, who I was better than . . . didn't need to listen to.

I can't touch Mel . . . I just listen to low talking in the next room.

This is so good. People rap about how Mel is on an ego-trip, blowing himself up with self-importance. He is important, but it's not for him that you say it. You say it for yourself . . . he doesn't need it. He knows.

We all need Mel.

Candy's letter was quite different from mine, although, like mine, it also gave Mel the kind of full and easy access to the deepest aspirations of the reader-writer that he loved to work with and respond to. She wrote:

Dear Mel,

You have always touched me and reached me and probably stood watching over me during all those times when I tore my guts out and screamed and clutched because I was nothing and there was nothing but blackness and emptiness everywhere. I could take nothing though much was offered. I could only ask for love because I couldn't take it. Every moment was one quake and I was surrounded. And I surrendered. I was nothing but a scream—and so was the universe. I knew that I was the universe and I didn't want it. This was the nature of the battle.

I started writing this letter because you spoke so closely to what I had gone through and I don't seem to know how to relate my past to my present. I have rejected dying while alive and have chosen peace but I don't have it completely. Peace? If there were any forever it would have to be everywhere. The hands are always ready to grab your guts again. I know them so well. I always end up shrugging and saying "on with it" and denying a whole bunch of it but I also keep being haunted and I can't decide what to make of it. There, that's it! Is there ever an end to it? To anything? This is the always and forever question—is there an absolute? Do I need an answer? I keep living without one but I'm writing this letter and I may bake bread or move up to the hill or do lots of things before I ask the question again. So it's shelved for a while and it will haunt me intermittently, perhaps until I die, as in "What is the ultimate use."

I love you.
Candy (Cancer)

The Only Absolute

Mel loved talk like this, as he had made clear in previous responses to such letters. He responded to Candy with one of his favorite aphorisms, "The only absolute is 'MORE.'" In other words, don't push for meaning or clarification of the questions that bother you most deeply; just keep doing "what's right in front of you," step by step, and meaning and understanding will come in their own time. This aphorism turned out to be one of the basic tenets of Fort Hill philosophy, something we would come to have drummed into us over and over in a thousand different situations; but sometimes it was hard to see it being practiced, even by those most in a position to be doing so.

For instance, Mel was even now, in the same issue in which Candy's letter and the response to it were being published, declaring a major change in the structure of the game, for reasons that were certainly not clear. A note at the front of the tabloid section of no. 21 announced that Mel would no longer be writing his several columns for the *Avatar*, although the paper would continue printing and reprinting articles already written. He would no longer write answers to letters; these would be answered by his "friends."

On the next page, under a picture of Mel with impossibly wide-open eyes, looking haggard and world-weary, was his "Declaration of Creation":

I am going to burn down the world
I am going to tear down everything that cannot stand alone
I am going to turn ideals to shit
I am going to shove hope up your ass
I am going to reduce everything that stands to rubble and then I am going to burn the rubble
and then I am going to scatter the ashes
and then maybe SOMEONE *will be able to see* SOMETHING *as it really is*
WATCH OUT

On the next page, his "Telling It Like It Is" declared,

The only thing I know is that people have to get together and love one another. I mean really FEEL each other. People have to look so deep inside themselves and inside of each other that they see the SAME GOD, and we can't stop looking until we KNOW we SEE it. Just knowing it's there isn't enough because it might NOT be, you've got to look until you're OVERWHELMED with how much it is there. . . . Please, whatever you do, don't bless ME. . . . . CURSE me! HATE me! Do SOMETHING real!

For some reason, Mel was raising the stakes of the game he was playing with his readers. He was sounding like an angry and impatient teacher who thinks his students are defective. The next article illustrated another consequence of his mood. Mel and some of his followers had been invited—and according to advertisements had accepted the invitation—to conduct a Sunday-morning service at Arlington Street Church, one of the prominent Unitarian Universalist churches in Boston. The date had been kept, but not by Mel. Eben Given, David Gude, and another of Mel's longtime friends had shown up instead, to a mixed reception, as exemplified by two letters from members of the congregation, one harshly critical and the other warmly favorable. In a third letter, to David, the minister who had arranged the event complained of the awkward situation that Mel's absence had created for him.

David's answer is especially revealing of the outlook from Fort Hill at that moment. He begins by calling the minister a "hypocrite." Mel Lyman, by contrast, is "Truth," "Life," "Love," "Consciousness," and "Christ." He then explains why the minister wasn't told about changes in Mel's itinerary, and even attempts to extract some guilt from the minister: "But neither Eben, Bob nor I could say any of this to you or your congregation because YOU DIDN'T ASK. If you had sincerely wanted to know we would have sincerely answered you. You say, "But I did ask, I asked you twice." But there was no depth to your question and so there was no depth to the response that we gave you. And it did hurt Eben and Bob and me, believe me."

A second letter from the minister good-naturedly tried to bridge the gap between the two views of what had transpired; this was clearly a doomed undertaking.

A few pages later, under a picture of himself sitting on the grass on Fort Hill, Mel gave his own version of what was happening in a letter to "Dear Readers":

I want you to understand what I have been trying to do in *Avatar* and why it is time for me to do something else. So far I have only written what I HAD to write, I have been driven to say certain things in certain ways and I have said them, and now I am no longer driven. If I continued my writing in *Avatar* it would only be because I felt obligated to all the people who are following what I say so closely but in all honesty I must tell you that I no longer have anything to say, at least not in the present form. I have come, I have delivered my message, and now I am taking my leave. Those of you who understood me need no more words from me. Those of you who RESISTED me will find me in other people. I am the Truth, wherever, however, in whatever form it appears. As Mel Lyman writing in *Avatar* it appeared very simply and very directly.

In the "Letters to Mel" section, along with Candy's letter, a young man describes his coming to believe that Mel is indeed God, but asks whether others could be God as well. Mel's answer speaks to the "spirit that is":

The world we see, hear, touch is one aspect of that spirit. The world we feel, sense, aspire to, is another aspect. I am totally at home in both, in me they are the same. I seek to unite them in others. I am God only in the sense that I am one with the spirit of God. The Father is in me and I know Him well. He is my leader as I am yours. I can only lead you to Him and then you are me. I am building a road into the wilderness, all other roads lead to my road, it is the LAST road, it BEGINS at the crucifixion.

The next page was devoted to yet another untitled, unsigned declaration of Mel's faith, this one faith in loneliness as "the sole motivation, the force that keeps man striving after the unattainable, the loneliness of man separated from his soul, man crying out into the void for God, man eternally seeking more of himself through every activity, filling that devouring need on whatever level the spirit is feeding, the arena of conflict, be it flesh, thoughts, aspiring to ideals. . . ."

The issue ends with a final note from George Peper: "On Fort Hill, with Mel Lyman, our principal task is communication, to master every instrument necessary for us to become totally conscious in what Mel describes as 'the World of Sight and Sound.'" He explains that henceforth work in films will supplant and "contain" all the previous expressions of Fort Hill in music, newspapering, and other media. He says that, for more than a year, Mel and others have been working and experimenting with inadequate film equipment, and solicits donations of equipment, funds, skills, and any other items that can be put to good use, in order to help them move into full-time work in their new chosen medium.

Imagine our surprise, Candy and me, invited to move from Michigan to Massachusetts to work on a newspaper we admired tremendously, in the belief that meaningful work was waiting for us, only to find ourselves walking into this turmoil of change, polarization, and redirected energies, in which it wasn't clear whether there would even be a newspaper for much longer. We didn't know what was happening, and we certainly didn't feel in control of our destinies at that point. We didn't have any way to predict what would happen next, and we weren't necessarily feeling very aligned with each other either.

CHAPTER 6

Two Different Worlds

I was noticing that the people on the *Avatar* staff who were based in Boston and Cambridge, rather than Fort Hill, were feeling rather threatened by the sense of impending change, in ways I didn't quite understand. I liked those people, and as I heard their versions of the story, I found myself sympathizing with them and becoming confused about where my allegiance was. There was, for instance, Ed Jordan, also known as Ed Beardsley, who had been involved in the artwork and production end of *Avatar* from its beginnings, and who was the central figure in a collective household around the corner from the office, very reminiscent of my collective household in East Lansing. Ed would wonder aloud, "If Mel is God, then what about me and all of us, aren't we God, too?" This attitude didn't make him popular with the Fort Hill folks, but the question seemed like a good one to me. Besides, I enjoyed working on layout with him, with his irreverence and his zany sense of humor.

And there was Charlie Giuliano, who had known Mel for years, since the early days of psychedelic experiments at Harvard and later in Waltham, around Brandeis University. Charlie seemed sincerely interested in building *Avatar* into an alternative news source, and seemed hurt by Mel's putting him on the spot to declare his allegiance this way or that. I felt for him in his ambivalence.

Candy, however, had no such problem; she was clearly prepared to align herself with Fort Hill and its needs, whatever they would turn out to be.

Also, much more than Candy, I was enthusiastically absorbing whatever details I could about the lifestyle of the people we were getting to know. This activity filled a fair amount of my available time. I had never before thought much about the concept of "voluntary poverty," although the idea had had a certain vogue for a while among New Leftists. But here at Fort Hill, even though the phrase was seldom used and would not have been universally accepted as a description of what was happening, clearly most of these people, one way or another, had had access to lots of resources and privileges and had chosen to forego the easy life in favor of a life of principle that happened to be taking place in a poor neighborhood, in rundown houses, following a set of priorities that did not include money and what it could acquire as the primary goals. Looked like voluntary poverty to me.

Having lived for several years on relatively small amounts of money (mostly gleaned from my share of my father's rather small estate, and from Social Security income that was available to me from the time he died until I turned twenty-one), but not having had to struggle to support myself, and having been able to remain in school as long as I wanted without worrying about where the tuition would come from, I now felt somewhat flush and embarrassed by comparison to the Fort Hill folks, with their flocks of children and their patched clothing. At the same time, many of them had given up lucrative careers to live on the Hill, and they did own their houses and have some pretty nice material possessions around them. The houses had a tattered, almost magical elegance about them that fascinated me, that seemed to transcend and transform the mundane modesty of the furnishings.

And there was a certain self-righteousness to the self-imposed frugality of Fort Hill. An article in February 1968, in the local newspaper of Roxbury's black community, the *Bay State Banner*, described the attitude of this band of new white immigrants into the mostly black neighborhood: "[L]iving without financial security is an important part of the philosophy of the Hill People. They believe that what they need they will find, and that their security comes in living for the moment at hand. 'This is a way of life where you do away with everything except the moment,' says Faith Gude. 'The secret is to lose everything. I have to become everything that's going to happen. And then, the thing that happens is you. That's not something you can lose.'"

On the other hand, when I had mentioned my misgivings about my own financial status to Wayne Hansen, he had let me know there was another, seemingly less voluntary side to the apparent poverty of Fort Hill. On that side of the issue, the lack of material goods was a real problem to be overcome, and the idea was to take advantage of whatever was available from whatever source and to make the most of it, because the need was enormous. Again, this left me confused.

I did enjoy participating in the rituals of salvage and make-do that had developed under the circumstances. People from the Hill were in the habit of going to the open-air produce market that filled Haymarket Square in downtown Boston on Friday evenings. The usual practice was to go shortly before the market was to close, scout out where the surpluses were at the various stands, and make bargains for case lots or damaged goods just before they would be discarded anyway. Frequently, we would fill entire cars with huge amounts of inexpensive or free food and would be greeted as heroes upon returning to the Hill. Other types of inexpensive food, less dramatic but no less fascinating, included bulk purchases, dented cans, and day-old bread. We were clearly demonstrating the well-known and observable principle at the time that America produced huge, wasteful overabundances of everything, and that there was more than enough to go around if you knew where to look.

I learned also that the abundant supplies of building materials used to refurbish the houses on Fort Hill were also to a great extent the result of this waste and surplus. Boston's neighborhoods at the time were filled with abandoned houses, factories, and other commercial buildings—sometimes burned out in fires and not rebuilt, sometimes just abandoned for urban renewal projects that hadn't happened, or for who knew what other reasons. In any case, plenty of usable construction material—frequently very attractive Victorian-style decorative moldings, stained-glass windows and mirrors, built-in cabinetry, and similar wonderful stuff—was available for the taking, and the Fort Hill men took frequently. Sometimes a slight risk would be involved if you had to break into a building to get the goods, but often doors and windows were open; all you had to do was walk in and start dismantling. I found this occupation perfectly fascinating. I had a longtime interest in architecture and construction, had in fact nearly chosen to study architecture rather than journalism in college, and had already taught myself some basic construction and remodeling skills. Hooking up with this gang of folks who had a living laboratory of half a dozen houses that they were constantly renovating, making beautiful homes for themselves, and doing it with free, salvaged construction materials—well, this was just wonderful, as far as I was concerned.

I also had a strong desire to become familiar with the culture of these people. In my mind, and in my prior experiences, the reason for choosing to live low on the economic ladder was to free up more of one's time to enjoy the pleasures of friends and of life generally. Now, here was a group of fascinating and accomplished people, many of whom were musicians, poets, visual artists, historical philosophers—all of whom had an interest in astrology, spiritual and occult matters, and personal growth. They all seemed to be in relationship with each other, and they were raising more than a dozen kids together, with more on the way. There certainly was plenty to do to fill up the time when one was not working a nine-to-five job. I did what I could to pick up on all these activities, but curiously discovered a certain sense of pressure, of time scarcity that kept most of the folks on the Hill from being comfortable just hanging out and sharing all these pleasures. By contrast, I found the people in the South End contingent of *Avatar* more available for this kind of pursuit, but generally less accomplished and interesting. Another paradox.

Waiting for the Revolution

I was not the only one struggling to make sense of these subtleties. Numbers of people around *Avatar* were considering whether or not to move to the Hill; people were examining their own lifestyle choices and were looking at the demands Mel was making on the people close to him, and at the implied possibility of becoming closer to Mel if they could adapt their lives to these demands. And there was all this talk in the air of the Second American Revolution, a sense that history was moving faster and faster, that we were right on the verge of becoming active agents in one of the big historical changes, and that there wasn't time to dawdle with these little personal decisions.

Wayne wrote an article for the front page of the news section of *Avatar* no. 22, entitled "Gospel of the Good News." In laying out the page, we set an excerpt from the middle of the article in large, bold type, almost a headline itself, above a picture of Mel deep in conversation with Owen de Long, one of his close friends, a former Harvard doctoral student in international relations with connections to the Kennedy family political establishment. Owen was Fort Hill's candidate for president "in about ten years," Jessie would say.

Wayne's headlined excerpt read, "Men are coming, great men who are among us now, who will unite the extremes in to an unshakable structure, unshakable not because of its suppression of the will of the people, but because of its perfect expression of that will. And from the present bewilderment, anger and chaos a true will must arise to replace that shadow of will, that vacant greed which is now called the will of the people by the clumsy dwarves who stumble where graceful giants ought to stride."

He writes about his experience working for *Avatar* and for Mel Lyman—being besieged by offers of help and advice, but only really appreciating the contribution of those who immediately recognize the need and go right to work, without fancy talk or good ideas about how the work could be done better. He talks further about the need to sacrifice one's personal vision in preparation to do the larger work demanded by the needs of history. He makes comparisons to the time of the original American Revolution, "when a few men, who most felt the need for independence from the nation which held the great force of this nation in check, took those first steps to risk that necessary separation," and created the format for the rest of the population to follow. "[I]n our time, our revolution shall differ only in that it is a subtler thing, for the need is of a deeper nature, but its fulfillment shall be manifest outwardly at every level, in life-style, in politics, in science and in art. Men are coming, great men who are among us now. . . ."

He compares the struggle to that going on in the black community at that time, and among young whites and politicians who recognize that change is inevitable and necessary. He predicts a season of political polarization and the preeminence of the likes of Nixon and Reagan, even though Robert Kennedy and Eugene McCarthy could do more to unite the country if it was ready for that. "Among politicians, Robert Kennedy is the avatar," which means "the bridge between heaven and earth . . . pure spirit manifested in everyday reality." And this, "if you'll allow me, brings us right back home." With Mel no longer playing an active role in producing *Avatar*, "*Avatar* will not be less Mel Lyman. No, there will be more Mel Lyman in every issue, whether by that name or not, for there is no separation between us from where you stand. God is not dead, my friend, just now more uncreated."

He concludes optimistically with a clear statement of Fort Hill's recommended moral stance: "The greatest change humanity has ever known is upon us. Each of us must give up what we have to further that change. Evaluate your thing in that light, check it genuinely, and see what falls away and what remains. Bring what remains to us, and together we shall recreate the world."

A Season of Riots

Helping Wayne put together this front page and the rest of Issue 22, I experienced a clarity and sense of purpose that cut through a lot of the confusion I had been feeling. I felt envious of Wayne, who clearly had been living close enough to the source of all this inspiration to be able, himself, to express some of its values in terms that I found inspiring and meaningful. And change certainly was coming quickly. The "Good News" issue of *Avatar* was dated March 29–April 11. While it was still on the streets, Martin Luther King was assassinated in Memphis. I was in the *Avatar* office working on layout for the next issue when the radio announced the news. Cities across the country exploded with rage and unleashed racial tension. In Boston, a mayor named Kevin White and an incomparably popular black entertainer named James Brown (I was struck by the coincidence of their names matching their roles in the political drama) collaborated brilliantly to keep community tempers in check by canceling a live concert

Brown was to perform and televising it instead. Boston, well known as a racially polarized city, rode out the season of riots unscathed.

On the front page of the next *Avatar*, we featured an essay Wayne had written—two days before King was shot—on the impending and inevitable social upheaval in America, under an oversized picture of a political demonstration on Boston Common, and alongside a headlined quote from Lyndon Johnson, of all people, who had just announced he would not run for president again: "We have talked long enough in this country about equal rights. We have talked 100 years or more. It is time to write the next chapter."

Wayne's essay discusses the tendency of society to offer diversions to the mass of the population, meaningless rivalries and preoccupations that keep people from confronting the deeper internal questions, all based in people's own desire to avoid what is real. He concludes:

> They will not wake up until all they have is gone. The choice today is simple, give it all up today, or have it all taken away tomorrow, there's little difference, it feels the same either way, he who tries to hang on until tomorrow is just putting off the inevitable.
>
> Yes, go out there and hang out in the street for an afternoon, look at the faces, if you can stand it. Then go home and look at yourself. Where do you stand in the midst of all this and what difference do you make? Precious little, I'll wager. Better get to work on yourself, my friend, become a tool of what's happening, it's willingly today or like it or not tomorrow. Nobody gets left out, there's not a way out of this one. We're all up against the same wall, and the poison gas we've been making all this time has now completely filled the air in this little room, and in a moment we shall all have to breathe.

This rather Calvinist message drew the connection between the steamrolling events in the world at large and the emerging philosophy of Fort Hill. Wayne seemed to be saying it was time to give up the hedonism and self-indulgence that had characterized the flowering of the hippie culture, in favor of a more purposeful and self-aware participation in the reshaping of history. I took this idea seriously, though rather innocently. It seemed to give meaning to the path Candy and I had chosen, in contrast to the aimlessness of our last days in East Lansing and of our arrival in Boston. It put the struggle for relentless self-improvement that seemed so central at Fort Hill into a context that made sense to me, joining it with the political struggle with which I had so long identified. And, it gave Candy and me a new belief to share. This would come in handy soon, as the pressure mounted on all the Fort Hill hangers-on to make a choice.

Incorporating as Mel

The magazine section of Issue no. 22 had featured the "United Illuminating Charter," a document created and handwritten by Eben Given and signed by him and eleven other mainstays of the Hill, declaring formally their solidarity with Mel and his purposes. This was accompanied, behind the scenes, by legal incorporation into several interlocking companies, to promote the community's media work, to hold the real estate, et cetera. (The name "United Illuminating" was borrowed from the power plant in New Haven, Connecticut, whose big red neon sign

"United Illuminating Company" lit up the highway on the route between Boston and New York.) Eben's charter reads:

> Dear Friends,
>
> I have written a charter that includes and defines everything I know. I have lived a thousand years in a day and a night, talked with you all, been still, slept, gotten up again and written—knowing through the sharpest pains of my own inadequacy and limitation—the greatest that I have ever known in all my life—that what must finally be written and signed by all of us today, can only be written as my first picture of Mel could only have been drawn—when the last resources of my own separate talent had been exhausted—when I had seen so deeply, and suffered so deeply that there was finally nothing left of me to draw WITH. And the picture came.
>
> It is not my own private pain. I suffer it as each of you has suffered it and will continue and must continue to suffer it. It is the pain of being consumed, of having every last vestige of separateness between that which we have felt and come to know more deeply than all else, which is incarnated forever, for all of us in Mel which is our heart, burned away that we may be free that HE may finally be freed. It is the pain of being born.
>
> Today we simply incorporate ourselves as Mel Lyman. The definition rests with all that we can attest together as the larger embodiment—through us to all men—of the purpose and the practice of one pure man. Today is our birthday—March 21st, 1968.

The charter includes a horoscope for the moment of signing, high noon of the spring equinox, with the sun high in the sky in Aries and the moon in Capricorn. Not coincidentally, Mel's chart also had the sun in Aries and the moon in Capricorn.

The same issue included a lengthy transcript of a conversation between Mel, David Gude, Jim Kweskin, and Joey Goldfarb—a far-ranging conversation that occupied four pages of the magazine under the heading "The Structure of Structure." In it, Mel elucidates for the others his way of keeping his behavior present in the moment, always feeling where the energy is attempting to move, and always ready to drop whatever prior notions he may have had in order to respond to the immediacy of the emerging situation. This idea, later summarized by Ram Dass in the phrase "Be here now," was rather novel in 1968, and Mel engages in some mind-warp on the other three in order to get them to understand it. He goes on to relate this to the purpose of the Fort Hill Community as he experienced it, contrasting the community to the general population, who did not yet know how to respond to Mel's way of reflecting back to them their own limitations:

> [L]iving amongst men is like cosmic asthma, it's hard to breathe, and I want to BREATHE. So I have to expand the structure of man, the mind.
>
> . . . . There just is NOT ENOUGH LIFE on the planet EARTH for me. And I don't have any other choice, I've got to LIVE here.
>
> . . . . [T]he world is a dead shell on the outside and a volcano on the INSIDE. I want all that feeling OUT, I want it all AROUND me, I want it so thick I can SWIM in it, I like it THAT STRONG. Now for most people that is sheer agony, for ME it's joy. It CANNOT GET too strong. And the more structures I break down the more life there IS. That's what most

people are AFRAID of, to have their structures broken down, because it HURTS. Breaking down structures is PAIN, but there is no other way to make room for more life, and I FEEL that pain, more than ANYBODY, because I am capable of so MUCH life, I KNOW that life, I FEEL it, it is ME, so I feel the limitations more than anybody does, which is why I'm gonna DO something about it, I don't have any choice.

. . . . [A]lready I've cleared a LITTLE space, I've broken down the structures of the people on the hill, almost to the point of being comfortable. I'll never STOP doing it, because I can't IMAGINE too much life.

Along with Wayne's two articles on the front pages of *Avatar* nos. 22 and 23, this conversation gave still more urgency and meaning to the challenge to become part of the community, as quickly and full-heartedly as possible. We certainly didn't want to be left out of the opportunity to travel with Mel as he brought more life to Planet Earth. But I, at least, had misgivings. Mel liked to speak of his people as his creation, who in turn served as his mind and his hands, the mechanism to bring his message to the world. I didn't really know what would be involved in becoming part of his creation.

There's Always Room for Sacrifice

The magazine section of Issue no. 23 illustrated again the depth of personal exploration and sacrifice that were implied by Mel's ethic and the Hill's attempt to manifest it in the world. After completing the United Illuminating charter, Eben Given had spent several days in New York helping Brian Keating fix up an office space in a Soho loft, from which to publish the New York edition of *Avatar*. While he was there, Eben had painted a mural of the tower on Fort Hill, in order to bridge the seemingly great gap between the Hill and the New York outpost. Then, after reaching a state of ecstatic creative intimacy with Brian, he had told Brian to destroy the mural by painting over it, because he had realized his reasons for wanting to create it were no longer relevant or valid, and had returned to Boston. Brian had done so, leaving only a star hanging in a blank sky as a reminder of what had been. The magazine contained this story in the form of an exchange of spacy, visionary letters between the two of them, explaining to each other the mysteries of what they had just experienced, accompanied by a series of photos George Peper had taken of Eben creating the mural.

Reflecting again in yet another form the idea Mel had discussed in "The Structure of Structure," that each moment needs to be free to create itself in its own way, Eben concludes his letter by saying, "It's always seemed to me that the greatest truth of a picture is had in the painting of it—what it took to make it happen, what it felt like at the time. That's the part we don't see. There are museums and they are full of pictures, but they're frozen and lifeless nearly all of them. A bad movie moves with more life than most of the famous paintings of history. But we didn't make it either. The life was there at the time and the picture is gone. The great picture is made with what we gave and so much more and most important, it must endure."

I remember that my gut reaction on reading this for the first time was to mourn for the beautiful lost picture. But the correct reaction, in terms of the lessons we were being encouraged to learn, was to forget the picture and instead to celebrate the bond that had grown between Eben and Brian, and the growth they had each experienced in the process.

Candy and I were struggling, internally, to get with the demands of Hill life. In this mood, we participated in the next escalation of the struggle to make the Hill and the planet a more suitable home for Mel.

Issue no. 24 was a kind of declaration of spiritual war by Mel on the others who felt they had some claim to the paper but were not ready to move into the routine of sacrifice and blind creativity that he was advocating. Abandoning the two-section format, the larger news section wrapped around the smaller magazine, without discussion, Mel instructed those of us producing the paper to reintroduce the earlier format—a single, tabloid-sized paper. This time, though, there was a difference. This issue had an uncompromising uniformity that allowed no space for any other viewpoint. On the front page was a large, bold headline (I remember setting the press-type and thinking, "Whoa, the shit is really going to hit the fan now!"):

You know what we've been doing up here on Fort Hill? We've been building a wall around Mel's house out of heavy, heavy stone.

This headline was wrapped around a picture of a Fort Hill work crew celebrating after raising a heavy lintel stone over what would become the entranceway of an eight-foot-high stone wall around the front garden of Mel's house, Number 4½. Such an action had become necessary because some visitor to the Hill, unaware that the red signal light meant to stay away for the moment because Mel was working, had managed to make it as far as Mel's front door at a moment when his presence wasn't welcome, and Mel had become furious. For weeks, all the available energies of the Hill's men had been devoted to learning masonry skills and building the wall, big and strong and impenetrable. The raising of the lintel was the symbolic completion of the task, and another opportunity to celebrate the unity of effort it takes to accomplish such work. Thus, four more pictures of the stages of the process appeared on the next two pages of the magazine. But that was just the beginning.

Rounding out the issue were the following features, in the sequence listed:

- a letter to Mel from a teenaged admirer, broken-hearted at the announcement of his departure. His answer compares himself to the sun, shining brightly during the day but disappearing at night, giving us the opportunity to find its light in ourselves;
- a photograph of the sun in a recent eclipse;
- a page devoted to one of Mel's "Diary of a Young Artist" passages;
- a large photograph of Alison Peper in a moment of exclamation during a recent LSD trip guided and photographed by Mel;
- a letter from Mel to David Silver, a local television programmer—who had interviewed Mel and whose work Mel admired—congratulating Silver on a recent program for its ability to convey real feelings and experience through the medium of television;
- five more full-page pictures of Alison, expressing a variety of moods at various points in her trip;
- a reprint of one of Mel's "To All Who Would Know" columns: "How much you feel is an exact measure of just how alive you are. Every time you feel pain it is just that much more of you that is trying to be born. Every time you express what you feel it is that much

more of you that has just been born. We are constantly surrounded by the opportunity
to give birth to more of ourselves . . .";
- twelve more pictures of Alison's trip, each one occupying an entire page; and
- a final picture of Mel on the back cover.

Like It or Lump It

What appeared in Issue no. 24 could only be interpreted as Mel and the Hill thumbing their
noses at the other members of the *Avatar* alliance, challenging them to get with the Hill's
program or split. I remember finding it embarrassing taking the new issue out on the streets
to sell, somewhat at a loss to explain to readers why the format had changed so dramatically,
so suddenly. But I guess I accepted the challenge, another early opportunity to face difficulty
and let go of old ideas in Mel's name. I found it more difficult to confront the likes of Ed
Beardsley and Charlie Giuliano at the *Avatar* office, quite unable to help them understand
why their contributions were being undermined in this way, quite unsure of what would
A meeting was called to bring together the Hill community with representatives of *Avatar*'s
"downtown" component, which took place around the big dining table in Eben and Sofie's
house, Number 4. Candy and I attended—our first chance to share in the process of the Hill
in one of its moments of yearning for a collective solution to a problem. I was struck by the
intensity of the conversation and the emotions being exchanged, and by the seeming contempt
in which the non-Hill people were being held. There seemed to be no room for compromise.
I remember saying something about the difficulty of a person, such as myself, who didn't
necessarily feel ready to commit to what was being asked, intending my comment to also
apply to others in the same situation, and being cut off by Jim Kweskin, who angrily spat
out, "Michael, you just want to know that you're all right," as if I were foolish and wrong
for wanting that. At the same time, I could feel Candy, next to me, moving closer and closer
to the Hill position and attitude, ready for anything and unquestioning of her willingness to
give up whatever was necessary.

That meeting was our first encounter with Mel in the flesh. He sat around the table with
the others, obviously feeling intensely whatever it was that was making this crisis necessary. At one point he insulted Jessie, telling her she was full of shit for some comment she
had made. I was struck by how vulnerable he seemed, how his rather high-pitched voice
sounded like that of a very young person. I had trouble integrating this with my notions of
Mel the Great Man. Finally, the meeting ended, in anger and frustration, with no resolution
whatsoever. I don't know how there might have been resolution, short of the "downtown"
people saying they didn't really want to publish a newspaper after all and were now willing
to give up their private lives and move to the Hill to do Mel's bidding. They clearly weren't
ready for this. As Mel stomped out of the house, I attempted to introduce myself to him,
wanting a personal encounter of some kind with him, and blatantly violating the rule he had
recently been teaching about, to stay in the present and leave behind prior ideas of what
might happen. He was in no mood to talk and brushed past me to leave.

An *Avatar* Here, an *Avatar* There

As a result of that meeting, the Fort Hill mainstays encouraged those of us who were equivocating to declare our allegiance to Mel, and everyone on the Hill was encouraged to rededicate ourselves to building him a more perfect media laboratory in which to develop his people and his films. From the "downtown" point of view, the meeting was further evidence that Fort Hill had declared war on them. They proceeded to pull their resources together to publish a non–Fort Hill newspaper, not exactly using the name *Avatar*, but not not using it either. They laid out a newspaper that looked a lot like the metropolitan-size news section of *Avatar*, but that had no flag on the front page. On page 2, in reverse, was the familiar *Avatar* logo, so the page could be held up to the light to reveal its true identity.

In addition to the confrontation of wills that the fight over the name represented, there was a question of whether Fort Hill had a legal right to deny use of the name to the others, based on who had been a member of the board when, and similar details.

For his part, Mel was furious. In retaliation, he ordered his "boys" to take action. On the night the new, renegade *Avatar* was delivered to the South End office, which we from Fort Hill had all but abandoned to the other staff, and after that staff had gone home for the night, several carloads of us from Fort Hill raided the office, stole all the printed copies, and took them up to Fort Hill, where we locked them in the small room at the base of the tower. (I remember having to simply put my own free-press, pro-Constitution values out of my mind in order to tune in to the adventurous spirit of the raid and the camaraderie of working with the other Fort Hill men on something that was obviously important to them. Was this a sellout or a betrayal, or was this an oblique way of protecting the truth? I was confused.) The next morning, the downtown staff had its turn to be furious, and there ensued several days of negotiations and angry recriminations between the two factions. In a final deception, the downtown staff were invited to Fort Hill ostensibly to work out a deal. While representatives of the two sides were meeting, others of us from Fort Hill took the papers out of the tower and sold them for recycling. A coup!

Both sides consulted lawyers, and the legal situation was worked out in favor of the downtown staff's keeping the rights to the name *Avatar*, while Fort Hill retained the right to use the word "Avatar" in other name forms. Between June 1968 and the end of the summer, the downtown staff published, on their own, about half a dozen issues of a completely reconstituted *Avatar* Vol. 2, whose contents were more typical underground-newspaper material—antiwar, countercultural stuff, music reviews, commentary on public events. During the same period, Brian Keating's New York *Avatar* also continued publishing, at least for a while. And on Fort Hill, after a few months' break, there would soon appear the first of four more-or-less quarterly issues of a newly manifested magazine version of Mel's *Avatar*, under the name *American Avatar.* In other words, for a brief period, there were three different *Avatars* all publishing simultaneously.

CHAPTER 7

Time to Get a Life

With the fiction of working on the Hill's newspaper set to rest once and for all, it was time for Candy and me to figure out what else to do with our lives. She readily moved into the sisterhood of Fort Hill women, with their flocks of babies to tend and their men to take care of and make fun of. I knew then and know now little of what went on among them, other than that they were ingrown in their little society and traditional in their viewpoint. I found it strange to watch Candy, who had been as rebellious and modern a woman as I had known, relax into traditional roles and dress, but that was the Fort Hill way. The "battle of the sexes" was very much alive at Fort Hill.

The men, too, had a tight little society based on traditional roles and expectations, but I found it far from easy to merge with them. I had never had any notion whatsoever of living out a traditional man's role of any kind, didn't even have concepts like that in my mind, and certainly had no plans of playing a traditional blue-collar man's role, performing physical labor and hanging out with the boys, complaining about the women but otherwise accepting my limited lot in life. To a surprising degree, in the absence of the occasional uplift provided by association with some work of creation inspired or produced by Mel, this was all there was to the day-to-day life of the Fort Hill men. I was also surprised to find how much racism was expressed in the everyday conversation of the men—how little regard they had for the black community that surrounded us, and even for the occasional black seeker who would come visiting or looking to join the community. Sexist language was also the order of the day; the standard phrase indicating a tiny measurement was "cunt-hair," as in "Move it to the left just a cunt-hair." I had never heard or used such talk.

My first real experience with the men's society had come when I was drafted into working on the stone wall around Mel's house while we were waiting for the newspaper wars to resolve themselves somehow. I was pleased enough to be learning a bit about cutting and setting stone. I asked one day, during a fairly demanding work session, why Mel wasn't out there with us, building this wall around his house that he had asked for. The answer, delivered in a tone of condescension, gave me one of the basic Fort Hill truths: Mel didn't work on these demeaning physical tasks because he spent his time and energy keeping us all together by doing his creative work—taking care of our spirits, as it were. Well, that made vague sense to me, but it didn't tell me much about what I could expect for myself. That lesson was to come in other ways.

In the course of working on the wall, I made the acquaintance of Richie Guerin, another of Mel's closest lieutenants. Richie had come to the Hill as a dropout from architecture school, the son of a construction worker from New York, and a bit of a musician, too. He was young and brash, and talented in both design and construction supervision—a valuable asset to Mel as he imagined rebuilding the row of houses on the Hill into a multimedia production facility. The stone wall was just a necessary preliminary project. Richie was also one of the Hill's astrologers; when I learned that the graceful hand-painted charts I had seen in a number of people's private spaces had been created by him, I decided I wanted one for myself and asked for a reading. I found Richie easier to relate to, as a fellow Taurus, than Joey Goldfarb. Finally, we had our evening to discuss my chart.

Too Many Planets in Aries

I already knew that my sun—representing my essential self—was located in Taurus, a sign that denotes stability and consistency, determination, and earthbound, practical wisdom; and that my moon—representing my personality and my way of presenting myself to others—was in Aries, a sign that suggested inspiration and creativity, individuality, and unpredictability. (Remember, Mel's sun was in Aries.) This combination indicated an interesting counterpoint, a dynamic tension between my Taurus "center" and my Aries exterior. In fact, I already had developed a certain fear of what my chart would reveal because one of my first experiences of astrology, something I had in common with most visitors and newcomers to Fort Hill, was from a book called *Heaven Knows What* by Grant Lewi, one of the most successful popularizers of astrology to Americans over a period of several decades. His book enables readers to do quick, approximate personal horoscopes based on the aspects formed by the various planets in their signs, using simplified charts in the book that eliminate virtually all the calculations required for more precise horoscopes. *Heaven Knows What* focused significantly on the 144 possible combinations of sun and moon positions, as indicators of the main dynamics of the personality. In my case, Taurus-Aries was described as a sign of great power, likely as not to walk all over other people accidentally unless held in check by a conscious discipline, which Lewi recommended if there was going to be a productive life and the possibility for relationships in which the Taurus-Aries person would not dominate. Coming out of my East Lansing phase, in which I had become a fairly charismatic personality among my circle of friends, some of whom had had difficulty with that characteristic of mine, I was taken aback by this view of my potential and made to feel I had to watch myself carefully. But I was ready to learn more about myself through the lens of astrology, and hoped Richie could guide me toward positive directions of growth.

I learned from Richie that in addition to my moon, I also had my three inner planets—Mercury, representing communication skills and mental ability; Venus, representing sensitivity and appreciation of beauty and harmony, basically feminine values as those are traditionally understood; and Mars, representing assertiveness and physical energy, basically masculine values in the traditional understanding—all in Aries. Altogether, I had four of ten planets in

Aries, all but overwhelming my sun in Taurus. (In most popular versions of astrology, the sun and moon are considered "planets," but the earth isn't counted because that's where we're looking out from.) Richie didn't point out to me that my four planets in Aries equaled the number of planets Mel had in that sign, or that among members of the Fort Hill community only Owen de Long also had four planets there, including his sun and moon. He didn't emphasize my inherent birthright in the realm of creativity and self-direction. I learned instead that I had lots of personal potential but a difficult path to follow, with lots of aspects indicating limitations and challenges, and that my own impulses could not be trusted much because of the way my energies were balanced one against the other. I had a nice tight square, an aspect representing difficulties and limitations, between the moon and Mars, both strong in Aries, and Saturn in Cancer, the planet representing discipline and an ordered life, located in one of the signs where it expresses most poorly. This aspect suggested a continuing struggle between creativity and spontaneity on the one hand and worldly responsibility on the other, an aspect suggestive of a personality that needs guidance from others.

Somehow Richie looked at the array of my planet placements and aspects and synthesized it into a single injunction: Writing was clearly not the occupation for me; practical, physical work would serve me much better. I don't know how he found this in my chart. Certainly it wasn't simply that my sun was located in Taurus, frequently considered a sign of builders and bankers, but also of artists and sensualists. Historically, Taurus has produced huge numbers of prominent writers, philosophers, artists, and composers—including Shakespeare, Brahms, Kant, Marx, Freud, Tchaikovsky, and Dali—as well as numerous political leaders and prominent entertainers. I think he may have been extrapolating from his own chart and his own experience as a person with both sun and moon in Taurus, and Mercury in Aries, living in the shadow of the dominant personality of Mel Lyman.

Or he may have been interpreting my chart more closely, using a method of interpreting the meanings of particular planets in a chart based on the individual degrees of the zodiac where they are located. This method, the "Sabian symbols," was a popular interpretive tool at Fort Hill. The symbols had been developed over several decades by Marc Edmund Jones, one of the most significant modern astrologers, who distilled the meanings of the 360 rough images delivered to him by a psychic medium into a cogent method of applying these images in individual chart interpretation. Jones didn't publish his version of the symbols until 1953, long after the symbols were adapted and popularized by his protégé, Dane Rudhyar, in *The Astrology of Personality*, which was published in 1936 and revised and reissued in 1963, and became one of the seminal texts in the reinterpretation of the ancient science of astrology to incorporate contemporary values and psychological understanding. Rudhyar called the resulting method "humanistic astrology," and it became the dominant trend in the field during the 1960s.

Rudhyar's book was undergoing a vogue on Fort Hill about the time I arrived and got my reading from Richie. There was one little glitch in using Rudhyar's book in interpreting charts, however. The recommended method for interpreting degree symbols, as given by both Jones and Rudhyar in their respective versions of the Sabian symbols, was to round each degree of the zodiac upward to the next whole number for purposes of interpretation. Thus, Mel's sun position of three degrees, four minutes into the sign Aries would be rounded up and interpreted as "fourth degree of Aries"—"two lovers strolling through a secluded walk," in Jones's version, a symbol of personal expression without the burden of responsibility. But on Fort Hill, it was a given that Mel was God, or at least a fully realized man, most likely an avatar for our age. And, lo and behold, there it is, in the third degree of Aries: "a cameo profile of a man in the outline of his country," as Jones put it—and Rudhyar's description is even more precise: "the individual self as an avatar of greater collective reality." Mel's moon position, on the other hand, made sense if rounded upward. Six degrees, 39 minutes into Capricorn became "seventh degree" Capricorn: a hierophant, or prophet, "leads a ritual of power," explained by Rudhyar as "gathering together of the power of a group to one purpose and into an individual will. 'Avatar'-ship." There was that word again. In Fort Hill logic, then, Jones and Rudhyar must be wrong; the correct way to interpret the symbols must be to round the numbers both upward and downward, as dollars and cents are rounded both upward and downward to estimate whole dollars. This forced misinterpretation of the Sabian symbols, extrapolated from a misinterpretation of Mel's sun degree as that of the avatar, became the basis for all the interpretations of charts of people on Fort Hill. Of course it was a long time later before I saw through the scam.

For the moment, I learned my chart according to an incorrect method of interpretation, and lived with a sense of my sun degree—for example, as a "symbolical battle between swords and torches, "an image of the struggle between might and enlightenment," quoting Rudhyar's version of 17 degrees of Taurus, when it really is Taurus 18, whose symbol implies continual spiritual renewal, a woman "airing a linen bag through a sunny window." In a time when I was trying to take such symbols and subtle messages deeply into myself, this misinformation encouraged me to feel afraid of my potential, and to seek guidance from others rather than from my inner self. This happened to mesh well with my state of mind at the time—hesitant and confused after my long experiment with drugs and political activism, anxious for new role models and priorities to present themselves—and with the community's need for willing, compliant servants. Richie's declaration that physical work and not writing was the path for me fit this need, too, and came to me with the force of law, albeit mysterious and incomprehensible law. I assumed it meant my future would be filled with more work on the Fort Hill houses, and I prepared for that. I also started becoming accustomed to being "Michael Taurus," the name that would be used almost every time I was mentioned for the next several years. So much for the balancing influence of my Aries planets.

A Place of Our Own

A little bit of East Lansing business remained to be taken care of, and that first spring on Fort Hill, I handled it. Having given up my student deferment and lost my bid for conscientious-objector status, I had to do something to guarantee that I would not be drafted into the army. I had received a notice to turn myself in for a physical. At Fort Hill I had heard several stories of people who had given themselves physical injuries or had managed to fake mental incapacity in order to be disqualified at their draft physicals.

This tactic sounded like a good deal, and the Boston Army Base sounded like a good place to use it, unlike the draft centers in Detroit and New York, where I could otherwise have chosen to turn myself in for a physical, but where it was reportedly difficult to get away with any kind of goofy tactics (Arlo Guthrie's "Alice's Restaurant" notwithstanding). On the appointed day, I woke up and took a small dose of LSD to make sure I would be a little disoriented and uninhibited. I wore no underwear under my clothes, so they would either have to make me go through the physical-exam line naked or with long pants on; they chose the latter option. For the written exam, I declared I had five years of college, and proceeded to answer nearly every question wrong; I scored 3 out of 100. I volunteered that I was both gay and a Communist, and was unresponsive to the psychological interviewer. He made it clear I was not the kind of person they were looking for. The result was a 1-Y classification, ineligible for the draft for reasons of *physical* disability, except in times of declared national emergency, which Vietnam wasn't. I did not get the 4-F I was hoping for, but it was good enough.

Candy and I were feeling the need to create a Fort Hill house of our own, and were itching to get out of the apartment we were sharing with Rachel Brause, two blocks from the Hill, where the urgent growth of the Hill seemed far away and somehow became abstracted by talk. We wished for a place close to the main rows of Hill houses; what we found was a ground-floor apartment at 49 Beech Glen Street, facing the opposite side of the hilltop from Fort Avenue. The apartment was really just a two-minute walk up a path to the Fort Avenue Terrace houses, but it felt like another world. Our challenge was to make it feel like a Hill house. We settled on a few housemates, other newcomers to the Hill like ourselves, and painted the rooms in bright colors. I don't know what we were using for money.

I imitated Eben Given by building an oversize table for the kitchen using salvaged material. I asked David Gude if I could borrow a rasp to smooth the edge of the table, a task that would take about an hour, and was hurt by his reply that he didn't like to lend tools "off the Hill." I was also hurt by George Peper's failure to respond to my request for a print of a picture of Mel to use in our house. Every house on the Hill and all of the satellite apartments I had seen had prominently displayed on their walls large black-and-white photographs of Mel, usually full-frontal portraits of him staring directly into the camera or looking spiritual and exemplary; many were from a particular series shot by George and used frequently in *Avatar.* I wanted a picture for our new house, too, but I had a different idea. In George's darkroom one time, I saw a contact sheet with a shot of Mel standing in a circle with several of the other men, obviously planning a work project. I liked its democratic feel and asked George if he would make a print of that for our house. He simply said, "Hm, strange choice," and never made the print or mentioned it again.

One night, inspired somehow to try to put my current thoughts and feelings in writing, I stayed up late working at the big table, writing a group letter to all my friends from college and elsewhere, trying to convey the intensity of what I felt we had discovered at Fort Hill. I headlined it with a line from Paul Simon's song "America," off the new Simon and Garfunkel album, *Bookends*: "Michigan seems like a dream to me now." The truth is, most everything seemed like a dream, and I could not easily tell what was real and what wasn't, but in the letter (of which I do not have a copy) I remember being explicitly insulting and abusive of some of the people to whom I was writing, whom I perceived as not having something as important or powerful going on in their lives as I now had. I wanted to impress them with the significance of what I was doing, and to inspire them to move closer to it, but I think all I did was turn them off and make them think I was crazy. Char Jolles, my journalist friend and colleague from college, wrote back a succinct postcard: "Oh, come off it. Love, Char."

Soon, both Candy and I were feeling restless again and unsure how to move closer to our destinies. We settled on a plan—either individually or together, I don't remember—to ask Mel to guide us on acid trips. Like the astrological reading I had coveted and finally received, this was one of the initiation and transformation rituals of the Hill, which one sought only when one was ready for anything. The pictures of Alison Peper in the controversial "stone wall" issue of *Avatar* exemplified the wide-open emotional state that was considered the goal. I think Candy was probably ready for anything, as that notion would be understood by the Fort Hill people, and her trip with Mel bonded her closely to him in a childlike way (anticipated by her letter to him in *Avatar* a few months earlier); she came home feeling closer to Mel and to the Hill than to me. She was feeling independent and I was feeling fearful. We quarreled. Trouble.

CHAPTER 8

A Purpose Finds Me

My trip with Mel a week or so later made it clear I was feeling needy and unsure, but probably not ready for anything—though I would have liked to be. As I was ushered into Mel's private space, he showed me his instruments, explained a bit about how he worked with them, and said something about how I would learn to work with tools and learn more about the process of creating—and eventually feel myself compelled to do real creative work—sometime in the future. It was one of several cryptic and off-putting statements he made that night. But as I lifted off on his very good acid, lying on his floor looking to experience something familiar from my previous acid trips, assuming that Mel would do something amazing when he was ready, he just sat in his chair and watched me, and I felt small and unimportant. Mel apparently experienced me that way, too, and just waited until I came around enough for him to talk some sense or some wisdom into me. When he did, it was about work. He told me that when he was younger, he had had to do a great deal of heavy physical work, even though he didn't have the constitution for it, and that with the kind of body I had (I'm quite small but sturdy; at that time I was also soft, but had the potential for strength) I really had no excuse to not be working and making money. This wasn't quite the elevated message I was waiting for, but it was definitely, and literally in my eyes at the time, a "dancing lesson from God," to borrow Kurt Vonnegut's wonderful phrase. I left Mel's space with a purpose, a bit let-down but ready for something, if not for anything.

I stumbled home in the early morning to tell Candy this little bit of news gleaned from what I had hoped would be a major transformative experience, but to my surprise, something else was happening at the house. Our gay friends Will and Larry, from Michigan but now in New York, had shown up for an unannounced visit while I was tripping, and what a weird time it was to try to be nostalgic with them. We just couldn't pull it off. I found myself telling them (I don't know where this came from, because it had not been said to me in words by anyone) that the gay explorations I had shared with them the previous year were just not relevant to me anymore, that that wasn't my life now. Since they had come to express concern for our welfare, probably curious and a bit horrified after the letter I had sent to them and all my other friends, this was not the warmest message for them to hear, and they left rather disillusioned and worried about us. Candy wanted nothing further to do with them, and I couldn't see myself maintaining the friendship given my current beliefs and the all-encompassing nature of Fort Hill life, even though I felt a deep loss. Many years passed before we communicated again.

I was ready to get on with my new life as a worker. Another Fort Hill man and I found jobs in a furniture warehouse a short walk from the Hill, in Jamaica Plain. Was this the future? At the age of twenty-three, I had never held such a job before. People on the Hill were fond of saying you couldn't skip any steps in your personal growth. I guessed I was making up for lost time.

Candy was also making up for lost time, in her way. She was becoming more and more a part of the inner social scene on the Hill, and finding me more and more irrelevant. Before long, she moved into Number 1, Jim Kweskin's house. Soon she was involved with one of the men and took to offering me pointed little lessons about Hill life. I was quite unhappy. I returned to her a shirt I had given her that she had left behind when she moved out, along with a short note critical of her "social climbing"; that comment briefly became the joke of the Hill gossip circuit.

The warehouse job soon got old, and I quit to do some favors for my relatives in New York. Both my mother and an aunt needed help redecorating their houses, and helping them seemed like an opportunity to make money "for the Hill" in surroundings a little more familiar and less intimidating. It also gave me a chance to visit my old girlfriend, Carol Schneider, on our home turf and update her on the latest strange developments in my life. She was between terms at Albany State and getting restless again herself. I made several long trips to New York over a period of weeks. I told Carol she had "always" been "my wife" despite our respective adventures apart. That comment came from someplace I couldn't identify, that didn't even feel like me talking. All I know is that as the words came out of my mouth, I somehow felt more like a Fort Hill person for saying them.

Then I got a phone call in New York from one of the people living in my apartment on Beech Glen. She told me Mel had announced that the Aquarian Age was about to begin, on the date of a particular astrological configuration that most others didn't interpret that way. It was time to "come home," she said. I went "home" on the appointed day and watched the sun rise over Fort Hill at the beginning of the Aquarian Age. I think it might have been September 15, 1968, when the sun in Virgo was conjunct Pluto in the early morning. (Pluto in astrology symbolizes cycles of death and rebirth, thus all deep change and unpredictable turns of events; it was one of Mel's favorite planets and concepts, and in that season, lots of planets were moving through Virgo and making aspects to Pluto and each other.) Nothing seemed any different, but I was back in Boston, single and unemployed.

The Whole World Is Weeping

That summer, while I had been learning to be a blue-collar worker for the first time, and while I was getting used to living on my own, without my lady and in a rather harsh psychic environment, the nation as a whole was also going through some rather severe trauma. Robert Kennedy, by some accounts the front-runner, and by any account the most exciting candidate to replace the retiring Lyndon Johnson as president, had been assassinated in June, in the moment of winning the primary election in California.

The resulting leadership vacuum had given the Democrats virtually no choice but to nominate their lackluster vice president, Hubert Humphrey, as their standard-bearer. At the same time, the Neanderthal response of the civil authorities in Chicago to the presence of thousands of antiwar and countercultural demonstrators (Abbie Hoffman's Yippies) outside the Democratic convention there had focused the world's attention on the convention and the accompanying riots. The now-familiar phrase "The whole world is watching" was born, and the whole world was saddened and disillusioned by what it saw. At the same time, the Republicans chose to resurrect their most morally questionable, but somehow inevitable, candidate, the eminently hatable Richard Nixon, to oppose Humphrey. At Fort Hill, the writers and editors among the inner circle, and some of their friends, but not me, were busily at work planning the newly conceived *American Avatar*, a magazine-format reinvention of the magazine section of the earlier *Avatar* newspapers. The first issue appeared in October, in a tabloid-sized form on slightly better than newsprint paper. On the cover was a cow-eyed picture of a beautiful teenaged woman, Paula Press, who had gravitated toward the community and been wooed by Mel to be one of his many part-time "wives," but who had somehow found it in herself to resist his overtures and was attempting to be just a normal person in the community. She was living in my household on Beech Glen. Most of the issue was devoted to the community's response to the political events of the summer, mixed with a declaration of intent for this new form of the publication, under the headline "When Was There Greatness in History?"

> We, the old staff of the original *AVATAR*, are back once again. We are here under the Name, *AMERICAN AVATAR*. Before *AVATAR* fell into the hands of vermin we had a purpose, we are back with that purpose. Before AMERICA fell into the hands of vermin it had a purpose, we are back to fulfill that purpose. We are sick to our stomachs of counterfeit *AVATARS* and counterfeit AMERICAS, we are here to do something about them both, to DWARF them with a REAL standard, leadership.
>
> The *AMERICAN AVATAR* does not cater to any specific sociological group, do not confuse us with "hippies" or "liberals" or any of the other current titles designating qualities of understanding and areas of congruity. We belong to no group, party, race, religion, or fervent hope. We are on the side of what is right and that, my friend, changes every moment. We will represent the right side on every side even if we are wrong. . . . When was there greatness in history? When a man lived up to his ideals in face of the strongest opposition, there is greatness only when there is courage and courage relies on no security other than its faith in God. All great men had that courage and had that faith. It makes no friends, it transforms the world. We are here to transform the world and we begin with ourselves. We are a group of very courageous individuals. We will gladly face anyone who dares to challenge our devotion, and if they are men they will join us, and if they are boys they will follow us unwillingly.

This is clearly Mel's writing style, although the piece is unsigned. The next page features Eben's hand-drawn version of the phrase "The whole world's watching," followed by a photo of Mel looking stern, under another unsigned piece that asserts that the "Democratic system" is outdated because the people operating under its banner no longer carry the vision represented by the idea. "Democracy" can now survive only through force, but "real men" can reawaken the spirit of democracy by the force of their conviction.

This is followed by several articles of commentary on the events of the convention and the summer by some of the community regulars and a few of their intellectual friends. My personal favorite is by Skip Ascheim, a Cambridge intellectual who had relocated to the newly acquired house, Number 3 Fort Avenue Terrace, just in time to watch the convention on the television there, in the company of most of the enthralled and horrified community. His article "All Kinds of Stuff Passing through Your Body All the Time" was written shortly after the convention in July:

> Tonight Friday there's a silence from Chicago. What's happening there, are the kids in the streets, are the spades still lying low, is anyone dead? The distance wasn't there while the convention was going on television. For four days we were in the future. The country grew even more in those four days than it did during the assassinations. It was an unbearable amount of self-revelation to take; it had to blow.
>
> No one but the muse of history could have orchestrated the week, the event grew and shaped like an organism that knew its job. Theatre putting on life, with a script from the deepest channels of blood in the race. A very few of those delegates really knew where they were; probably not many of the demonstrators either. Certainly not the cops. Yet it was all there, the right emphasis to each gesture, everyone coming in on cue. And always in the wings, the unmentioned threat of the black uprising, a constant suspense.
>
> . . . . We have finally begun to use television, or rather television is beginning to understand its own use in this period of the nation, to connect us all to the same place and time, to coalesce our separate wills into energy with which to act upon the event. To focus us sharply enough to inspire the action. One of the very last gasps of the old order will be the shock of losing the myth of objectivity in television reporting. It is going fast.

He goes on to discuss the interaction between live television coverage and the unfolding of the Vietnam War and the public's reaction to it, then continues:

> The old ideology will give way when there is new life to replace it; that's what's happening in television. The cameras follow where there is life, and life, in revolutionary times, favors what is being born. Sometimes, as in Chicago, there is so much birth going on that the proud life spirit rides mercilessly over what is dying.

The Media People Are the Message

Skip's article offers a succinct statement of Fort Hill's view on the interplay between media and history, which was really the subject at hand on Fort Hill. Mel saw himself as creating a company of diversely talented people in a variety of media, and he saw that company as playing a key role in the phase of history that was then unfolding, in which a return to basic moral values and idealistic reinvention of the society would dominate the public awareness.

As a lowlife observer of all these trends from my newly acquired status as a worker and hanger-on to Mel's scene, I found what was happening here all very stimulating and heady. Some of what was published in the new magazine was familiar to me from my earlier days under the influence of Marshall McLuhan's ideas, and some was so new I hardly knew how to begin thinking about it. But there could be no doubt Mel was thinking about it. He made it explicit in an article entitled "Some Enlightening News":

> There is a great illusion going on in this country and that is the illusion that the govern-ment is supposed to provide leadership, supposed to set the example to the people of how to live. That was only true when government was new, when it was great, when the greatest people in the country were the statesmen. Today the great people are the musicians, the actors, the filmmakers, the COMMUNICATORS! The spirit that begat this country is playing a new instrument.
>
> All things begin as inspiration, on the highest level, and must necessarily descend to the needs of the lower levels. A truly successful song is born of the heights and is only fully realized when it has reached the dullest ears of man. This is organic development. . . . There are thousands of men today who are MUCH too great to be the president of the United States, that office can only be properly filled by much lesser men. Our new leaders will not be statesmen, we don't need a great new government to be great, we've already DONE that. We need a great new direction but not in the area of politics, we need it in the area of communications. That is where the new leaders are gathering. Let the Nixons and Humphreys and Wallaces keep house for us, we have a lot of work to do.

On Fort Hill, we undoubtedly had a lot of work to do. Mel took seriously what he was saying in this article, and he wanted to waste no time in getting ready to be there to transform the world when it was ready to be transformed, or maybe sooner. While most of us were on the street again selling the new magazine, Mel was making plans to accelerate the rate of change on the Hill, to intensify the internal struggle each of us was going through, and to undertake an ambitious building program to help manifest his vision. The word went out that fall that "the rocket ship is taking off," and one fact is clear about a rocket ship: if you're not on it when it takes off, you missed it. We found clues everywhere.

During that season, we received a large number of advance copies of the Beatles' mind-blowing new "White Album," filled with four sides of songs on every conceivable subject they hadn't addressed earlier, but lacking any central vision or theme. This was, of course, a harbinger of their own impending breakup, but we didn't see it that way; these guys were the future speaking to us. Of course, like Charles Manson, who later said the song "Helter Skelter" on that album gave him the inspiration to pursue the mass murders he masterminded, we heard in the background babbling in John Lennon's psychedelic patchwork song "Revolution No. 9" a message: "Here's to Mel, king of the world." I haven't any idea what the words really were, but they probably were not an homage to Mel, any more than Mel was really "the fool on the hill" the Beatles had sung about earlier. By this time, as weird as all this was, I was feeling distant enough from my former life and concerns that I certainly didn't have any plans other than to be on Mel's rocket ship; but I wasn't too sure I knew how to be on it, either.

One Man's Family

One person who was only too glad to help me know what to do was Jon M., a brash young newcomer to the community who moved into my house during that time. A Sagittarian by sun sign, like many of Mel's favorite players, and direct and unsophisticated in a way that lets you know he couldn't possibly be lying to you because he's too simple and ingenuous, Jon quickly became a favorite among the longtimers. In their eyes, he was the person in charge of our household, even though he was new and ill-informed. On Fort Hill, emotional directness was the currency of exchange, not age or experience or information. A competitiveness developed between Jon and me that quickly dominated affairs in our little family.

Into this environment, one evening in November, came a little surprise. A taxi pulled up in front of the house and out stepped Carol Schneider, my former girlfriend from New York and Michigan to whom I had been proselytizing about Fort Hill the previous summer. She had given me no indication then that she was ready to drop out of school and begin a new life. Now, here she was, bags in hand. It seemed I wasn't single anymore, but I was disoriented.

Carol quickly adapted to life in the community and, as she had done in Michigan several years earlier, found a job and settled into the scene effortlessly. I was still having a harder time and feeling very vulnerable. Jon instinctively knew how to take advantage of this state of mind. First, he started complaining that the living room of our apartment, which Candy and I months earlier had painted in a very traditional mode, with Victorian-style dark green walls and white trim, was too drab and boring to reflect our Fort Hill creativity. Attempting to please, Carol and I, who had decorated a bunch of rooms and houses together in the past, worked evenings with him and the other housemates painting each bit of wall and trim in the room a different pastel color, probably twenty or thirty shades in all. It certainly wasn't drab and Victorian anymore. I boasted of it to other people on the Hill, hoping to make them curious enough to come visit.

Then one day, shortly after it was done, Jon came home and started complaining about the room again, saying we had been self-indulgent and had been stealing energy that belonged to Mel and the community in order to make the room a monument to our own egos. Since the paint job had been his idea in the first place, I felt betrayed and confused. We spent the evening trying to puzzle it out, to no avail, and shortly before midnight one of us, perhaps Jon, suggested we take the problem to Mel, who we knew would still be awake. It made sense to me; if the question was whether to use all our energy directly for Mel's purposes or to somehow create a lifestyle influenced by his values, why not ask him what he wanted from us? So the whole household group, five or six of us, walked up the hill and knocked on Mel's door.

We found him and a few others sitting around his kitchen table, and they allowed us to tell them the conflicting sides of our family problem. Basically, they told us to go home and work it out among ourselves. The rest of us left, but Jon stayed behind. What they hadn't told us was that Mel was suffering from a toothache that night, and the last thing he wanted was to have to resolve interpersonal difficulties among his disciples. That became clear the next day.

That day, I went to work at my job helping to repair electric motors at a small shop in Cambridge. As I worked, I tried to figure out what had happened the night before. I trudged home after dark, hoping to gain some clarity from the folks in the household, but when I walked in, I found the living room filled not only with the entire household, but with a dozen or more of the Fort Hill heavies, men and women. At first I was pleased by the visit, although confused, but I soon realized they were not happy to see me. This was my first encounter with the "karma squad," which had recently emerged as Fort Hill's method of inner discipline for those who were having trouble getting with the program.

The phrase came from William S. Burroughs's spaced-out writings on the drug-crazed fringes of the counterculture, but the methodology was much more basic: physical and mental intimidation with no room for ambiguities or doubts. I sat down and attempted to respond to the barrage of questions and accusations, but I couldn't figure out how to be "real" in the way that was being demanded. I really had thought we were doing a good job of establishing a new household in the Fort Hill mode; these charges of ego-tripping left me again feeling confused and betrayed. Suddenly, in my confusion and paralysis, I found myself being attacked by Jon, who came flying across the room to punch me out and scream at me, while everyone else looked on. I had never before been in a physical fight with anyone, and I didn't know how to react. Out of the corner of my eye, I saw Carol freaking out, too, being comforted by one of the women.

When the mood finally settled down a bit, the heavies told us what was now expected of our household: We were to find a way to purchase for the Hill a good, sturdy work truck. Maybe having a simple purpose in common would give us the means to unify ourselves, and anyway the construction projects on the Hill needed such a vehicle. This seemed a large demand, but at least they didn't ask us to leave or kill ourselves. I started looking around for possessions I could sell, unable in my guilt to imagine raising new money any other way, and feeling ashamed for wanting possessions at all. I gathered up and sold much of what remained of my book and record collections. We all resolved to work more hours. When Ian Franckenstein, one of the few people on the Hill who expressed any sympathy for our plight, offered to help me search for a truck, I felt less isolated. He and I tracked down a used Jeep pickup, and somehow we arranged a loan so we could get the truck before raising the cash. Ian became the official truck driver for the Hill, and the rest of us started making payments.

Hit the Road, Jack

Within a few weeks, something was wrong again. I don't remember the details. It was probably another confrontation with Jon in the house, or something like that, but somehow I was persuaded that I just wasn't making it on the Hill, even with the new commitment to pay off the Jeep truck. Maybe it was time for me to try the "real world" again. With regret and a twinge of excitement, I found myself hitchhiking out of town late one Friday night, heading north for no particular reason. I was picked up by some teenagers in the northern suburbs of Boston, who took me to a deserted area and roughed me up, gave me a black eye, and threatened to hurt me more, until one of them decided to call it off. They put me back on the highway, where I made it to Portland, Maine, the next day, then changed course and hitchhiked back into New Hampshire. A friendly couple delivered me to a college campus to find a room for the night. I found myself in a dormitory social where the privileged young people of the next generation were flirting with each other and dancing to Marvin Gaye's "I Heard It through the Grapevine." I felt really old and disconnected, almost from another planet.

Next stop Stowe, Vermont, where I guessed I could find work at one of the ski resorts, since it was by now January 1969. I spent the next couple of weeks washing dishes, moping, eating kitchen leftovers, and hiding my heartbreak as best I could. I also exchanged letters with Carol, back on Beech Glen Street. She advised me to get out in the sun and snow and try skiing to make myself feel better, but I knew that was hopeless for me in the mood I was in.

Finally I left and dropped in on my friend Dale Walker, who had written such wonderful articles for *The Paper* during his graduate-school days at Michigan State, and had then returned to Vermont to do draft counseling as a conscientious objector. Now he was in Brattleboro, working a counseling job at the college there. He gave me access to the arts-and-crafts room at the college, where I couldn't quite cut loose and express myself; I did better in the evening, where I took on the job of painting the kitchen in Dale's apartment in gratitude for his hospitality. When the room was done, I hit the road again, heading for New York. I was in the mood for some urban despair, so I rented a tiny, cheap hotel room near the Bowery and found a temporary warehouse job.

A few nights later, I was walking in Greenwich Village and ran into—who else?—Jon M. and a bunch of other people from Fort Hill, selling the new issue of *American Avatar*. They were staying in Brian Keating's loft in Soho, home of the now-on-hold *New York Avatar*, and were doing such missionary work as they could on the streets of the Big Apple. My little hegira obviously had not produced much tangible change in my outlook; I wanted nothing more in the world at that moment than to join them. Reluctantly, they let me give up my hotel room and return with them to the loft. Jon especially was hard on me, testing the strength of my intention to be with them. I was not comfortable, but I had a connection, and it was my ticket back to the Hill after a few days.

The new issue of *American Avatar* was Mel's way of presenting to the world his own account of how he had created a community around himself. In the mythology we heard later, the "Fort Hill Community" piece was created over a period of many days, the paper sitting in the typewriter waiting for Mel to come up with the next thought or phrase. He did so, in perfect order, never correcting or changing a word, just unfolding it in sequence. This was an example of the "conscious" writing we were told Mel engaged in.

When the piece was done, he proceeded to wrap the magazine around it, starting by offering to Eben an acid-trip photograph of Faith Gude in wide-eyed adoration of Mel, to be touched up and worked into a cover picture for the magazine's new, ever-changing format. This time it was large pages, glossy coated paper, lots of white space and wide borders, and stapled at the fold, unlike all the earlier issues. On the inside front cover was a short poem by Mel, hand-lettered by Eben, evoking the feeling we were to glean from the cover picture: "and in all that time we were together / only once did I ever / see that look in her eye that gave me me /. . . . and it's lasted me a lifetime."

Below this was a long letter from a reader, Patti Ramsay, who writes of reading a book entitled *The Flower People* by Henry Gross, whose slightly fictionalized account of Fort Hill, under the name the "Lynch family," especially appealed to her. She had obtained from the author more information about the actual "Lyman family" and now was asking Mel to tell her more about it. "I want so bad, Mr. Lyman," she writes, "to know that there are other people who feel that there is a place for gentle love, and that there are others who not only share my belief in basic goodness, but who live it every day." Mel tells her to keep living according to her own values, regardless of the isolation this may create for her. "Continue to be an example of all you believe in and someday you'll FIND what you're searching for, don't get in a hurry, just LIVE it."

This was followed by one of Mel's poems, entitled "Contemplations," in which he explains how he applies this principle in his own creative life—"The world is a cold empty room that I seek to fill / with a life I do not own"—and by a reprint of Mel's question from the previous issue, "When was there greatness in history?" under a tranquil-looking drawing by Eben of Mel's profile, and the answer to the question: "When a man lived up to his ideals in face of the strongest opposition, there is greatness only when there is courage and courage relies on no security other than its faith in God. All great men had that courage and had that faith."

The next article, by Owen de Long, comments on the aftermath of the fiasco of the year's political campaign, which culminated in the election of Richard Nixon as president. "Perhaps all Ronald Reagan and Richard Nixon say shall come to pass for us, but it has nothing to do with my idea of leadership, nothing to do with my dream for America's future."

Another Absolute

The magazine then moves on to yet another of Mel's "Contemplations"—this one on the subject of loneliness, and followed by a poetic postscript under a photograph of Mel, folded into a birdlike position and quietly contemplating something off-camera: "To carry loneliness with grace is dignity. / To carry loneliness with grace requires patience. / A breach of dignity is an act of impatience. / A breach of dignity is a lack of grace. / Loneliness is an ABSOLUTE."

A section of reprints includes an old poem by Faith about "the beauties of the Atlantic" coming to visit and stealing the affections of the men of the Hill, leaving the women lonely and dependent on their own resources, as well as Mel's article from the previous issue about the communication workers as the next generation of leaders. A new article by Mel on "The Democratic Process" again attributes all movement in a time of social change to the influence of the great man whose ability to contain the aspirations of the people affected makes him the leader for that time. Such a leader, Mel says, comes into being when he chooses to feel the will of the people as his own and lets himself be transformed by it.

Among these articles was a full-page photograph of one of the Fort Hill men, dark and shadowy and almost undistinguishable, standing with a rifle at night in a garden. No explanation. It was a representative photograph of a process then occurring in the Fort Hill community that was to severely test its unity. The garden was behind Mel's house, surrounded by a high fence and until recently used to cultivate marijuana. The rifle and the man standing guard were a response to a late-night rip-off, by someone from the surrounding area, of a nearly mature eight-foot marijuana plant Mel had been nurturing for months. It was decided that Mel's most trusted lieutenants would guard the garden overnight until things calmed down.

Since we were the white and relatively affluent newcomers in a racially mixed neighborhood in a racist city in a time of rising political tensions throughout the country, this promised to be a while. In fact, the guarding of Mel's garden by his closest friends grew quickly into the guarding of the entire Hill by all of the men who could be enlisted, each serving in two-hour rotating shifts around the clock. The Hill became more and more militarized, with the front-entry porch of House Number 4 serving as the guard shed. We used walkie-talkies to communicate between guards in the front of the houses and others watching the rear, where the community had recently bought a set of garages with a driveway opening to the street behind, to serve as workshops and overflow storage space. (It was up this driveway that the marijuana thief had most likely come.) We had meetings to train guards, we had the usual competitions to decide who qualified to serve, and we sent delegations to attempt to build alliances with the incipient Boston Black Panther group, hoping thus to stave off racist attack on our turf. Guard duty started that fall and winter to protect one marijuana plant, but it continued for years and became part of the fabric of community life on Fort Hill. Only men stood guard; it was a privilege and responsibility of the gender, proof that we were "real men" after all.

CHAPTER 9

A Simple Man

But Mel himself was gradually emerging as something both more and different from a "real man." The "community" issue of the magazine included two articles under a joint headline, "There are a lot of illusions surrounding any truth." In these articles, both Wayne Hansen and Brian Keating present Mel as the Christ. Wayne writes as "John Wayne the Baptist" describing the out-of-this-world perfection of his friend Mel: "And if you think me exquisitely eloquent in placing in your hearts these pictures of this perfectly united god and man, then your hearts would weep and your tongues melt into universes to tell of what passed when Mel Lyman spoke simply of himself." Brian simply shares an adventure with Mel and Owen in midtown Manhattan, during which Owen buys for Mel a pair of Italian leather shoes. A picture of the shoes accompanies the article, which begins, "It took the passionate Latin soul to shoe Christ."

This is all an omen of things to come in the next issue of *American Avatar* a few months later. For now, the Mel who is offering the world his version of community-building presents himself as a simple person who followed his impulses step by step to wind up where he is. The first paragraph of his article on the community is printed in the sky of a two-page panoramic photograph of the tower and houses of Fort Hill against the backdrop of the rest of Roxbury and the hills beyond: "The largest community I am aware of is the universe but that is a very abstract kind of awareness. The community within that community that I am most familiar with is the United States, that is a much less abstract kind of awareness. The community within that community that I am most aware of is Fort Hill Community, I have to deal with that one every day. The community within that community is me, I have to deal with that one every moment. So I will start with myself and attempt to work back."

He describes his childhood and early life as a sequence of discoveries, first of his essential loneliness and then of his ability to fill his loneliness by reaching out and finding companions, beginning with his mother, then his schoolmates, then his wife and family and their friends. The text is punctuated by photographs of Mel's early life and of life on Fort Hill.

After six years of marriage, he sets out "into the wilderness again" because "I didn't know what I wanted but I DID know that what I had wasn't enough." Through becoming a musician, he begins "to feel close to perfect strangers."

> Thousands of people enjoyed my music, hundreds felt very close to me, and a handful wanted to be near me all the time. They loved me and I loved their loving me. Soon we were all living together in the same house. At first it was wonderful, I played and sang and everybody sang with me. But you can't play music all the time. We had to learn to share other things. Some had to earn money, others had to cook. . . . We all had to give things up and that was a struggle. . . . We began to criticize each other. I found that often people were afraid to tell each other what was bothering them and would instead come to me with their problem and I encouraged them to work it out with the people involved. This brought us closer together. . . . Now we all know each other so well that we have become as one person. We have a block of houses and we all work together on whatever needs to be done at the time. We do not need a set of rules to guarantee that everyone does his part because we trust each other and we are able to trust each other because we have come to KNOW each other.

He goes on to tell about the expansion of the community through the publication of *Avatar*, and the way in which communities, either large or small, depend on people knowing each other and telling the truth to each other. "What we have evolved together is a family structure, an ideal example of the natural order inherent in the family of man," and this is a microcosm of what is going on everywhere. "We are here to create a world together, the Family is building a home," and this in turn leads to the development of systems for governing, which usually lead to restrictions of the freedom they were meant to ensure. But at Fort Hill, "Our government is changed daily. Not without a struggle for conflict is a necessary step to greater understanding but it just doesn't take us very long to figure out what's wrong and then DO something about it. Things move very quickly around here, we're a fast crowd."

He continues with a rambling dissertation on how every pattern eventually is outgrown and yields to a pattern of higher order, illustrated in the article by his shifting to a very different voice to make this point, and by writing about the process of writing, in order to reach across the emptiness to touch people's hearts with his words: "If I can move you deeply enough then there will be a communion between us and we will be a community, it makes things so much easier when people understand each other, then there is no need for tiresome explanations."

Sometimes people make themselves unavailable because of their own fears and doubts. Mel makes it clear that he does not put up with such limitations. This helps explain the atmosphere on Fort Hill.

> That is prison. If you cannot see beyond your own wall then you cannot see that my door is open. I will not let you shut me out, I will leap through my door and tear your wall down. You will resist me to the bitter end but I will get through because I have nowhere to go but into people. My self is YOUR self. I am inside of everybody in this community, we are as one person, that is what a community is. We all feel each other as ourself and so we all are totally responsible for each other. That is why the policy of

open criticism, we are criticizing OURSELVES. . . . It requires a great discipline to do your best. We discipline each OTHER. We drive each other NUTS!

Every community needs a leader, Mel continues, "someone who best knows the potential of that particular group of people and how to bring it into actuality. A guide. I am that leader and guide, the father at the head of this family." Further, the people of the Fort Hill community know themselves well enough to know and trust him, he says. He is all things to all men. Newcomers to the Hill usually are awed by Mel and their preconceived concepts about him. "It always comes as a pleasant surprise to them when they discover that I am so easy to get along with. My relationships with people are solely dependent on how close they are to themselves, the closer they are the more intimate our relationship. I do not know any bounds on intimacy, if you do they are yours. All life yearns to be one."

The issue concludes with a little fictional story—by Mel, of course—about living on a life raft for months and months, just "the wife" and the writer, taking whatever comes along in the simplified environment of ocean and sky, even running out of complaints after a while and learning to accept their lot, learning to laugh uproariously about it all, not all serious like they were before. "You wouldn't believe it was really me & Margaret. It's not Margaret anymore, of course, it's Maggie the Sea Dog . . . or sometimes 'Lady Margaret, Queen of the Sea.' Can you imagine the things we get into together." This little non sequitur, I suppose, is meant to illustrate the central principle of life in the Fort Hill community as Mel had just explained it: that no matter what experiences befall us, the main thing, the only thing, is to get to know ourselves better.

I remember feeling grateful for Mel's explanation of what was going on in the community, even though it didn't much match the experiences I was having. At least now I had some words and concepts against which to measure myself. I enthusiastically hit the streets with the others, selling the new issue to the people in town, who were learning not to be surprised by whatever form the published output from Fort Hill might take. I sent copies to relatives, too. If I couldn't explain to them what was happening to me, maybe Mel could.

I had one of the strangest momentary experiences of my life with this new issue shortly after returning to Fort Hill from New York. I was standing with a copy on the front steps of House Number 4, ostensibly doing an evening guard-duty shift, but really lost in contemplation of the community article. Suddenly I found myself upside down on the ground next to the steps, on my head. It was as though some force had picked me up, turned me over, and dropped me. I never have figured it out. Maybe I just fell asleep standing up. But it was a perfect metaphor for how my life felt in those days. I just accepted it, like the people in the life-raft story.

Advertisements for Our Self

It's worth noting that the several pages around the centerfold of the community issue were filled with advertising—some of it national music ads similar to those found in all the underground papers, but most of it ads for local businesses with whom the Hill felt allied, and some of it ads for the community itself: Joey Goldfarb's astrology, Eben Given's artwork, George Peper's photography, Mel's book *Autobiography of a World Saviour.* A letter to readers took the place of a subscription appeal: "Dear Readers, Our purpose was stated in the last issue, it is created in this one. . . . We need to have more people know about us, we need more ways to do that, we need contributions, we need a national distribution. And you need these things too, for you need us, just as we need to do what we have to do. *Avatar* is the compassionate conscience of America. Nobody likes their conscience, but everybody has to deal with it. We're waiting for you, *American Avatar*."

There is a full-page ad for upcoming appearances, "courageously presented" in Worcester and Boston by a producer friend of the community, of "Jim Kweskin and The Lyman Family, etc." In those days, performing members of the community appeared in public as musicians only rarely. When they did, as likely as not they would not perform any music, preferring instead to dialogue with the audience until they felt confident that the audience was really present, really open-hearted and ready for whatever was to happen. The music thus became a reward for the audience for making the musicians feel welcomed and understood spiritually, far from the usual relationship between performers and audience. Not surprisingly, some of these appearances had resulted in quarreling between audience members and performers, and the reviews had grown harsh and nasty. Instead of embodying good feelings and old-timey music as they used to, Jim and the other musicians had come to represent argumentativeness and unpredictability reminiscent of the misunderstandings surrounding the scheduled appearance by Mel and others at Arlington Street Church nearly a year earlier. I attended several of these appearances at clubs around Boston, playing the role of acolyte and enthusiastic fan, but confused by how they were choosing to present themselves.

An important part of living in the Fort Hill mode was proselytizing, or what was called "learning how to talk to people." The notion was that what was happening on Fort Hill was more interesting, more important, more "real" than anything happening anywhere else. When people showed up, curious about our community or wanting more of the energy they had felt through our various outreaches, talking to them consisted of learning enough about them to then use that information to make them want to stay around and learn more. The men were invited to join the work crew, for a few hours or a lifetime. The women were introduced to the numerous children and encouraged to help with meal preparation and other chores. Little time was wasted by anyone, although hanging out with visitors was itself considered a job and a responsibility, and if a person was clever, he or she could practically make a career of it.

Follow the Leader

Some of the most sad and disorienting times I had during those early days on Fort Hill were when friends from East Lansing would show up and either fit into the scene or not. I felt obliged to give them as true a Fort Hill–type experience as I could, even when I was just reciting the lines, and this feeling at times produced strange results. Larry Tate, my longtime roommate and cofounder of *The Paper*, got tired of graduate school in Berkeley after less than a year and came to Boston to check out what we were doing and to visit another friend. He visited Fort Hill a number of times over a period of months, beginning when Candy and I were living in the apartment we shared in our early days there. Predictably enough, he was not at all interested in joining the work crew, even for an hour, or in being converted to our proto-religious adoration of Mel, or in being measured against some standard of realness.

This was really okay with me, but it was not okay with the others who observed our interactions, and eventually I was put up to challenging Larry on his "resistance." When he wouldn't budge, I accepted the inevitability of forcing him and delivered a slap across his face, which surprised and saddened both of us, and wimpily fell far short of what was expected of me. Larry left in a huff, nurturing hurt feelings and a permanent rupture in our relationship.

On the other hand, Eric Peterson, who had introduced me to Candy when he joined the staff of *The Paper* and then remained behind to help publish *The Paper* after we left town, graduated from Michigan State the next year and visited Fort Hill during that summer, before starting graduate school at Yale. The hierarchical authority structure, the inexorable necessity of doing "what was right in front of you," the clear truths that made it unnecessary and even undesirable to think for oneself from moment to moment—all these suited him perfectly, and he fit right in. Almost from the moment he started graduate school in New Haven, he was spending his weekends in Boston with us, and it was just a matter of time before he dropped out and moved to Fort Hill permanently.

This happened sometime during the spring of 1969, roughly a year after Candy and I first arrived. Eric and I began, with some discomfort, functioning as a working unit within the larger work crew; we seemed bound to each other, which made both of us rather uncomfortable, but we remained so for years. Always obedient, he took to reminding me of the dicta of Fort Hill discipline when I would seem to be lapsing, and it made me want to scream, or kill. But on the surface we remained friends, as best we could. The work required it.

A former girlfriend of Eric's from Michigan, Linda Kendrick, also showed up during that season to see what we were up to. She quickly became involved with Randy Foote, who had moved to the Hill about the same time as Candy and I, after apprenticing with *Avatar* for quite a while, dropping out of Harvard in order to sell copies on the street and get busted during the censorship struggles. Randy and Linda set up another satellite household on Marcella Street, a few blocks downhill from the main block of houses on the way to Jamaica Plain. Somehow, their household didn't go through the struggles our household on Beech Glen Street did, continually trying to figure out whether we were a Hill house or not. It was clear theirs was not, and it was equally clear Randy was destined to become part of the Hill inner circle.

For now, their place served as a stopover point for people curious about the Hill, but not yet with it. One of these, an unstable young man named Sandy, took a liking to Linda, and a complicated three-way relationship developed. One day, Sandy flipped out at Linda and beat her nearly to death, leaving her in a pool of blood with a badly broken jaw and numerous other injuries. Randy discovered Linda that way and rushed her to the first emergency room he could find, which happened to be at Boston Children's Hospital. There, Linda spent several months playing with the other patients, all of them young children, and gradually recovered both her health and her sanity. Her mother came to fetch her back to Michigan, but eventually she returned to Fort Hill to stay.

Another young woman from our East Lansing circle, who had been a freshman advisee of Candy's and mine in our psychology-department tutoring jobs during our last days there, came to visit and never left. She was another one whom the discipline suited well, and who was ready to move into the traditional woman's role that was the only option offered her. She eventually had a child by one of Mel's musician friends who lived at the Hill intermittently.

She also played a key role in setting me up for one of my several encounters with the "karma squad," but I'll save that story until its own time.

Then there was Nancy Platt, a friend from the East Lansing countercultural circle, who arranged to spend the summer of 1968 at Fort Hill before starting graduate school somewhere. She was simply too independent to fit in well, but her visit was pleasant enough.

And there was Dale Walker, whose curiosity brought him to Fort Hill numerous times, but who was really too traditional in his own values to be taken in by the Hill's futuristic rhetoric. Eventually he stopped visiting, but we remained close enough friends that I was able to use his home in Brattleboro as a stopover when I was wandering through New England looking for myself.

All in all, so many of our friends visited and came to stay, from various phases of our past, that our East Lansing circle became an object of considerable interest and curiosity around Fort Hill. This endless supply of visitors and curiosity seekers made it clear that we had had something fairly powerful going on in East Lansing, too, and that people there had looked up to us and learned a lot from us. Thus, it was even more mysterious that I couldn't seem to find the same thread at Fort Hill. I had these clear memories of having been a focus of community energy in the past, of having been right on about what was happening and able to move with the flow of events no matter what those events were. But at Fort Hill, I couldn't seem to figure out how to be anything but a coolie, a laborer, a follower, and not a very good one at that. It was very disconcerting and disheartening, particularly in the presence of so many people who had known me before.

I remember a brief conversation with Jessie in which she said Carol had told her about the old Michael in East Lansing, who was "full of piss and vinegar." "What happened to him?" she asked. I didn't know how to answer, but the same question was plaguing me. I used the oracle of the *I Ching* frequently for guidance and consolation, and sometimes it would help me find some direction. But with alarming frequency, it would offer me the hexagram "Holding Together": "Holding Together brings good fortune. . . . Those who are uncertain gradually join. Whoever comes too late meets with misfortune." Had I already missed my opportunity to bond with the people of the Hill? I wanted to see myself as "the superior man" mentioned throughout the *I Ching*, who understands the significance of each moment and senses the appropriate way to behave to achieve a good outcome. But I didn't seem to fit that description. I didn't want to accept that the light that I believed was shining at Fort Hill was simply too bright for me to be comfortable in its presence, even though that did seem to be what was happening. And events on the Hill were certainly moving in such a way as to test that theory.

CHAPTER 10

Christ, You Know It Ain't Easy

A few months after the "community" issue of *American Avatar* was published, Mel was feeling the urge again—and this time he was in the mood to really put people through changes. A third magazine-format issue was put together, again looking different from any previous one. The "Christ" issue was on heavy, matte-finish paper, the pages wider than they were long, so that the cover could be a close-up photo of Mel surrounded by a border resembling a television screen, in working-class getup, holding a cigarette and staring into the camera. The title *American Avatar* is printed in white block letters across his chest; no ambiguity here. The next two pages are a glittering array of white stars on black background, painted by Eben, with a corner of the earth at the lower left. Floating nearby is a photograph of Mel in his work clothes, sitting cross-legged on a painted-in nebula, holding a drink and grinning, with a halo around his head, and next to him is a "Message to Humanity" in white letters on black background:

Hi gang, I'm back, just like the book says. By God here I am, in all my glory, I thought I'D NEVER come. But I'm here now and getting ready to do the good work. Maybe some of ya think I aint Him. You'll see. I aint about to prove it for you, much too corny, I'm Him and there just aint no question ABOUT it. Betcha never thought it would happen like THIS did ya? Sorry to disappoint you but I've got to make the most of what's here and there sure as hell aint very much. No turnin water to wine and raisin the dead this trip, just gonna tell it like it is. You've waited a long time for this glorious moment and now that it's actually HERE I expect most of you will just brush it off and keep right on waiting, that's what those damn fool Jews did LAST time I came, in fact they're still DOING it. Oh well, what's a few thousand MORE years to people who've been suffering for MILLIONS. So while most of you turn your heads and continue sticking to your silly romantic beliefs I'll let the rest of you in on a little secret. I'm Christ, I swear to God in PERSON, and I'm about to turn this foolish world upside down. . . .

Love, Christ

Mel's "Message to Humanity" is followed, on the next few pages, by

- a page devoted to a painting of the "whole earth";
- another picture of Mel staring out from what looks like a small box inside a television set, telling readers that "As Christ appearing in this modern day and age I am going to take advantage of all mediums of communication," and promising his readers "another even GREATER surprise for you";
- Mel's surprise: "The Buddha is with me" for the first time "in the history of this planet. . . . I am going to operate as the heart, the CENTER, and Buddha is going to serve as the World Mind. He will put into effect, as World Government, all that I am." Mel does not reveal his identity, but above these words is
- a large close-up picture of Owen de Long;
- another picture of Mel, in farmer garb, holding a devil's trident instead of a pitchfork, looking in Owen's direction out of the corners of his eyes;
- a silhouetted picture of the Fort Hill tower against the sky, with small figures drawn in on the ground, seeming to be a crew of workers setting up crosses for a crucifixion; and
- a tongue-in-cheek article by Les Daniels, one of the Fort Hill hangers-on, who charges, but only humorously, that "Most people who claim to be waiting for the second coming are actually perverts who are just waiting for a chance to get in on the second crucifixion," and predicting "that the twentieth-century savior is going to outfox them all by, yes, he's going to crucify *himself*," while "his loyal followers" do the same. He describes a scene of Mel's followers attaching themselves to the ground with spikes and then ascending the heavens, dragging the earth along behind them.

The issue continues with a book review written by Mel, an excerpt from Mel's *Autobiography of a World Saviour*, a couple of short poems by readers, two full-page ads (both conveniently illustrated with pictures of Mel), a sarcastic meditation by Mel on the wonders of getting lost in his television set, a lengthy semi-real autobiographical ramble, "co-written" by Wayne Hansen and Mel, about the process of getting hooked on Mel's writing and music, et cetera, that gradually turns into an angry put-down of Mel and his arrogance (just a joke, of course), and Mel's "Essay on the New Age," on the need to have discipline if one is to handle increasing amounts of freedom.

Then come a picture of Jessie with Daria, her and Mel's infant daughter; another picture of Mel alongside an exchange of letters with a reader on the nature of being God on earth; another picture of Baby Daria; and another "Essay on the New Age," on Mel's role as the bearer of a new spirit for our age.

It goes on: a picture of Mel seeming to hold the earth in his lap; an untitled essay that begins, "Patience is the test of character, you can find out just exactly how deep your understanding is by seeing how long you can wait for something you really want"; a picture of Mel looking rugged in a heavy sweater; a long poem called "Contemplations" that concludes: "God creates me, I create the world. / Deep within myself I know unity, all my understanding / flows from a perfect order. In the world about me / I see fragments of this order, how can I help / but seek to unite them"; and two pictures of Mel, one of him silhouetted against the ocean at dusk, the other of him playing banjo and looking deep. End of opus.

A Test of Faith

Needless to say, the "Christ" issue was not an easy one to sell on the street. I had managed to stay with all the changes up to now, but this one was really hard for me. Having grown up in a home that was both Jewish and agnostic, and having found my own reasons as an adult to hold the Church and Christianity in high disdain, it was confrontational for me to find my hero presenting himself as Christ, whatever one perceived that to be. It was even harder to find enthusiasm to purvey this version of Mel Lyman and Fort Hill to strangers, although I did dutifully work at it. Now I really felt like a weirdo from some cult. I knew that the idea of "Christ" was not the same as the historical person Jesus. One of the popular astrology books on the Hill at that time was *Meditations on the Signs of the Zodiac*, by John Jocelyn, a dense and thoughtful consideration on how a person born under each of the twelve signs could consciously evolve himself to his highest potential, which in the book is called the Christ essence. This idea was okay with me, but to aggressively say to the world, "I'm it, ain't no doubt about it" was sort of another thing. And that, of course, was exactly how Mel wanted it. You're either with us, he seemed to be saying, or you're agin' us.

By this time, early summer 1969, I seemed to be spending all my time trying to keep pace with the shifting and changing priorities of the Hill. My mind simply couldn't keep up with it all or make sense of it, and my heart was more and more saddened and confused, but I couldn't admit that. I tried to make sense of it somehow by keeping track of information, such as who was living in which house and why, who was in relationship with whom, which baby had been parented by which parents. (In the "serial monogamy" mode of Fort Hill, in an atmosphere in which people's spontaneous urges toward private experiences were considered suspect and risky, liable to deflect them from carrying out their responsibilities or, worse, from their devotion to the pursuit of pure spirit, lovers often got separated from each other, and parents from their offspring, and couplings were constantly realigning; keeping it all straight was not easy.)

I tried to learn more about astrology and become more fluent in using it as a language of interpersonal communication—even managed gradually to acquire a set of astrology books of my own—but I was not encouraged by the others to pursue the study. I was required by peer pressure and expectations to spend more and more of my "free" time working on the building projects, and, along with most of the other men and a small number of the women, was picking up more and more skills as I did so. (The women took responsibility only for a limited range of tasks, such as removing old wallpaper or resurfacing and painting the walls.) I was trying to maintain something like a normal relationship with Carol, with whom I was still living. And both of us, and virtually everyone else who didn't have some specific defined role and responsibilities on the Hill, were going off the Hill every weekday to jobs in Boston or Cambridge to earn as much money as we could to help fund the building projects and Mel's other creative works.

The pace was quickening. There were more houses now to take care of. Number 3 Fort Avenue Terrace was bought back from Kay and Charlie Rose, who had bought it the year before to make it part of the community's holdings. Now they were leaving, and Mel directed the community to buy the house from them. Faith Gude devised a scheme to connect Number 3 to her house, Number 2, so the two of them together could serve as a special house and school for the growing number of children; Richie designed it, and the rest of us started building. Numbers 5 and 6, the duplex at the end of the row, had been bought; at first they were used as apartments for members of the community, but soon it became clear that their interiors had to be gutted and rearranged in order to fit into a grand scheme to combine them with Mel's house next door, Number 4½, and have the resulting complex serve as a media center and multipurpose living and entertainment space in which Mel could produce and display his various creations. On Fort Avenue, the set of apartment buildings—Numbers 27, 29, and 31—were being purchased and turned into full-on Hill houses, which meant still more gutting and rehabilitating, but this work had lower priority than the Fort Avenue Terrace houses; it was done in people's "spare" time.

No one, in fact, had any spare time. When we weren't off the Hill working to bring home money or selling the magazine, an endless array of tasks had to be done. Every weekend day and most evenings almost everyone worked on the construction projects, except for those women who were taking care of the houses and children, or cooking to feed the crew. We had work meetings each morning to assign tasks and plan the shopping and salvaging trips to collect materials. Visitors were enlisted into the work as quickly as possible so no time would be wasted. We were encouraged to put our personal feelings aside in order to participate more efficiently in the work. Everyone was encouraged (or badgered or driven or forced, as necessary) to learn basic skills and tricks of teamwork and group effort. We all became efficient at moving furniture and appliances. We learned to pace ourselves through heavy work, such as digging or demolition. Large tasks would be set up in lines, when possible: A truckload of lumber, or bricks, or sacks of cement, or whatever could be unloaded and moved onto a building site in a matter of minutes by ten or twenty people in a line, passing the load from one hand to the next. We learned to watch out for each other's safety, and for the quality of each other's work. We learned to notice when too much material was being used, and to encourage frugality. We centralized collections of all materials to minimize redundancy; often one or two people would be responsible for keeping a particular collection in order and doling it out to the others.

We were all expected to maintain a set of our own tools, and to continue learning new skills. Like most aspects of life, this was used as a parable to teach a moral lesson. In this case, it was that one started with the tools that were basic and readily available to do a job, and then, as one developed more skill and took on more responsibility, one could get in a position to have more subtle and refined tools to work with. My hammer and saw might eventually become recording equipment, for example, as Mel's had. How one could learn to work with the more refined tools before one had access to them remained a mystery to me. But when it came to construction tools, access became less and less of a problem. The Hill was well equipped, and new tools were always being added. One of the garages was turned into a well-equipped woodworking shop; increasingly ambitious cabinet and furniture projects were undertaken by ever-increasing numbers of skilled workers. But lots and lots of basic grunt work also had to be done. Each of the Terrace houses needed its sewer lines dug up and rebuilt. Several of the houses needed major foundation repairs. Since the backyards of the Terrace houses were a hillside that overlooked the garages behind and below, retaining walls and fences and staircases had to be built. And every house had rooms that needed repair and remodeling, sometimes more than once as the plans changed and grew. The work never seemed to end.

Hello, Central, Give Me Jesus

Increasingly, all aspects of our lives were becoming centralized. A first-floor room in Number 27 Fort Avenue became an office for the entire community. Mail delivery was coordinated from here. Finances especially became more and more centrally controlled. Everyone who worked "off the Hill" would turn in his or her paychecks to a bookkeeper who monitored all contributions and doled out money for construction purchases and other necessary expenses. Those of us still living in households outside Hill property would handle our expenses first, then turn the balance over. Our income tax returns would get filed for us at the beginning of each year, and our refunds would simply be deposited in the Hill accounts when they arrived. A switchboard was installed in the office to connect all the houses and to receive and send all calls to the outside world. As the men rotated guard-duty shifts through the twenty-four hours, the women took turns on the switchboard. Thus, someone always was on duty to receive visitors or handle emergencies, and also to monitor how much time anyone spent talking to people off the Hill.

There was a fantasy going around of all the houses being interconnected with sound and even video systems, the idea being that when something particularly "real" was occurring anywhere, it could be broadcast as it was happening, so everyone else could share in it. This simulcasting never happened, but everything short of it did. The details of everyone's private lives were increasingly the subject for community interest, concern, and control. As Les Daniels had anticipated in his metaphor in the "Christ" issue, members of the community were nailing not only ourselves but also each other to the ground repeatedly, holding ourselves and each other to impossible standards of perfection and guarded morality, ever-vigilant for any infractions, which were perceived as opportunities to help each other live up to the standards it was assumed we all wanted to maintain.

Even our recreation became more and more directed as time went on. Mel or one of the other central figures would discover something, and suddenly it would be all the rage for everyone, or it would be a mandated necessity. We tended to read books in fads, usually biographies or memoirs of the kinds of people who embodied spirit as Mel understood it—such as *Instant Replay* by football coach Vince Lombardi, or *The Movies, Mr. Griffith and Me* by actress Lillian Gish. We all read *The Godfather* when it first appeared. Mel spent a lot of time watching old movies on TV, and the ones he especially liked became required viewing for anyone who could break free to spend time watching. Over time, we all filled our minds and our conversation with images from these classic movies and became knowledgeable about the stars and directors who made them. When Mel discovered professional football, everyone began watching the games on TV and learning the horoscopes of the players. For a while, all the men played frequent touch football around the tower on the hilltop, whether we wanted to or not. (I was never one for team sports of any kind and particularly loathed football, but I was given no choice; I have a slightly gimpy finger from my required participation in one of the Hill's games, from an unfortunate encounter with a forward pass.)

Holidays and other special events were usually celebrated in large groups, often with big dinners or dance parties in Jim's house, Number 1. Thanksgiving dinners would be giant potlucks where the women would pull out all the stops to make us feel well taken care of. But despite these efforts, there remained a hierarchical and manipulative aspect to it all, to which I was very sensitive, since I never did find the way to feel like an equal participant in the Hill's social circles, despite wanting that very badly. On one memorable occasion, during a summer season when a lot of random and frustrated sexual energy was floating around on the Hill, Jim and a few others put out the word that there would be an "orgy" in Number 1 that night, and we were all invited. Well, that would certainly be a first, and I don't think I really believed it was true, but I thought at least there would be some attempt in some form to confront and defuse the sexual frustration. At the appointed time, the more curious among us showed up at Number 1 and found Jim and a few of the others walking around wearing giant oversized genitals and breasts made out of balloons; apparently the whole purpose of calling the "orgy" was to tease us, and maybe themselves, for wishing to relieve our sexual energies.

Mel's role in all this was paradoxical and confusing. On the one hand, he always said, both in person and in his writings, that what he wanted most was to be surrounded by people who, like himself, could take responsibility for themselves and help develop an atmosphere of creative spontaneity and inventiveness. On the other hand, he seemed to find it necessary to guide that process closely, to intervene with lessons and instructions and demands that, I felt then and am convinced now, interfered with the process. The mythology of the Hill held that Mel was in effect the source of all the riches and opportunities we enjoyed. This was understood quite literally—as though, for example, the old movies we watched on television would never have come to our attention if Mel hadn't pointed them out to us, or as though we would never have had the imagination to experiment with living in groups and alternative families if it hadn't been Mel's idea, and we certainly wouldn't have had any success in doing so if he hadn't told us what to do. I found this all contrary to the obvious truth—every one of us had arrived in the community specifically because we were actively looking for alternatives in our lives, and many of us had identified ourselves as creative, innovative people before we arrived there—and also contradictory to Mel's stated intention to have us outgrow his leadership and eventually become his equal in spiritual stature. How could we do that if we were constantly urged to follow his example and instructions rather than our own impulses?

Mel had little patience for our differing personal needs, particularly our needs to learn different lessons at our individual paces. When problems made themselves known to him, often he would use them as opportunities to issue directives or to teach particular lessons to the entire community. He might write a letter that everyone had to read. Or he might call a meeting, or direct someone else to call a meeting, to explain some need that the Hill had now, or some behavior that would no longer be tolerated, or that would now be required. Or he might throw a tantrum in private and then insist that whatever it was that set him off never occur again. One time Mel got angry because one of the women had become unexpectedly pregnant, when he had decided without warning that there were too many children on the Hill. He ordered an abortion for her and six months of sexual abstinence for the entire community. Incredibly, people did their best to obey. For me, this entire process of being told to take care of ourselves and then being told how to do that made it more and more difficult to know who I was, or where I ended and the community at large began. But trying to fit in gradually became all that seemed to matter.

In retrospect, it seems so superficial and futile, trying to adapt our behavior to some notion of how certain other people were living, pretending to be something we weren't in order to gain acceptance—especially when the standard of comparison kept shifting and changing. It was a hopeless, Sisyphean task. Whatever behavior standard one attained, by the time one attained it, the role models had moved on—sometimes for no reason other than to keep the race going, or so it seemed.

I was one of a sizable and ever-shifting population of hangers-on and hopefuls around the Hill, people who for one reason or another wanted to attach ourselves to Mel Lyman's energy, and that of the glittery, resplendent people he had gathered around himself. My two lady friends, Candy and Carol, both moved easily into the inner circle and remained there (to this day, as far as I know), but I never could find the secret. One could watch certain people show up on the Hill, win the attention of the longtimers, and suddenly be part of the gang—while others, such as myself, could hang around for years struggling to be respected and appreciated, to no avail. In one particularly poignant case, a man who had been hanging around *Avatar* and Fort Hill for a couple of years simply couldn't make it, got sick and had injuries all the time, couldn't get anyone to care for him, and then his younger brother showed up and was instantly ushered into the inner sanctum, literally into Mel's presence, and figuratively into the circle of people whose energy somehow matched that of the Hill regulars. He made as many mistakes as anyone, but he was tolerated and encouraged.

Sometimes someone who had struggled for months or years to fit in would reach a limit one day and just leave. Leaving, however, sometimes involved advance planning. For instance, a person who felt the need to have some money when leaving the Hill might go off to a job on a payday and simply never return. Or, someone who was feeling pressured to perform beyond his or her limits might decide that the only way to get out was to run away in the middle of the night. Or there might be an argument or a fight, and the person would be allowed to leave in disgrace. Others would leave surreptitiously and then somehow let the community know where they were, and people would go out into the world to retrieve them. It was very erratic and unpredictable, but the overall effect was to make all of us know that our presence was noticed and valued, especially if we were productive workers, even if we had to put up with intolerable demands and pressures as the price of being appreciated. The operative principle was a kind of survival of the fittest. You could almost see the pyramid of hierarchical authority around the people who got to determine what happened on the Hill, and you could equally well see it shift and change from day to day. I saw all this clearly, but could not find the way to succeed at the game.

CHAPTER 11

Superstars

After returning to Fort Hill with the sales crew for the "Community" issue, I was again given the responsibility of finding a decent job off the Hill, as a source of money and, therefore, respect. After a series of short-term jobs, I answered an ad for a delivery driver for a major architecture firm in Cambridge, The Architects Collaborative (TAC)—professional home during his last years of the world-famous Bauhaus architect Walter Gropius, another great man in whose shadow I could hang out for a while, delivering blueprints to major construction sites all over the Boston area. After a few months in that capacity, I moved to a different role in the same firm, doing odd jobs in its maintenance department. This is the role I was in when "Grope" finally passed on that summer, at the age of eighty-six; the firm hosted an afternoon celebration of his life instead of a funeral, fulfilling a clearly stated wish of the late genius.

TAC was also where I was working when, one evening that summer while I was doing a guard-duty shift, I attempted to enter a conversation that was going on near the Fort Hill tower between David and Faith Gude. In my imagination, they were just sitting on the Hill appreciating the weather and the view of Boston, and I wanted to share that, too. It turned out they were negotiating the end of their long common-law marriage and felt invaded by my arrival. But instead of simply saying so, they waited until I left on my own to return to the guard shack and then continued their conversation. After a while, David joined me at the guard shack and, without ever saying what had been wrong with my behavior (I figured it out myself long afterward), told me in cold anger that I was not making it on the Hill, was clearly missing the point, and should probably move off the Hill, try the "real world" again, fall in love, fight for causes, do something real. I took this to heart, and within a day or two had arranged housing in Cambridge, first with one of my coworkers and then in a small apartment in a working-class part of town. I took one of the cats from the Beech Glen Street house with me for companionship, but after a while he disappeared.

After six weeks of living and working in Cambridge, trying to reframe my life on that small and individual scale, I couldn't resist visiting Fort Hill one Sunday afternoon. Inevitably, the first person I encountered was David Gude, who asked me if I was ready to return yet and if I felt badly about how he had treated me. How and why these things happen continues to seem a mystery to me, but I said yes, I was ready to return, and of course I harbored no ill feelings toward him. (What a missed opportunity!) I immediately made arrangements to rent a studio apartment of my own facing the hilltop, in Number 23 Fort Avenue, one of several apartment buildings adjoining those owned by the community. About a third of the units in Numbers 21, 23, and 25 Fort Avenue were rented by community members. I liked the apartment a lot and enjoyed having my own vantage point for observing the tower and the activities of the community houses, but I think I only lived there for a month, maybe two. The household on Beech Glen Street where Carol and several others were still living was ready to break up, and Carol and I and Eric Peterson wound up inheriting a third-floor attic apartment around the corner on Highland Avenue, probably as a way to house more of us for less rent expenditure. The apartment had previously been the home of Mark Frechette, a peripheral member of the community and an avid reader and admirer of Mel's writings in *Avatar*, whose life had taken a dramatic turn, and who no longer needed a small apartment on the backside of the Hill.

Mark, young and rugged-looking in a sensitive sort of way, with a quick temper and little use for fancy language, had found himself in a shouting match at a bus stop in Boston, intervening in a quarrel between two lovers. Miraculously (this is a true story), he had been observed in his anger by a talent scout for Italian filmmaker Michelangelo Antonioni, who had exclaimed something like "He's twenty and he hates!" and had immediately whisked Mark off for a screen test for the lead role in Antonioni's upcoming made-in-America film *Zabriskie Point*, a fictional story of the revolutionary career of a Berkeley activist who runs off to Death Valley to escape the law and winds up confronting his destiny in the desert. Mark had indeed been given the role and had immediately pledged his devotion and the bulk of his earnings to Mel Lyman, who for his part immediately welcomed Mark into his inner circle. Mark's costar, aspiring actress Daria Halprin—daughter of two famous creative parents from California's Marin County, landscape architect Lawrence Halprin and choreographer Anna Halprin—during the course of the filming had also become his lover, and before long they were living uneasily together in one of the Hill houses. Mark loved being one of the Hill workers, when he wasn't planning future filmmaking endeavors with Mel or going off to act in a couple of Grade-B movies; Daria had a harder time fitting in, and was really out of her element. Mel and Jessie named their baby after her, but that didn't help.

The summer afforded those of us on the work crew, the "dummies" of the Hill, two opportunities to travel out of town, feeling like emissaries from Mel's universe. For some reason, Mel and Jim Kweskin decided to try showing up one last time at the Newport Folk Festival in Rhode Island, a couple of hours' drive from the Hill, with the entire performing "Lyman Family" and a gang of fans and helpers in tow. I remember that the musicians of the group were scheduled to appear at the end of one of the afternoon concerts. They started doing their make-the-audience-prove-they-really-want-it number from the stage, while Mel waited in the wings, unwilling to appear until and unless he sensed the perfect moment. The audience didn't go for this and started loudly demanding entertainment, especially some of the familiar Kweskin Jug Band songs. As the mood got worse and worse, into the breach unexpectedly came Joan Baez, no fan of Mel Lyman, suddenly assuming the role of peacemaker by singing an a cappella version of "Amazing Grace" to calm the audience down and give them some of what they wanted. Jim and the others were furious and walked off stage, cursing Joan and recalling how much bitchier she could be than her more pleasant sister, Mimi Fariña, an old friend of theirs. For my part, I thought it was a delightful, subtle allusion to Mel's spontaneous "Rock of Ages" performance in a similar moment a few years earlier, when Bob Dylan had pissed off an audience that expected him to do one thing when he was in the mood to do another. In any case, we piled in our cars and headed back to Fort Hill.

Not too many weeks later, we were off again, this time several carloads of us heading for the Catskill Mountains region of New York, to represent Mel and Fort Hill at the Woodstock Festival. I haven't any idea how or why this trip got organized. I think we must have been wanting to sell copies of *American Avatar* and otherwise proselytize to the assembled masses. I remember that in preparation for the trip, I bought myself a new pair of used bell-bottom jeans, white with light blue stripes, and a pale red shirt; I fancied myself looking like a sort of off-beat Uncle Sam to go with our "Second American Revolution" mythology. We arrived at the festival site (nowhere near Woodstock, as everyone knows, but farther into the Catskills, on Max Yasgur's dairy farm near a town called White Lake; it happened to be just a few miles from a poultry farm where some cousins of mine had lived for many years, so it was a weird kind of homecoming for me) after the huge crowd had already gathered and established its impromptu villages and campsites, and as the now-famous rainstorm began. Our official position was that the music happening on stage was of no interest to us, and we were there to sell magazines or whatever. But with the rain coming down in buckets, Richie Guerin, who was field-marshaling the operation, decided the best thing we could do was position ourselves on the roadways and help direct traffic, because he could see mass confusion in the making. That is what we did, and it's all we did for the two or three days we were there—twenty or so of us getting muddier and muddier, directing traffic in the rain while one of the great cultural events of our generation went on all around us. Needless to say, no magazines got sold and no music was heard by any of us, except dimly in the distance.

Also during that summer, Mel started what became a long campaign of physical expansion of his community, one that went on for some years. He accepted an invitation for himself and several of his closest associates to spend the summer on Martha's Vineyard Island, off the southern coast of Massachusetts, where Jessie's father (the artist Tom Benton) and his wife had a summer home and studio. Mel needed a rest from his world-savioring, and it seemed to be time for Mel and Tom to become better acquainted. In fact, they began making a little film of Tom working in his studio, and developed a friendship and mutual respect that inspired Tom to, in effect, give a portion of his summer home to Mel and the community. (I don't know the details, since I was never invited to visit the Vineyard; were there separate houses on one large property? separate quarters in one large house? adjoining properties?) The effect was to give the Hill insiders a permanent second home, to which they would retreat from time to time during appropriate seasons, inviting along those who needed a break, or with whom Mel wanted to spend more time, or, occasionally, those who needed the discipline of living in close proximity with The Lord for a while.

A Last Hurrah

While Mel and company were at the Vineyard, they began work on the next issue of *American Avatar*. This time, the magazine transmogrified into a large-format, relatively slick imitation of a journal of general culture and trendiness that was dated Summer 1969. (I believe it appeared in late summer or early fall, but it might have been earlier, in time for us to take it to "Woodstock.") It was numbered "Fourth Cycle, First Issue," and was priced at $1, a high price for that era. On the cover was a photograph, by Mel, of David and Faith Gude's young daughter Clothilde, and headlines announcing three of the articles inside, including an "Exclusive Interview with Antonioni's Newest Superstars." The first page of the magazine included an elaborate staff listing with no fewer than thirty-three members of the community listed in various positions, from editor in chief (Mel, of course) and executive editor (Jessie) all the way down to director of maintenance. A table of contents listed twelve articles and features, only a few of which were by Mel Lyman, and a box of publication data promised bimonthly publication. The magazine had not yet been published bimonthly at any time, and never would be. This was the first issue of the "fourth cycle," and the last issue ever of *American Avatar.*

The first feature was an "Editorial," untitled and unsigned but obviously Mel's work. It was yet another restatement of Mel's political philosophy of the time, and appeared facing a photograph of a statue of a Revolutionary War soldier, perhaps Paul Revere:

> Only in this country could such a wondrous revolution take place. . . . This revolution is the test and the fruition of true democracy, of the people, by the people, for the people. There is spirit in the air again, and without a world war yet! That is encouraging. We are not uniting against an alien power, we are uniting against each OTHER! Not even north against south this time, even that won't work anymore, we are virtually eliminating geographical warfare, we are fighting man against man, we are fighting for something bombs can't buy, we are fighting for LIFE! America is getting stale, we are fighting for LIFE!

Revolution or Bust?

The next article, "No Solution to Revolution" by Wayne Hansen, tries to place Mel's message in a larger historical context. Generally speaking, Wayne describes a dialectical model of historical change in which opposing forces become more polarized through the unfolding of events until there is no choice but for a great leader to emerge spontaneously, uniting the opposites from a completely new vantage point. He attributes such a role to Hitler, whose unexpected violence in storming over Europe forced the United States and its allies to confront him, thereby ending the historical isolationism of this country.

He then discusses the early deaths by assassination of John Kennedy, Malcolm X, Martin Luther King, and Robert Kennedy—all of whom, he says, had the potential to unite and lead the country out of its despair and confusion, had the country been ready to follow their examples, and had the forces of the status quo not been so strong. Next he talks about the generation that developed the hydrogen bomb and, as an afterthought, went to the moon, and the generation of its sons and daughters, the young people who were now attempting to develop a new language and a new worldview that could transcend the limited world of their parents.

> To a sensitive idealist it is a time of such universal agony, he must pledge his total understanding to alleviate it. . . . The conservative pragmatist sees only the destruction of his values and his society. . . . With these forces separating further and further every day, with men being continually thrown back upon themselves and forced into acting from the depths of what they hold most dear, the time is coming when every individual will be absolutely real, when words and concepts will be unable to mask ulterior motive, when everything will be reduced to exactly what it is, and only then will there be room on earth for entire and true creation.

I never understood what Wayne was talking about in this article. The catchy title sounded like advocacy for revolution as it was then understood—that is, either violent or nonviolent thoroughgoing opposition to existing social and political structures. But the article doesn't seem to support this notion, focusing instead on cryptic generalizations about recent European and American history, and offering after-the-fact rationalizations for how things had turned out, ignoring the power plays and manipulations that had produced those results. This was not my view of history.

Wayne's concluding reference to Mel's "Declaration of Creation," in which Mel promised to "burn down the world," only confused me more, unless one assumes Mel himself is the great man, the historical force who can polarize society so thoroughly that something truly new will result. I was not convinced.

Mel himself did little to clarify the issue with his latest "Essay on the New Age," which followed Wayne's article. It's a garbled statement about the place of law in governing society, and the moral authority some people have to act outside the law when they perceive a higher necessity.

> These people are on the way to becoming the new legislators of this land, the poles are shifting. . . . They have conceived of a wiser way to live. So far they have no legislative power, they can only resist. But they have a power far greater than the power to control action, they are invested with the future of the world.
> BEING A REAL AMERICAN IS A STAGGERING TASK

Following Wayne's article is an allegorical fable about two animal kings who confront each other annually in a ceremonial war-for-a-day. Next comes the feature interview with Mark and Daria, which is actually the partial transcript of a conversation between them, several members of the community, and a visiting Italian journalist who found himself unexpectedly sitting with the American stars of the latest film by one of Italy's most successful and controversial filmmakers. Over many pages of dialogue, little clarity emerges about Antonioni's film or about Mark and Daria; what does come through is that Mark and Daria (who had only been on the Hill for three days at the time of the interview, even though she reports having had powerful dream visions of it in advance) are struggling to integrate their experiences with Antonioni, Mel, and the community. Jessie and Owen seem to be doing a lot of their talking for them, fitting their comments into some prior notion of how it all fits into what is happening on the Hill. The interview ends as Mark is about to tell of a major confrontation with Antonioni during the filming; the continuation is promised in the next issue, the one that never appeared.

(My recollection from Hill gossip is that at a certain point in the months of filming, Mark, feeling compelled to bring Antonioni and Mel together, walked off the set in California and returned to Boston to rejuvenate himself with a hit of Mel. Mel, in effect, ordered him back to the filming—otherwise, all that fame and fortune would go out the window—and Mark reluctantly returned to Antonioni's influence, but never gave up trying to bring Antonioni to Fort Hill to meet a "real" filmmaker and some "real" revolutionaries. That meeting never happened. *Zabriskie Point* opened to tepid reviews; it flopped financially and critically.)

The magazine continues with several articles about current affairs and foreign policy, drawn from diverse sources. The section appears to be an attempt to present the magazine as a serious and balanced commentary on world affairs, despite its highly idiosyncratic character in other articles.

Messages from Beyond

The political articles are followed by several pages of letters to Mel, and his responses. In the first letter, Paul Williams—former Cambridge resident, precocious editor of *Crawdaddy* magazine, and long-time friend of Mel and the community—spells out his excitement and joy at Mel's announcement that he is Christ. "I can feel no envy of your greater strength, but only great joy, knowing that you, like me, continue to choose to expand, knowing that any strength you have is my strength & my strength in turn is so much the greater because it can contribute, does contribute, to yours. . . . Jesus, brother, you have my undivided support!" Mel responds, "[Y]our letter is the first real reply to the meat of last issue, 'The Dread Proclamation.' No one knows what it has meant or who was compelled to do it. It is a man who never knows what he will have to do next."

Mel's responses to several other letters emphasize the same point, that greatness and true creativity and spirit are only found when one pushes oneself beyond one's own boundaries and capabilities.

The magazine's major feature follows. At long last, Mel and company had chosen to explain and present the "Box Poems" to the world. An introductory essay by Eben Given discusses an experience of the great psychologist Carl Jung, as described in his autobiography. Jung had found himself one day chiseling, into a large piece of stone, a poem he did not compose but that came through him automatically. The voice in the poem is of a disembodied spirit whose perceptions transcend and rise above those of mortals on earth. "It is the voice which he listened for, all ears, throughout a long and discerning life—a voice which became at times the voice, beyond words, beyond images—the voice that speaks when all the meaner voices are momentarily stilled."

He goes on to introduce the thirty Box Poems that appear in this issue:

Written down in the early 1960s, they are as authorless as the poem at Bollingen [Jung's home at the time of his automatic writing experience]. The phenomenon of their making, which at the time attracted certain scientific minds at Duke University, is still for that factual and over-documented world to discover. To those of us who only attempt to live more closely to the message of the poems themselves, in consciousness of that place from which all whole truths, like great poems, emerge, it would be as silly as attempting to dissect the writings of Mel into vowels and consonants and saying, "Here it is—this is how he does it."

He then explains further how the Box Poems were created, drawn one word at a time from a box into which hundreds of words on little slips of paper had been placed, in a moment of mysterious creativity shared by Eben himself and several of his friends. The poems had subsequently been entrusted to Mel, who, I believe, had done some editing and rearranging to make them come out as literate as they appeared, but this part of the story was not told in the magazine. The poems were presented as though complete from the moment of their creation; they speak in the same otherworldly and spiritual voice as Jung's disembodied poetic source. Many of the images seem to be Christian, that is, concerned with Jesus Christ and his life and its meaning as interpreted down through the ages.

It's easy to see from reading the examples (see sidebar 4) why these mysterious poems had won the hearts of Mel and Eben. The poems speak in such a similar voice to theirs, and probably were among their teachers when they were wandering artists during the hectic and unpredictable days before they settled on Fort Hill. Laid out here on many pages of *American Avatar*, printed against photographic backgrounds of stormy and dramatic skies (photographed by Mark Frechette), they were at last being presented to the world in a cogent form. As mysterious and obfuscating as I found the rest of this issue of the magazine, I found the Box Poems a welcome and illuminating counterpoint. I had my own favorite, one that was not included in the magazine, but that Eben had painted in floor-to-ceiling glory on the living room wall in House Number 4. It was another retelling of part of the Christ story, from the mother's point of view. I think it appealed to me not because of the Christian imagery, but because it reminded me of my own life story then in the making, and whose motivation neither my mother nor anyone else from my past could figure out.

My son has found truth
somewhere in a sky
that looks like one grey weeping eye to me

I bore him under a blinding star
but he comes from some land not in me

What piercing sorrow not to know
Where your one child must go.

THREE BOX POEMS

No poem is this . . . a shadow on the page
that could have held his song
if blazing death had not seared down through all
*   his bones*
to bring his requiem out

I wish I could give glory to this man
but words are like the pebbles on the shore
dead
to the endless living ocean of a soul

Bear witness gates of death
that I have never ceased to knock at doors
I know will never hear

Bear witness
heaven
that my love has been as great as I could bear

And know my love
I sing of you

And always will

      *   *   *

My face is sheeted with tears

I say
I say
that all my saints have gone

Does any other god have ears for me
or must I
unredeemed
stalk through this world wondering
why men live on and on
and gods die fast

            *   *   *

Will you never risk me

Not ALL things live in the light
or hang in a silver sky
like a cross
A past age will tell you how beauty was hidden
in a circle of thorns

The origin of the nightbirds song
and nights kisses
and tomorrows snow
ivory bones
revolting thoughts
unsuspected love
and blazing vision
all these strange things are known only in finality

You must dare to live in darkness

SOURCE: From *American Avatar*, "Fourth Cycle, First Issue" (Summer 1969): 28–41.

The magazine ends with a "Contemplations" piece by Mel, in which he gives what appears to be the moral of the entire issue: "All that really matters in this life is a man's inner worth, what he still has left when all the chips are down. . . . When a man is alone with himself and all his deeds are behind him what is there left that he can truly call his own. If there is nothing then he is nothing. If there is understanding then he has made good use of his time here."

Life is a struggle for everyone, Mel says, and no one knows how life will unfold as we take one step after another.

CHAPTER 12

Another Visit from the Karma Squad

About the time this new magazine was published, a mysterious impulse overtook me, as suggested by Mel's essay. Mine wasn't an impulse to produce a great creative work, exactly, but it was a bold step out for me at the time. Something possessed me to give notice at my job at the architecture firm and become a freelance handyman and carpenter. I was impressed by stories of the longtime Fort Hill men occasionally hiring themselves out around town, and I felt, because of my job, I now had enough skill and personal contacts around town to successfully fill my time with freelance work. In this way, I could both bring home more money for the Hill, and possibly create employment for other men from the Hill. All this easily came to pass. I put up a few signs around Cambridge announcing "The American Dream," as the little enterprise became known, and before long I was employing myself and several of the other low-status men from the Hill work crew most days of the week. I had my first-ever conversation about astrology with Joey Goldfarb, who assured me that the Mars-square-Saturn aspect in my chart was perfect for what I was doing, an aspect that would keep a person like me from ever acting boldly unless the action was perfect for the moment in which it occurred. My new venture seemed a long way from making music or films, but it did seem to give me a purpose and a role that I could play that fit in with what was going on around me.

Haltingly at first, and then with more confidence, I found myself behaving more like a standard-issue male human, with all the accompanying mannerisms and expectations. Finally, the blue-collar role seemed to fit. I found myself remembering and identifying with my father, who worked unhappily as a machinist and equipment designer all his life, never feeling he was getting ahead fast enough, and always wishing he could in some way be a writer and raconteur instead, and who finally died of injuries incurred in a work accident. I seemed to be recreating his experience, the last thing he or I ever expected me to do. Some group of us guys—as many as were needed for the day's assignment—would go off in the morning with a car full of tools and materials, and would do whatever sort of work the day demanded of us: painting, carpentry, plumbing, digging and trenching, plastering, demolition, apartment fix-up, you name it. The pleasures of the day were simple: a coffee and doughnut break from time to time, the chance to get to know a new neighborhood, sometimes a conversation with people living in the places we were working. We took pleasure from proving to ourselves that we could credibly accomplish some task we weren't sure we knew how to do. Sometimes tempers would flare, and it would suddenly seem like Fort Hill again, with clashing egos and power struggles. I tried to keep the operation upbeat and simple, but, of course, sometimes I made planning errors or got us into projects over our heads, and this would elicit challenges from the others. But all of us were focused on bringing home as much money as we could with as little hassle as possible.

I changed homes a few times during that fall and winter period. Carol and I, and then Eric, were living in Mark Frechette's old apartment on Highland Avenue part of the time. We made a weird, bold decision to remove several of the partitions between rooms of the apartment to make a bigger, more flexible space, without asking or telling the landlord, who lived downstairs. We used the resulting pile of scrap wood as firewood to burn in a wood stove we installed, also without his permission. (My mind reels now at the arrogance of this maneuver.) I remember all of us being under stress at the time, such that I found myself hitting and yelling at Carol a few times—another step into the world of male-patterned behavior that I hadn't experienced before. When our landlord figured out the damage we had done to his building, he evicted us, and the three of us moved back onto Fort Avenue, this time into a small rented apartment in Number 23. Carol and I had the only bedroom; Eric's space was a portion of the kitchen/living room. In these cozy quarters, I remember listening for the first dozens of times to the Beatles' *Abbey Road* album, whose enigmatic lyrics somehow came to symbolize for me the whole time period.

Then, for reasons I can't recall, our little household group broke up. Carol moved into Faith's house, Number 2, mirroring Candy's "social climbing" of a year and half earlier; Eric moved into Number 27, which was still undergoing remodeling; and I moved into Number 29, which was only now starting the remodeling process. At last, we were living in buildings owned by the community, a small step toward assimilation. I lived for a period in the top-floor apartment, which had been gutted and now had exposed framing and brick exterior walls, with my bed in the middle. I also lived in the basement apartment and a couple of other places in the building, as the several apartments were disassembled, and a single kitchen and living room and numerous bedrooms were carved out of the space. Gradually, a loose family unit came together in the house, which served as an anchor for me during an upsetting time.

I had another encounter with the karma squad during the winter. I was still running a work crew five days a week and working on the Hill houses with everyone else most evenings and weekend days, trying to be a good member of the team. My crew was dependent on an old station wagon I drove, and one Sunday I felt a need to work on the car to keep it running, rather than on my appointed project of the day, which happened to be completing a portion of a decorative picket fence around the Terrace houses, obviously not an essential task. One of the men found me and insisted I work on the fence instead of the car, which I did, resentfully. Later that day, I wrote a note questioning the rigidity of the priorities and left it on the table in one of the Avenue houses, seeking support or feedback from whoever read it.

The next day, several of us went off to work in my station wagon; predictably, the car broke down during the day, and we had to call the Hill to be rescued in order to get home from where we were working. Ian came to collect us in the Jeep pickup and was inexplicably sullen as we rode home. When we arrived on the Hill, he directed us into House Number 5, which was at that time still in a stage of being remodeled for Mel's visionary use, and whose large living room was serving as a community meeting space. Practically everyone on the Hill was there waiting for us, and Richie was at the front of the room ready to pounce on me. I couldn't figure out what was happening until Richie read to the group the note I had written the day before. My former tutoring student from East Lansing had read the note and, for reasons I never have figured out, turned it over to Richie during the day. He decided to make it an example of something or other—insubordination, I guess. Now that he had me on display, he wanted me to confront the person who had insisted I work on the fence, but I wasn't even willing to name who it was. To me, his behavior wasn't the problem; the problem was that the work priorities were so inflexible that we were disallowed any initiative even to choose to take care of problems for which we had assumed responsibility, such as my car. It was obvious to me that I was correct, given that the car had in fact broken down that day, but I couldn't frame this thought clearly enough to protest at the time, and I was confused and terrified being put on display that way. I simply froze and could not give Richie and the others what they wanted, any more than I could successfully defend myself. The meeting finally broke up with nothing resolved, but my status in the community was diminished again.

Suspend All the Rules

Other incidents happened during those days on the Hill that I also just couldn't accept or rationalize. The abuse of relationships shocked me repeatedly. Couples would be thrown together or ripped apart at the whim of someone with higher standing in the community. Any withdrawal from the main group for the purpose of exploring the possibilities of a relationship was considered a violation, and if this happened to occur in combination with what was perceived as disrespect, there would be hell to pay. Children were treated the same way, and were often separated from their parents or disciplined for what seemed specious reasons. I attempted a couple of times to intervene in such situations, and suddenly found all the anger and frustration focused on me. Once, in a moment when Brian Keating's former wife, Pat, was being told to leave the Hill, but to leave her two young children behind because they belonged to Mel even if she didn't, I spoke up in her behalf, defending to Jim Kweskin her right to keep her family together. Jim was furious with me and stood by while one of the other men, who saw himself as the head of our household in Number 29 and who was a great deal larger and stronger than me, punched me hard in the face, giving me a black eye that required medical attention. Pat left the Hill, with her children.

Another time, I happened to speak up in defense of Rita W., the space case who had borne one of Mel's babies (who was being raised by Faith), and who periodically would wander back to the Hill from her sojourns in the larger world. This time, she was showing up homeless and pregnant, and I felt an impulse to offer her space in Number 29. I barely knew her, but I believed she obviously was part of our family, like it or not. No one took my suggestion seriously, and Rita was told repeatedly to leave, that there was no room for her in the condition she was in. After a couple of weeks of this, Jessie finally pronounced that "we have to take care of our own," and Rita was given a space in (of course) Number 29. No one but I saw the irony in this turnabout, but now crazy Rita, and later her new baby, were part of our household.

Jon M. was the central figure in two dramas that horrified me, mainly because he was perceived as being in the right in both incidents. In one case, he reacted to what he saw as disrespectful and separating behavior on the part of one of the women, and he responded by barging into her room and raping her, and then boasting about it. Another time, he got angry at similarly "disrespectful" and inappropriate behavior on the part of two of the children, two boys about four or five years old, and he beat them up, one of them quite seriously. In both cases, he was not criticized for what he had done; instead, he was praised for following his impulses so uncritically. I found this incredible, and impossible to condone. (I did entertain a fantasy for a time of treating another of the women, with whom I was having a running argument, the same way, but I couldn't bring myself to use force deliberately in that way.)

Equally incredible was the way in which two babies who were born to a particular couple during that period were received. They were the half sisters of one of the boys Jon had beaten, born a year or two apart from each other. Both were born with birth defects—I don't know exactly what, but they involved certain internal organs functioning irregularly, and promised that the babies would need extraordinary care for a long time, perhaps permanently. The first baby was tolerated on the Hill, but when the second one was born, it emerged as a necessity that both girls be given up for adoption because they were "monsters" and there was not room for them on the Hill. The babies went; the parents stayed.

I was experiencing life as more and more irrational. I was living in an authoritarian hierarchy in which the rules and priorities and power relationships were constantly shifting, and I repeatedly found my values challenged and undermined. All around me, my peers seemed to think everything was just fine, and all we had to do was keep working for Mel. In fact, that's practically all we were allowed to do, so we did. In such an environment, it goes without saying, the work was all that counted. It didn't matter if we had the right tools; it certainly didn't matter if the work was beyond our skills, or was physically risky, or exposed us to chemical fumes or other hazards. Getting it done, somehow, and winning the attendant approval was the most important thing. We were still finding some of our building materials in abandoned houses around the area, and this opened the way to an amoral view of property ownership in which anything that you could get away with was okay.

One time, I took one of the Hill's vehicles on a lumber run, and the lumberyard personnel almost forgot to charge me for my truckload of goods. I paid, but when I told Richie about this, he said I should have run for it. I couldn't quite integrate this attitude, but I did try to do so another time. Several of the other guys and I had borrowed Jim Kweskin's van to go on a "scrounging" run, looking for building materials. We came across a new building site where some large space heaters caught our eyes. The Hill had a major construction project under way at the time, rebuilding the back end of Houses Number 5 and 6 as part of Mel's grand scheme to create a "Magic Theater" in which to display his various works and put people through transformative changes. At this stage of the work, the crew was laboring inside a two-story plastic enclosure that was very cold and unpleasant to work in. We decided to lift the heaters and some other materials from the site. As we were loading up the truck, being as invisible as we knew how to be, police came along and busted us. Of course, the stolen goods and Jim's truck were confiscated, and we were held in jail until the Hill's lawyer could arrange bail for us. Eventually, after some skillful plea bargaining, charges were dropped against three of us, and the two who had prior records were given light sentences, probably probation. Jim and the other authorities of the Hill lectured us on our transgression—not for attempting to steal things for the Hill, but for doing it clumsily and getting caught. Part of our "punishment" was digging a big hole in the driveway near the workshop buildings, in which to bury other stolen materials that were lying around, in the event that the police would want to search the place. So much for morality.

By contrast, the face that the Hill presented to the world continued to be unperturbed and self-assured. Now that the magazine was no longer being published, other endeavors were receiving the attention of Mel and his close associates. The story of these endeavors was featured in an article in the *Boston Globe*, Sunday, February 1, 1970, "Fort Hill: Re-inventing Life on a Hilltop in Roxbury." Under a picture of several dozen members of the community sitting on the lawn in front of the tower on the Hill, sternly staring into the camera, the reporter, Robert L. Levey, offers the community's rationale for its treatment of both members and visitors:

> The Fort Hill community has a single mind and a single heart. . . .
>
> [T]here is a severe authority structure on the hill. People are divided by function and they are all instruments in a plan for a new way to live that begins and ends with Mel Lyman. . . .
>
> [The] insistence that individuals continue to evolve and change leads to intense confrontations among those on the hill and between them and outsiders who come to visit or observe the community. There is a premium on persons being honest with each other to the point of insult. The motive is to bring people into deeper relationships of trust and common feelings.
>
> My own presence in the community as a reporter was greeted with some suspicion and hostility. I was berated for not having the capacity to participate fully in the Fort Hill experience, for remaining rigid and aloof. I was informed that one member of the community had said of me, "He's so empty I didn't want to sit too close to him because I might fall in." Twice, when I told people it had been good meeting them I was angrily accused of lying.
>
> This impatience with outsiders stems largely from the facts that Fort Hill residents have each gone through a series of intense changes and experiences in their own lives. They harbor massive faith in Mel Lyman and they regard most of the other three billion people in the world as infants who have not proceeded very far [a]long the path of real life.
>
> (Reprinted courtesy of the *Boston Globe*)

The article describes the ceaseless building projects on the Hill and the "standard of perfection," as it was known, to which we were working, as well as the traditional division of labor between men and women, and the devotion by which we were giving, typically, two-thirds or more of our individual incomes to support the Hill's projects. A new project of the Hill is mentioned as the latest creative work to take the place of the now-defunct magazine. The author seems unaware that the "new" work is really old work recently taken out of the can. The old recording done by Mel and others with Lisa Kindred, during the days when the Jug Band was intact and David Gude was the recording engineer for Vanguard Records, had resurfaced. Jim was offered a new recording contract with Reprise Records, and had asked permission to purchase from Vanguard the rights to the old recording. This was now being released by Reprise in the only version that still existed, the one with Mel's harmonica mixed to equal prominence with Lisa's voice, under the title "Love Comes Rolling Down," by the Lyman Family with Lisa Kindred. We on the Hill thought this was a wonderful turn of events, and we had grown quite fond of the music, which even the least of us had heard a number of times, but very few copies were sold. Much later, Lisa Kindred told another reporter she had not been consulted or even informed when the record was being prepared and released.

The *Globe* article ends with a mention of one of the more visible anomalies of Hill life at the time:

> Fort Hill people are the first to point out that Mel Lyman's influence on this growing group has parallels with the case of Charles Manson and his "family," the accused mass murderers on the West Coast.
>
> Pictures of Manson, in fact, are in evidence in some of the Fort Hill houses. Jim Kweskin was on the phone recently with an executive of the record company that will be putting out their album and the conversation got around to Manson.
>
> "Sure, we got a lot in common," Kweskin said. "But Charles Manson talked about saving souls and he went around killing people. Mel Lyman talks about destruction and he goes around saving souls."

We Buy Another House

The air of unreality about the record release and the *Globe* article, in the context of increasing irrationality in our daily lives, was pervading everything. The United Illuminating Realty Trust, the holding company that held title to all the buildings the community owned, had finally succeeded in acquiring title to Number 4 Fort Avenue Terrace, the original home of the community, which until now had been rented from a disagreeable neighbor lady toward whom Mel felt an irreconcilable enmity. During the negotiation process, Mel had a dream one night about fighting with Lena, the landlady. In the dream he was hitting Lena on the head; awake the next day, he interpreted this as an instruction to damage the roof of the house, so it would lose its value and she would be more ready to sell. This was done; some of the men drove nails into the roof and then complained to Lena that the roof was leaking and needed replacing. Or, she could sell to the community, cheap. To underscore the point, they removed the top of the chimney. Lena gave in and accepted the offer, one she could hardly refuse, and the house was bought for something like $4,000 (a typical price for the neighborhood at that time). As soon as we bought the house, Mel ordered it vacated and cannibalized for building parts. Before long, the instruction came to destroy the house.

The day this order came down was a special one for me, in a crazy kind of way. Feeling desperate and unable to understand why I couldn't fit into the community, I had built up my courage and asked for a second acid trip with Mel, hoping again to glimpse some kind of truth that way. I remember the moment of asking for the trip: I let myself timidly into

Mel's house and waited quietly in his living room while he finished a conversation in the kitchen with one of the men. They got talking about a mouse that had moved into the kitchen cabinets, and Mel said, "I don't mind a mouse." I was convinced the comment was aimed at me in the next room. But, whatever Mel was thinking, he agreed to arrange a trip for me. Coincidentally (or was it?) Eric had asked for an acid trip at the same time for a similar reason, and the two of us were guided through the experience one Saturday night—not by Mel, but by a group of his lieutenants.

I remember sitting in the kitchen of Mel's house during the most intense part of our rush, with Faith and Jessie and some of the others, who were teasing Eric and me about the way in which we never quite seemed to get along but couldn't seem to get away from each other, either. Later in the trip, we were upstairs in the large room we had recently created in the top of Number 5, intended to be Mel's recording studio and transformational journey site. I wandered away from the group for a few minutes to admire the city skyline through the unusual front windows, which had been reworked by Richie to resemble the cockpit of a giant airplane. David Lanier, known as David Libra, who was nominally our primary guide, came up to me and ordered me back into the group; looking deep into my eyes, he told me he finally understood why I kept myself so aloof from the community all the time. "You're afraid you might kill somebody," he said. It had never occurred to me. Then we were out on the hilltop in the middle of the night, running around the tower at top speed, flying above the ground, it seemed. All in all, a very strange night.

When the rush of the trip finally ended, very early in the morning, I went home to Number 29 to rest up for the coming Sunday workday. When I woke up, still early in the morning, I wandered over to the Terrace houses and encountered Wayne Hansen, who was doing some early morning carpentry work, and toward whom in that moment I felt a brotherly bond that I could not explain, but that feeling of mysterious brotherhood became the overriding emotion of the day for me. Wayne told me that during the night, Mel had ordered the demolition of Number 4 (did that have something to do with our acid trip?), and that everyone would be working on that project as soon as the workday began. When everyone else was awake and ready to work, we went at it full throttle. I think most of the house was taken down in that one day, while the women and children played on the hilltop and numerous strangers came wandering around. It was one of the first warm days of spring, and the hilltop park was full of baby carriages and puppy dogs, moms and dads and kids. The entire event had for me the air of an old-fashioned community celebration.

It happened that I had recently been reading one of Hermann Hesse's lesser novels, *Beneath the Wheel*, in which a socially retarded young German boy finds himself unable to fit into the vibrant life of his peers and his community and eventually dies an ambiguous death in the gutter. Is it accident or suicide? Is it inevitable or was there a choice? I felt on that Sunday as though the close-knit traditional town of the novel had suddenly come to life around me—and was I the misfit boy? I was certainly feeling disoriented, not just on that day but during all those months. A big question kept running in my mind that I couldn't discuss with anyone: Who would be the first person to die for Mel and the community? How would it happen? Would it be a work accident, or a suicide, or the result of a worse-than-usual physical fight? Would it be me? Would I find the strength of character to leave the community and expose its hypocrisies, and would I then be punished for doing so?

A Letter Home

A couple of months after the acid trip and house-demolition adventure, I was working at a fix-up remodeling project in Brookline with Eric and Danny Oates, who had been one of Candy's and my hosts during our first visit to the Hill more than two years earlier. Two events of note happened during the few days we were on that job. Danny persuaded both Eric and me to try smoking cigarettes, something neither of us had done before. He explained that it could be almost as pleasant a high as marijuana, which we weren't getting too much of in those days and which we missed. (He was lying, of course.) Because smoking was very much the thing to do on the Hill—we were among the very few nonsmokers—we gave in to Danny's urgings. For the next several years I smoked Camels or, later, roll-your-own Buglers when money was especially tight—about half a pack a day. Smoking helped me feel and act like one of the folks.

The home we were working in was that of a religious but rather disorderly Jewish family. In some ways it reminded me of my family's home, not because we were religious (we were anything but) but because our home had typically been disorderly, and because the Jewishness of the home we were working in made me think of my family. For reasons that are unclear, I attempted to put the mix of my feelings in a letter to my mother. The letter paints a picture of my confused state of mind during the process I was undergoing, which can only properly be called brainwashing.

After describing my experiences in the community and the memories stimulated by my current work situation, the letter goes on to rhapsodize at some length about Mel and his mother (about whom he had written and spoken a lot), about their relationship and the lessons Mel learned from it that he was now teaching to us, and about the experience I was trying to have in his community (see sidebar 5).

SIDEBAR 5

AUTHOR'S LETTER TO HIS MOTHER, JULY 14, 1970

Today has been an especially lonely day for me, and I spent most of it wishing I had something solid and comforting in my life to hold onto, but I haven't got that right now, and it seemed like the place to start looking to build that is inside myself and my feelings. I have so much frustration and emptiness in me, years and years of it that I have held onto and almost never been willing to show anyone, that when I get lonely I hardly know how to start telling of it. I don't know what I have to hide, but somehow I've always been a secretive person, and mostly I've learned to ignore my feelings instead of opening up to them and building on the ashes of my pain, as I know I should. But these things always come home, and now I am left with only myself and the same old feelings to work with.

I guess things aren't as bad as I am making them sound. I have friends, of course, when I want them and know how to use them, and I have more work to do, really rewarding work not just drudgery, than I could ever handle, and I live in a house full of women and children who need more of everything, especially love and caring, than I am ever able to give them, and of course nothing is stopping me from growing and being more except my*self*, because that is the way our lives are arranged here—but still there is a loneliness that underlies it all that each person has to learn to overcome, and at that I am just a beginner, and my personal life is really empty.

I worked today in the home of a very religious Jewish family in Brookline, and I listened to old records on the radio all day. In some ways it put me right back 8 or 10 years to when I used to paint our house all alone just because I wanted to see it done, wanted it worse than almost anything else in my life, worse than girlfriends, worse than peace of mind or wisdom or places to go at night—or at least I was able to turn wanting these things into the spirit to do the work, and that kept me going as long as it did. That's the same way we work here, building our home and Melvin's home out of the pain of lacking all the other things we don't have yet. In some ways I am still exactly the same person I was then, only little things have changed, but I don't have an awful lot more wisdom or ease of manner or anything—except that I am surrounded by purpose and when I am empty it can carry me. . . .

Mel had a painful and lonely childhood, but he learned things as a child that enabled him to grow into the most fantastic man alive, because he always had a clear and dependable love and strength to fall back on. A lot of what he has had to do here is to teach us first how to feel that thing coming from someone else and then how to create it and give it back to someone that needs it. Everyone needs it, everyone needs to be cared for, and it's such a simple thing as long as it doesn't get all muddled with misconceptions and as long as you accept that caring exists alongside pain and loneliness. . . .

[T]here's something I've always missed that I'm working on getting now, and it's going to be all right. I'm finally learning to look consciously for the thing I've always thrashed about in agony trying to find, so I guess I'll live and grow after all.

I'm really pretty lucky, anyhow. The people I've learned the greatest and deepest lessons from are here on Fort Hill or are connected with the Hill at our houses in New York and Martha's Vineyard. They're not far away, ever, especially if I need them. We are a great big family, and we're as close as each of us is able to make us be. I don't know what I was feeling so down about, in fact. But I'm glad I wrote this anyway, I hope it makes you feel good.

CHAPTER 13

The Colonial Era Begins in Earnest

It was unusual for me to attempt to put my feelings about my situation in writing. In fact, I hardly remembered how to write anything anymore. Once in a while, a directive would come from somewhere in the inner depths of the Hill, requesting or instructing that all of us write letters to tell Mel how we felt about some creative work he had produced, or about our gratitude for his leadership. I would dutifully write such a letter, but doing it would be like dimly remembering something from my distant past. Less frequently, I would feel an impulse such as the one that made me write this letter to my mother, trying to put on paper some of the essence of the experience. But by far the greatest part of my energy was going into staying current with the demands of Hill life; any impulses toward a personal life or individual expression were at best an inconvenience, and at worst the excuse someone else might need to humble or discipline me.

Increasingly, "dummies" like myself on the work crew were becoming just the means for Mel and his close associates to achieve more and more elaborate ends. We were no longer the "creation" that in earlier days Mel had said we were; now we were just used to produce work and money, while ever-larger projects were conceived. We were encouraged to find money wherever we could to help with the enormous expenses. During this period, the last of my inheritance from my father finally became available to me, about $2,500, the biggest single chunk of money I had had access to since shortly after his death. Unhesitatingly, I turned it over to the Hill, imagining it contributing to the studio and sleeping-loft portion of the "Magic Theater" project, into which I had poured a tremendous amount of work.

Mel decided we needed a more permanent home in New York than the Soho loft that Brian Keating had kept for a couple of years. A nice two-unit brownstone was found on a quiet block of West 15th Street near Seventh Avenue, on the edge of the Chelsea district. First one unit, then the second was rented, and after a while a deal was struck to buy the building, in the name of Owen de Long, and with an investment of our collective funds that equaled the total cost of all the houses on Fort Hill. We were moving into the big time, and the need for money was greater than ever. Mel started moving people between the Hill, the Vineyard, and New York—more opportunities to give people just the experiences they could use to grow in the way he thought they needed. The nicest accommodations in each location were reserved and upgraded for Mel's use.

The opportunity to recruit people in new places gave Mel the idea that some of his representatives should travel the country, seeking out souls ready for the Fort Hill experience. He dispatched Owen and a woman named Karen Poland to be the road crew. They traveled all over the country for a number of months, visiting campuses and urban centers, selling *American Avatars* and talking up the Hill and Mel. Eventually, they settled in New Orleans and established a temporary home base there in a rented apartment. Only one person joined the community from all their work: Chris Thein, known as Hercules.

Before much longer, the impulse arose to colonize California, too. I am not able to recall clearly the sequence of events, and of course no one was consulting me about any of it. But Mel's focus was definitely on collecting people and homes everywhere around the country that he felt was worth "saving," as though Mel directing energy toward a place was the only way it would be saved from certain dissolution. Definitely on his list was San Francisco, where he had settled as a very young man first leaving home, where he had met and married Sofie and become acquainted with her large and flamboyant family, where he had discovered himself as a musician. Shortly after initiating the New Orleans experiment, Owen was sent to San Francisco to rent an apartment with a view near Buena Vista Park, and a second home was obtained in the Outer Mission district with the help of the family of one of the community's mainstays, the ex-husband of one of Sofie's sisters, who also lived on the Hill. A crew was dispatched to Los Angeles as well, and a large house was rented in Hollywood. Before long, this house was outgrown and a second house was found, and purchased, I believe. Later, the first house was given up when a much larger house, really a mansion on a large plot of land in the Hollywood hills, was found and purchased. It was by far the most expensive and fanciest property yet added to the increasing holdings.

Mel was moving people around between the various homes at a faster and faster pace, and was doing a lot of traveling himself, getting to know the cities, houses, and people he was now working with in his expanding creation. Also, he was pursuing new creative projects. A strong impulse had overtaken him to reassemble the documents and memories of his childhood and his early career as peripatetic musician, laborer, and spiritual explorer. He was writing to old friends, asking them to return to him letters and other writings he had sent them. He conceived the idea of revisiting the places of his formative years and reacquainting himself with people from his past.

All this activity was leading eventually toward publication of an autobiographical collection of his writings, but that took about a year to manifest. During this time, as well, the opportunity arose to bring his current company of musicians to San Francisco to record a new album to be released under Jim Kweskin's contract with Reprise. A strange musical mélange was assembled: Mel and Jim and several other musicians and indispensable groupies from the Hill, along with two of the folk musicians Mel and Jim knew from the Jug Band days, bassist Reed Wasson and dobro player Mayne Smith. Together they recorded an album's worth of music in just a few days, attempting to summarize the range of the best of American popular and folk music. This, too, would take about a year to manifest commercially, but the mood of all of us now scattered around the country was excitement about the new burst of creative energy.

Back on the Hill, of course, we were noticing a severe shortage of personnel and money, as more and more of Mel's favorites were moved out to the other locations, in a time when new people were showing up only occasionally because the community was not doing a great deal of outreach. Mel himself was absent more and more. In fact, his absences also required further sacrifice and investment on our parts. Rather than continuing to spend more and more money on plane fares, he decided after a while that what he needed was a fleet of high-powered vehicles in which to drive from place to place. Over a period of a year or so, the fleet was assembled: a Lincoln Continental limousine, a Mercury Cruiser, a Mustang point car, a large Travco motor home—all of these customized and outfitted for Mel's very demanding tastes and needs, all connected with CB radios, all staffed and maintained by Mel's favorite traveling companions. The process of moving him between the various locations became a major undertaking in itself, really a traveling home for a portion of the community, leaving the work responsibilities of the people traveling with him to be taken up by others in their absence.

Topsy-Turvy Time

When Mel was on the Hill, it was often to rest up and concentrate on his own work. For this, he often preferred to work during the late-night hours and sleep during the day. Much was made of the fact that Mel, who despite his strong character and presence was paradoxically increasingly frail and sickly, took hours to wake up each day, gradually descending down to the mundane planes on which the rest of us hung out, and then reorienting himself there each day in order to accomplish his rarefied creative work. He was also constantly switching between aspects of his personality, which had differing needs and dramatically different appearances. He had all his teeth—the "rocks in [his] mouth" that had given him lots of pain and trouble—pulled, and thus developed a very convincing old-man persona. In fact, he had long been known as "the old man" by certain of his admirers. But he could put in his false teeth and switch back to his youthful self in minutes. All this changing and adapting, naturally, required lots of support from others, required the most detailed and exactingly maintained accommodations, required lots of privacy and insulation from other people's concerns, because anything was likely to intrude on his attention and break his concentration. And he had a way of homing in on anything that was out of place in his environment and immediately experiencing it as a problem. I remember, for example, a time when Wayne cut and polished a new piece of glass for the top of Mel's dresser, but he left a small portion of the edge unpolished by mistake. The first time Mel entered the newly redecorated room, he put his hand precisely on that spot on the glass and cut himself; it was often that way.

One creative solution Mel came up with was to have the entire Hill move onto his schedule, so we would all be working when he was working, sleeping when he was sleeping. Beginning late in 1970, all of us who did not have daytime jobs off the Hill moved onto a day-sleeping schedule to match Mel's so the major construction work could be done at night when he was awake. My role in this endeavor was to find a way to make money on this schedule and also to be available as needed to work on the studio, or whatever the current construction project was. I don't remember phasing out the "American Dream" handyman operation, but I must have, because during the period of overnight work I got a job as a cab driver with a company in Brookline, driving from late afternoon to midnight, then coming home to do construction work until morning, and sleeping days in Number 29, while the women and kids banged in and out of the house all around me.

I hope Mel got plenty of needed sleep during this time, because I sure didn't. I stayed on this schedule for over five months, as I recall, becoming more and more exhausted and frayed around the edges. Finally, one night, I fell asleep at the wheel of my cab on a side street in Jamaica Plain while heading back to Brookline to take a brief nap at a cab stand (the licensing agreements of the various cities in the area made it unacceptable for me to stop my Brookline cab within the Boston city limits). I crashed at slow speed into a parked car a few blocks from my destination. The manager of the cab company told me that repairing the car would cost him everything he had made on me in five months and then some, and he fired me. Once again, I was subjected to a disciplinary talking to from Jim Kweskin and the other men on the Hill, as though I was solely responsible for having willfully cracked up the car. In the aftermath of this, I was given something I had wanted for quite a while: I was allowed to remain on the Hill full-time as a member of the in-house construction crew.

Moving On

During this time, one day, I got to wave goodbye to Candy and Carol and several others, who were all driving together to Hollywood to live in the new houses there. Even though I hadn't had cordial relations with either of them in quite a while, and even though both of them had long since become involved with other men of higher standing than I (in fact, Candy was pregnant with Richie's baby at the time), their departure together for a distant home left me feeling somehow uprooted and disconnected. But within a few weeks, it was my turn to be transferred. Eben and Wayne had been in New York for some months, living in the house on 15th Street and working for a range of well-off clients, doing custom carpentry for high wages. Now it was time for Eben to move on (to Hollywood? I don't recall), and Wayne needed new partners. Les Sweetnam and I drove to New York in his little car in May 1971, there to make our fortunes for Mel. I have never been back to Boston since that time.

The first period in New York was exciting and gratifying for me. At last, I felt, I had a respectable role within the community, in an environment where I was fairly certain I could perform adequately. With only a few of us in New York at the time, I also had a nice room in a nice house; it felt quite civilized. And, of course, New York was in a way my hometown. Even though I had never lived in Manhattan before, I was familiar with the environment and how to function there. Wayne made Les and me feel welcome as part of his crew, and in no time we were busily working and bringing home the bucks. Quickly, though, the pressure was turned up. We weren't making money fast enough, we needed to be more scintillating conversationalists at home, Mel's rooms in the lower unit of the house needed to be fixed up, et cetera.

I had a chance to share some of my frustrations with one of our clients, an interior decorator for whom Wayne had done lots of work. She sympathized with my plight and offered to buy me a visit to a psychic friend of hers, a tarot reader with an apartment uptown. One day after work, I slipped away to keep my appointment, hoping I would hear something like "You're too good to be hanging around with that gang; here's what you should do instead." But

I couldn't bring myself even to mention the community until almost the end of the reading; maybe I was testing the reader on her prescience or something, although she probably knew my story already. When I finally, shyly mentioned my dilemma and my restlessness, she just said, "You're not done with them yet," and I took that as an instruction to go home and try to adjust. When I got home that evening, of course, I was soundly criticized for having gone so far afield looking for a kind of assurance the others believed I shouldn't have been wanting in the first place. Oops.

Within a few months of our arriving, the New York handyman operation was going well enough that more people were moved down from the Hill to take advantage of the profusion of available work and the relatively high wages. Eric was among the new transferees; we were thrown into working together again. Also new in New York was Jeremy, a longtime resident of the Hill from England who seemed to me to be willing to do absolutely anything in the name of spirit and spontaneity. He was currently in the country illegally because an earlier marriage to an American woman had fallen apart. Mel decided it was time for Jeremy to marry another American, and he moved Rachel Brause, my former housemate, back to New York, her hometown, for the purpose. Rachel's parents were led to believe their daughter had finally fallen in love, and a formal wedding was held in the house, in which they participated. Rachel and Jeremy proceeded good-naturedly to live as a couple, a very odd couple; her parents even gave Jeremy a job and hired our crew to paint their apartment.

The house on 15th Street couldn't accommodate everyone, so additional space had to be found. We sublet for the summer a small loft space on West 21st Street, and several of us moved there, living and sleeping and running a shop in the tight quarters, and heading back to the other house for occasional periods of cultural R & R. In addition to working as carpenters and handymen, we also started a second business. One of Mel's longtime friends, a taciturn, reserved inventor and mathematician named John Kostick, had spent a number of years developing designs for unusually strong three-dimensional structures based on principles of multidirectional symmetry. He even held a patent on the basic design, which he called a tetraxi (four axes), and he had developed a vast line of wire sculptures based on the tetraxi and elaborations of it, which he periodically attempted to market under the name "Omniversal Design." His "stars" were everywhere in the houses on Fort Hill.

The unusual characteristic of his designs was that they were simple to make out of ordinary materials, once a person learned the principles of weaving the parts together symmetrically. Suddenly, with an entrepreneurial community of us based in a wealthy district of New York, we (John, too, was living with us in New York) were using our evenings and other "free" time learning to make his sculptures. The shop space on 21st Street was outfitted with acetylene torches for spot-welding the bronze wire we used to make the sculptures, and vats of cupric acid and plastic coating material to clean and preserve the finished products. We would take collections of sculptures out on the streets and sell them to passersby, as in the past we had sold newspapers and magazines.

We also developed furniture designs using the same principles of symmetry, gaining maximum strength from lightweight materials. I remember two specific projects: a warehouse full of storage shelves in New Jersey that we built from very light lumber in a labor-intensive but material-shy scheme, and, quite the opposite, a heavy, carefully contoured bench made of walnut, to serve as the couch in the living room of a gentleman in Greenwich Village.

When the sublet ran out at the end of the summer, Omniversal Design seemed to be doing well enough to merit some further investment. We found a larger loft on West 18th Street, near Fifth Avenue, with large windows facing the street and a high rear space with a raised floor area that we could readily develop into a two-story living area for five or six of us. We built in a kitchen (my mother donated an extra stove out of her house on Long Island), improved the bathroom, and developed the upstairs area into several bedrooms. The front part became a shop and store for Omniversal Design, and our living room for those rare occasions when we weren't working. We filled it with samples of the furniture possibilities inherent in John's sculpture designs.

CHAPTER 14

Send Out a Lifeline

Meanwhile, back in the house on 15th Street, the New York community was receiving periodic infusions of news and cultural guidance from Mel and Fort Hill central. These infusions included the first of what would become a long series of music tapes prepared by Mel from a growing collection of 78 rpm records that he and Jim Kweskin were assembling in their travels around the country. The record collection was being lovingly preserved and stored in the Hollywood houses. The "Melzak" tapes were conceived as a compendium of the best popular music that had been produced in this country over the decades, carefully selected and sequenced. In choosing pieces for the tapes, Mel was looking for music that seemed to have been produced easily and spontaneously, when the spirit moved through the musicians and singers, without the labored effort of repeated takes and after-the-fact engineering. (The 78 rpm medium, in its simplicity, encouraged this possibility.) It was the same standard Mel used in evaluating his own music, and he was using the tapes to educate us in this principle, as well as to have ever more influence on what we listened to and thought about. The first tapes were of "race music," the black rhythm-and-blues music that Mel had listened to during his young adulthood, and which gradually evolved into rock and roll. Later tapes moved into numerous other styles, from country and western, to swing, to World War II–era pop, and everything in between.

Tapes of the evolving music for Jim and Mel's new album also came to us from time to time, and finally the finished album itself arrived: *Richard D. Herbruck Presents Jim Kweskin's America, co-starring Mel Lyman and the Lyman Family.* On the front of the jacket was a collage by one of the Hill women, composed of some of the community's favorite images of what made America special: Marilyn Monroe, James Dean, John Kennedy, Gene Autry, Henry Miller, Billie Holiday, Vince Lombardi, Jimmie Rodgers, Lyndon Johnson, Marlon Brando as Stanley Kowalski, Henry Fonda as Tom Joad, et cetera. On the back of the jacket, Richard Herbruck, the ostensible producer of the record, describes the excitement of the recording session and the interaction of the unlikely assemblage of musicians. "All in all it was a magnificent experience, one to never be duplicated. . . . And then we were done. The spirit of this once great country of ours had come and left its mark as minute little tracings on a plastic disc and the second American Revolution was underway." The liner notes also included a little essay from Jim, talking about the astrological sign of Cancer and its deep relationship with the musical history of this country:

American Soul, still flowing in deep strains of hope and conquest. That soul was the Freedom that the earliest American dreams of and fought for which was *the freedom to find God in themselves and follow Him*, and it was finally born on earth as the spirit of a nation which would live in men, in Cancer . . . the sign of the birth of God in Man.

[The American soul has been repeatedly expressed in great musicians born under the sign of Cancer] . . . and people who could truly hear them have felt history before it happened.

I am here once again to sing that song for you. And as this album was born in a burst of spirit and recorded simply in three days as it was sung . . . a new life for the world is bursting forth from the Heart of America.

The soul that is born in Cancer must always find its completion in Aries, when God and man become one. You can read the story of it in *Mirror at the End of the Road* by Mel Lyman. It is the story of life from the moment it doubts itself and receives its first intimations of immortality to the time it becomes God . . . as it grows from Cancer to Aries. You can hear that story in this album if you will step aside and let your soul listen. I am singing America to you and it is Mel Lyman. He is the new soul of the world.

Jim Kweskin

You might wonder what he is talking about here. This little essay is an even more general-ized, simplified, and romanticized version of American history than any that appeared in *American Avatar*. Are people expected to take this seriously? So much of the album and its liner notes is tongue in cheek, it's hard to know what Jim expected when he wrote this, if he wrote it. The truth is, Mel is everywhere in this album; Jim is no more than the vehicle through whom the album became possible. Jim sings every song, but Mel's backup vocals and harmonica are frequently mixed equally with, or even stronger than, Jim's voice. The selection of music is surely the result of Mel's influence. The album starts on an upbeat note, with Jim singing Gene Autry's part in "Back in the Saddle," and moves through several other country-music classics from various time periods, including Woody Guthrie's "Ramblin' Round Your City" and Merle Haggard's "Okie from Muskogee," the recently popular redneck anthem. The arrangements are uplifting and richly textured. The second side begins with a similarly rousing version of "Stealin'," a classic number in the jug-band style, but then moves to a long, slow, somber version of the gospel song "The Old Rugged Cross," and an equally heavy "Dark as a Dungeon," the coal miner's lament by Merle Travis. The album ends with a long, serious choral version of Stephen Foster's "Old Black Joe." Jim and Mel seem to be attempting to take the listener through a journey from simple, happy feelings into a confrontation with the real and the serious. Or something like that.

One Isn't Enough, Let's Have Two Mels

I have always found most of this album very pleasant to listen to, particularly the more upbeat songs. But I've never understood why it seems to take itself so seriously, while at the same time it's packaged in such a weird way. There are even two drawings of "monsters" adjoining the liner notes, credited to Anthony Benton Gude, the then-eight-year-old son of Jessie and David. And those weird notes by Richard Herbruck, describing the epiphany of the recording session. Who is Richard Herbruck anyway, and where did he come from to become the producer of this record? The truth is, "Richard Herbruck" was just another manifestation of Mel Lyman, inexplicably using a pseudonym as a joke. Richard Herbruck was in fact the name of one of the men in the community, a rich kid from Ohio who had arrived a few years earlier. He was known to everyone as Dick Libra and rarely needed his legal name, which came complete with credit cards and respectability. He happened to look a bit like Mel, too—similar coloring and body type. So during the days when Mel was traveling around a lot by airplane, he became Richard Herbruck in order to travel more anonymously. For some reason, it caught on, and he started being Richard more and more of the time. Soon, Richard was developing a public persona of his own.

In the period shortly before the appearance of *Jim Kweskin's America*, Richard Herbruck had a brief fling with fame, as well as notoriety, through the efforts of the Hollywood branch of the family. It's a complicated and controversial story, one that I know primarily through published accounts, but it contains a number of familiar elements. In an attempt to gain media influence in the Los Angeles area, Owen de Long had applied for and been hired as program director at KPFK, the listener-supported Pacifica station in L.A. He had no radio experience, but he did have his impressive academic credentials and his self-assured manner. Joey Goldfarb was simultaneously hired as maintenance person at the station, and as part of his conscientious performance had built and provided to the station some shelves on which to store the profusion of recording tapes there. For his part, Owen generously offered to provide to the station broadcast tapes of a series called "History of Rhythm and Blues," ostensibly put together by Richard Herbruck. These were the first "Melzak" tapes that Mel had been producing and distributing to the various homes of the community. (Or maybe they were tapes in the same style produced just for this purpose; I have no way to know.)

For some reason, there was disagreement between the radio station's engineers and Owen over the sound levels at which "Richard's" tapes were put out over the air, and after a couple of disagreeable episodes, Owen simply pulled one of the tapes off the air in the middle of the program and asked listeners over the air to complain to the station about its sloppy engineering. Apparently, this was a signal to community members, who obediently called the station to make the complaint. This in turn precipitated a physical encounter between Owen and a station employee, who claimed he was injured when Owen pushed him against a wall. Owen was fired on the spot.

The next day, a large crew from the community showed up at the station to reclaim their shelves and, as indicated by their behavior, to impress the KPFK staff with their seriousness. They did this by blocking all the exits, yielding only when station personnel called the police for assistance, and it was agreed the Fort Hill people would let traffic in and out of the station while they methodically removed their work. The whole episode was then exaggerated and boasted about in a column that "Richard Herbruck" wrote for the *Los Angeles Free Press*, part of a series of columns Mel as "Richard" was evidently writing in the *Free Press* and the *Berkeley Barb* at the time. These columns became controversial among the *Free Press* staff and were discontinued because "Herbruck's" defense of the KPFK episode included threats of further violence.

The facts as presented here are gleaned from two lengthy articles published in the *Free Press* by its longtime editor Art Kunkin, who made it his business in two articles, on July 30 and August 13, 1971, to investigate not only the KPFK episode but also the history and current doings of the community. He describes the commitment to excellence and perfection that he observed when visiting the community's Hollywood houses, and the pleasant interactions he had with the people there, despite their public reputation for violent and erratic behavior. He also includes "Richard Herbruck's" latest and last column for the *Free Press*, which occupies a full page of the paper, bordered by stars, with a tag line, "promises you everything, gives you nothing":

We should be entering the new world, all the preparations have been made, it has all been written about and everybody wants it, it is so easy to imagine. A world where everybody loves each other and all motion is towards harmony and there is no more war or hate or fear and everybody is together all the time. It is very easy to imagine.

Yet here we sit in a grey and tumbling world out of place and bursting with song! What happened? . . . Perhaps we didn't want ENOUGH. Perhaps we have settled for too LITTLE. Perhaps what we REALLY wanted had nothing to do with everything we THOUGHT we wanted. Perhaps the new world hasn't really even BEGUN yet!

Et cetera, et cetera. More of the same old diatribe against the pretentiousness and smugness of the New Age as it was emerging at the time. More complaints about the stagnancy of the government and the old institutions. A plea to stop infighting and unite against "the common enemy."

Get together with your friends, pool your resources, make some money, buy a house, take on some responsibilities, learn to FIGHT for what you believe in, stop doping yourselves up, stop looking for a Utopia, look around you with clear eyes and make some clear decisions, THE ENEMY IS WITHIN! We have to start a new life here, we cannot live in this dying structure, it will kill us, it has already killed itself. Our only weapon is inner strength, a small group of people with a great deal of determination can transform the world, be the NEW Christians, fight for your life, fight for love, fight for a new world, fight for room to breathe, the Heart of God is a vast darkness that only the brave can know, this is a plea for courage, WE MUST GET TOGETHER AND FIGHT THIS CREEPING DECAY!

So this was "Richard Herbruck's" message for the world of Los Angeles. Sounds a lot like all of Mel's earlier messages for the people of Boston and New York. I didn't read it until many years later—for some reason, the series of articles of which this was a part was not sent to us in New York—but it's easy to imagine such talk landing with a thud in the Southern California of the early seventies. In any event, by the time "Richard Herbruck" went public as the "producer" of *Jim Kweskin's America*, the entire KPFK–*Free Press* episode was in the past. The little bit of talk about it that reached us in New York focused on the spontaneity and unity of Owen and the rest of the crew as they confronted the wimpiness and low standards of KPFK. We didn't hear much about the violence, or the unwillingness to reach any kind of compromise. It was a typical adventure for the community during those days. Some outreach toward the world, often through the media, would be begun with great hopes but often with unspoken ulterior motives, as Owen's "offer" of tapes was really the reason he was at KPFK in the first place, to promote Mel's work there. Then something would go slightly wrong, or the situation would be exploited beyond its tolerance, and the whole thing would come undone. After the fact, the Hill people were always right and strong, and the other people were always weak and misguided. But almost always, the effect was that the high hopes would be shattered, and the plans for major influence on the world would be disappointed.

Doing It All with Mirrors

By the time the news of the KPFK adventure arrived, such as it was, we in New York were busy with a new project. Mel's autobiographical collection, *Mirror at the End of the Road*, was now published, as Jim had indicated in the liner notes of *Jim Kweskin's America*. The community had a distribution contract with Ballantine Books, under which they were placing it in stores, but we had the right to sell it as well. We had boxes filled with books and were spending all our available time hawking copies on the streets of New York. Imagine the scene: You're walking down the street in Greenwich Village or Times Square and this young stranger approaches you, neatly dressed and looking sincere, and tries to sell you a book that is the life story of someone you've probably never heard of, who claims to be the savior for our age. It was a difficult selling assignment, but we went ahead with it, day after day when all our other work was done. I remember one day being on the street on the Upper East Side, a trendy part of town. Suddenly, around the corner came, unmistakably, Janis Joplin with two long-legged, bell-bottomed friends. I looked at her and said, "I know who you are." And, just as quickly as it takes to read these words, she fired back, "I know who you are, too," and continued walking. It was the high point of my brief book-selling career. She died a few months later.

Mel's book represented to us at the time the best opportunity yet to present what was special about him to the world. It seemed like the culmination of a long evolution, of which *Avatar* had been a preliminary phase. The book was an assembly of his personal writings, letters and diary entries, poems, and photographs (as well as drawings by Eben of important scenes for which no photographs existed) of the years of Mel's development from a brash, frustrated young man to the spiritually accomplished person he had been just before the start of the community. Its moods cover an enormous range of emotions and diverse reactions to all kinds of situations, from silly wordplays and pornographic complaints about the injustices of life, to sincere love letters and reminiscences, to contemplations about the eternal questions, and little odes to his pets and his humble surroundings during difficult times.

It begins with a section called "Diary of a Young Artist" at the end of 1958, when he was first hitting the road to find himself, his marriage to Sofie on hold for the first of many times over the years. He wanders and rambles and suffers, moves his family of Sofie and a growing bunch of kids around the country trying to find some situation that works for them while he is becoming more proficient as a musician, and finds no peace. Then, in a section called "Judy," he lives through a devastating relationship over a couple of years with a young woman student at Brandeis, who eventually returns to her family in the Midwest and leaves him to "live with a broken heart," as he puts it in the dedication of the book. This experience catapults him unwillingly into a spiritual exploration, which is spelled out in the next section, "Dark Night of the Soul." As his musical career was finally taking off and he was making new homes for himself in New York and Cambridge, his longings for a higher understanding kept him restlessly seeking some meaning in life beyond the day-to-day adventure. Then in the last section, "Dark Night of the Spirit," it finally begins coming together for him, in the form of spiritual and personal strength to fill the emptiness all by himself if necessary, with no expectation of help from the outside or from God or anyone else. The "Contemplations" piece published in one of the *American Avatars*, the one that begins "Loneliness is the sole motivation, the force that keeps man striving after the unattainable," was written during this period. The book ends in mid-1966, with Mel's contemplation on the death by motorcycle accident—or was it suicide?—of his friend, folksinger and novelist Richard Fariña, and just before Mel and the people closest to him decided to throw in their fortunes together and move into the first house on Fort Hill. The epilogue is a playful letter to Eben, written as the book was being assembled, recalling the fun they had in their old days, of struggling unconscious with the big questions and the adventure of it all.

More Demands, More Opportunities to Grow

About the time Mel's book and Jim's record finally made it out into the world (to resounding critical silence and sluggish sales), while we in New York were struggling to make money by any means we could—when we weren't assembling "stars" to sell, or hawking books, or re-modeling one of our houses—a couple of events occurred to make life even more complicated for the entire bicoastal community of us. With more and more of his people moving to the West Coast, and with his creative projects increasingly centered in the Hollywood mansion, but with the roots of the community still based in Boston and a large crew of us in New York, Mel decided that keeping in touch with all of us spread all over the place was taking too much of his time, with too long a drive between homes. The solution? Get a place in the middle of the country and move some people *there*; that way it would only take half as long to get "home" when he was on the road. Besides, he had had a fantasy for a while of a country place where his citified followers could learn to get back to basics. He and some of the others looked at a map of the country; drew lines between Boston, Los Angeles, San Francisco, and New York; and decided to find land where the lines crossed, very near the geographical center of the forty-eight contiguous states, in northeastern Kansas. Coincidentally, the metropolis of northeastern Kansas and the surrounding area was Kansas City, winter home of Tom Benton, Jessie's famous father. Mel dispatched David Gude to Kansas to search for land there. Tom Benton offered to help fund the project, maybe in hopes of having some of his pet hippies closer to home more of the time. Before long, David had found the perfect place: 280 acres of rolling farmland with a big old farmhouse and a broken-down but serviceable barn and other outbuildings, in the economically depressed Flint Hills area of Kansas. Now it was time to fill the place up with people and bring it to life.

At about the same time, the community was contacted by a writer from *Rolling Stone* magazine, David Felton, who wanted to do a major feature on the community. Over a period of several months, which happened to coincide with the media coverage of the KPFK incident and the purchase of the Kansas farm, he visited most of the community's homes around the country (but not New York). Somehow, he ingratiated himself with the Fort Hill people he met, sufficiently so that they shared lots of their time and information with him, expecting him to produce an article generally favorable to the Hill and its view of its role in the world. He even got to interview Mel privately at the Hollywood house.

During the period when Felton was traveling in Fort Hill circles, *Rolling Stone* published an article on another large community based in Berkeley and Oakland, which had some similarities to Fort Hill. Led by a salesman-turned-guru, Victor Baranco, the More House group offered quick, materialistic solutions to personal problems, encouraging its followers to set themselves up as paid teachers of the methods used—sort of an early version of spiritual network marketing. Unlike Fort Hill, it also offered its adherents lots of opportunities for sexual exploration and other hedonistic pleasures. Reading and hearing about the More Houses intrigued Mel and some of the others, and Faith Gude, who was living in the San Francisco apartment at the time, was dispatched to Oakland to meet Victor Baranco and establish friendly relations with his community, if that seemed appropriate. Faith reported back that the extensive remodeling work of the More Houses fell far short of the standards to which we were working, and that the level of interpersonal confrontation and growth was also deficient by comparison. But one of the methods used in the More Houses to keep people focused on each other and their collective responsibilities fascinated Faith, and she brought it back and taught it to people in each of the Fort Hill communities around the country. It was a structured game in which people would sit in a circle and take turns being in a "hot seat," where each one in turn would get to hear criticisms and receive praises from the others. I don't remember what this was called, or what the ostensible purpose was (and I know that in the context of our overstressed and overexamined lives, out of the context of the superficial and ego-gratifying lifestyle of the More Houses, it seemed trivial), but I do remember that for a period of a couple of months during that fall of 1971 when I was in New York, we played the game frequently, several nights a week, adding one more burden to our already very full schedules.

On the Cover of the *Rolling Stone*

Mel got his picture on the cover of the *Rolling Stone* on the issue dated December 23, 1971. Under the headline "The Lyman Family's Holy Siege of America," for twenty pages of the magazine David Felton juxtaposed the community's glowing reports and hyperbolic claims about its greatness with interviews of people who had been burned or disappointed by Mel over the years, or who had memories of a time when Mel was just another explorer on the path, before he claimed his divinity so flamboyantly. Highlights of his article included:

- an interview with writer Kay Boyle, mother of Faith Gude and Ian Franckenstein, who was persuaded on two occasions to attempt living at Fort Hill, but found herself locked inextricably in a battle of wills with Mel and David Gude;

- a detailed story from several non-Hill veterans of the founding of *Avatar* and the faction fighting that plagued it from the beginning;
- some stories of the Hill's often violent confrontations with media people who had tried to report on the community, or with whom the community had tried to build alliances;
- the story, witnessed by Felton himself when on Fort Hill, of the persecution of a "dummie" on the work crew who was trying to decide whether or not to leave the community; and
- stories of several other people's departures under pressure from the Hill, and of the mysterious "vault" that had been rumored (correctly) to exist in the basement under one of the houses, where people due for a punishment were occasionally held in solitary confinement while they reformed themselves.

All in all, it was a detailed, well-researched, beautifully written, and less-than-flattering portrait of the life of the community. It was a big disappointment to the Hill, and this was only half the story. A second installment was due two weeks later. A chill went through the community; what stories would David Felton reveal next time?

The second installment again took twenty magazine pages to tell. This time, Felton was much more personal, and also more explicitly critical of the community in the stories he told:

- his visit to the community's compound on Martha's Vineyard;
- his attempt to make sense of something he had witnessed on Fort Hill in Boston, the sudden decision to disassemble the addition to the houses in which Mel's "Magic Theater" was to have been housed;
- his version of Mark Frechette's brief career in films and how it intertwined with Mel's decision to colonize Hollywood;
- his story from Kay Boyle of how the community had attempted forcefully to take over her house in San Francisco, and how she had outsmarted them;
- his attempt to ferret out the truth about the community's relations with Reprise Records and Ballantine Books, and with KPFK;
- his visits with George Peper to Mel's father and his former schoolteacher, in northern California, and the fight George had picked with him about questions Felton had asked them;
- his very own visit from the "karma squad" at the *Rolling Stone* offices, where they threatened to pull out of the interview project if the reporter didn't become more real and personal; and finally,
- his early morning visit, dinnertime at the big house in Hollywood, in which he had his long-awaited private audience with Mel, finding him both surprisingly accessible and predictably mysterious and off-putting, and in which he heard about Mel's exchange of letters with the imprisoned Charles Manson.

The overall impression given by the article is of a somewhat mad, incestuous conspiracy, a little dangerous to outsiders, and inexplicable even to its own participants. Rather surreal, you could say. It even contained a full-page paid advertisement for the new record and book, headlined "Mel Lyman Is the Soul of America."

Reading the articles from within the suppressed confusion of my life in the New York community was, for me, definitely surrealistic. I wanted to feel loyalty to the community and therefore outrage at what Felton had done, but in truth I felt a lot of respect for his investigative reporting and the skillful, seamless way in which he had woven together the complex story. (*Rolling Stone* later reissued its coverage of the Mel Lyman, Victor Baranco, and Charles Manson "families" in book form, under the name *Mindfuckers* [Straight Arrow Books, San Francisco, 1972, Library of Congress number 72–79032].) I was as mystified as Felton was about the demolition of the Magic Theater and the sudden shift it seemed to represent in the community's priorities, which had not been explained to us at all. And I was kept busy, to say the least, and always on the edge of burnout by the heavy demands on our time and energy. I kept my feelings to myself and continued trying to do what was expected of me.

But it was weird to feel so alone, while surrounded by my supposed friends. At one time, about fifteen of us were living between the loft and the brownstone house. Many were men I had known and worked with for several years, my peers. Some were people I had learned to admire and was pleased to be with up close. Others represented continual difficulty for me. Sofie had moved to New York and in her characteristic way, part Third World bumpkin and part jaded sophisticate, had become queen of the place. I had long been fascinated by her and welcomed the chance to connect with her, but even after we found ways to talk with each other, she was suspicious of me and frequently accused me of being "asleep" to the important things. Brian Keating was there with us, now completely out of his role as a writer and newspaper editor and instead directing, or you might say dictating, some of our work energies in a high-tech painting enterprise, for which he bought us airless spray equipment. On the other hand, I enjoyed the company of several of my male coworkers and several of the women who had transferred down from Boston, with whom I felt more equal. At a certain point, Les Sweetnam, the companion with whom I had moved to New York, staged a carefully planned runaway from the community, aided by one of his construction clients, a family of well-known rock-and-roll musicians who simply didn't understand why he was sacrificing himself as he was. The priorities were, as always, mysterious to me.

As usual, there wasn't enough of anything to go around. We had one van to use for all of us, including all the larger-scale pickup and delivery needs of the construction and handy-man business about half of us were running. Most of the time, we would travel to our jobs on subways and buses, carrying all our tools and materials with us. We would go off in the morning with just carfare and minimum food money in our pockets, often carrying a lunch of peanut butter sandwiches with us.

The financial needs of the community had grown so great that there was simply no room in the budget for personal expenses or luxuries (unless they were somehow part of some scheme mandated from above), and everything we did was milked for cash at the earliest possible moment. There were even times when customers would front us advance money to buy materials for specific projects, and that money would make a mortgage payment or be sent back to Boston to be used for some overriding need of the community, such as a land payment in Kansas or a down payment on some piece of equipment Mel wanted to buy, and then we would have to arrange other work to make some new money to replace the advance so we could get back on schedule with the original job — all this without telling our customer what was happening, making excuses as necessary.

As in all the other Fort Hill homes around the country, periodically Mel and his entourage would come through and everything would be turned upside down for a time. Work schedules would instantly be revised or reduced so we could be on call to do special projects around the house; there might be screenings of Mel's latest bits of film work, or a chance to listen to some of his music. The living room of the lower flat of the house had been outfitted as a small theater for this purpose. I used to call the preparations in advance of such visits "painting the roses red," in reference to the ridiculous behavior of the characters in *Alice in Wonderland*, but no one else seemed to get the joke, or to see the ludicrousness of these last-minute attempts to make things into something they were not. The crew traveling with Mel would use their visit to check out how things were among the locals and make adjustments as needed. Thus, the visits took on a fearsome aspect alongside their inevitable celebratory quality. On one such occasion, I inadvertently blew it one more time, and everything came crashing down again for me.

Late one night during a visit from Mel and the traveling crew, I was invited to join in a round of Mel's favorite card game, a variation of pinochle he had invented that he called—what else?—"Melvin." Group members had been playing the Game of Melvin at Fort Hill and around the country wherever he was for a number of months, and it was considered an elegantly simple way to practice the principles of cooperation and attentiveness, or something like that. We in New York had had very little chance to learn the subtleties of the game, and I felt honored to be sitting around the kitchen table in the 15th Street house with just Mel and two others. Things went along well enough for a while, although Mel did seem to be winning most of the hands somehow. Then I found myself with a hand that begged to be played as a winner; it seemed that not doing so would have been an error. So I did just that and won the hand, at which signal Mel threw down his cards and stormed out of the room, back to his private quarters downstairs. I didn't know what had happened, but suddenly I was being confronted by all the men who were present who had higher status than me; they were telling me I still hadn't learned anything from Mel and living in the community, that I was still trying to compete and win, letting my ego get in the way. I guess the message was that one was supposed to recognize that one *could* compete if one wanted to, and then back off and let someone else win instead, especially if there happened to be a World Savior present. I never have figured it out, and in an environment of almost continual competitiveness it didn't make any sense to me. In any case, I was being given a choice: I could accept demotion to the lowest position available in New York—living in the basement of the house, working all the time, no pleasures, et cetera, until I had redeemed myself—or I could leave the community immediately. As I considered the choices, I felt a physical rush up my spine, something I hadn't felt in years, and said I was ready to leave.

CHAPTER 15

Hit The Road Again, Jack

Within an hour or so, well after midnight, I was out of there, walking to midtown Manhattan to hitchhike out of town. I decided on the spur of the moment to head for East Lansing, where I expected I still had some friends, where I hadn't been for four years, and where I believed, incorrectly, I still had a box of treasured goods in storage in someone's basement. I was, needless to say, quite disoriented and despondent.

I made it to East Lansing by the next afternoon, barely more than driving time, and started walking around town, assuming I would run into someone I knew before long. I did, indeed, find friends almost immediately, and before long I was installed as a stay-as-long-as-you-like guest in the home of two longtime friends. It was April 1972, and I thought it was the beginning of the rest of my life. I still have a letter I wrote to my mother shortly after I arrived in East Lansing, telling her the truth of why I had quickly canceled a plan to have dinner with her and my brother. Apparently I had asked for that meeting in order to press them to "invest" in Fort Hill's anticipated purchase of the house next door to the existing one in New York. In my letter, I tell the story of my demotion and justify my sudden move ("This really seems like the right thing for now, even though my heart still belongs to Fort Hill and to Mel if he can ever use it again") and give the details of the investment request, which I say "would be about the kindest thing you could do for me, and for everyone in the New York community." That old fidelity dies hard.

After a few days of getting used to where I was and paying for my friends' hospitality by painting their kitchen for them, I started looking for work. I was quickly hired onto a crew that was framing a bunch of houses in Lansing, and borrowed money to buy a hammer and tape measure, the minimum tools I needed. Then came a phone call from my old friend and nemesis Eric, in New York, who had figured out where I probably was and had found me on the first attempt. He was authorized to invite me back to New York to get myself together and get ready to move to the community's farm in Kansas. Was I interested? It was another of those moments. If I had been just a little bit more established in East Lansing, or if I had achieved just a little more understanding of the psychic dilemma I had been in for years, I might have turned him down. But I did not. I immediately accepted and headed for the highway again. Back in New York, I got help from my family; my brother hired me to do some carpentry work to make traveling money, and my mother gave me an old car she no longer needed, a roadworthy Chevy sedan. I felt grateful for the chance to take "basic training" at the farm, to have an identity again. I spent a week or two getting ready, and then left for Kansas along with crazy Rita, Mel's former lady who had lived in my house on Fort Hill. Considering the unlikely twosome we made, the trip was relatively uneventful, and our reception at the farm was warm.

I remember clearly the all-American hominess of my first few days there, which made me believe, at last, the community had found a place where I could be comfortable and valued. Curiously, I have no memory of Rita after we arrived at the farm. My guess is she must have stayed only long enough to hitch a ride to one of the other "homes"; certainly she was not cut out for living in a place where one had to attend daily to the physical necessities of life.

I felt good being received into the comparatively low-pressure environment of rural Kansas, albeit Fort Hill's version of that. The few people at the farm were all familiar to me, to one degree or another, and the necessities of the moment were relatively achievable: make a home in this new place, employing simple, old-fashioned technologies as much as possible (for example, we removed an electric range from the kitchen and installed a big wood-burning cook stove; the neighbors thought we were crazy); get to know the locals; and in general, keep things simple. That was the point of "basic training" and it was okay with me. Wayne Hansen was there, once again acting as my guide into a new home, and we had plenty of work to do around the place. There were animals to take care of, old farm equipment to wrangle with, a big vegetable garden that the women tended, and large fields we were considering using to grow cash crops, imitating the locals. On one hand, it seemed more "real" than the concerns that had preoccupied us in Boston and New York; on the other hand, it was all kind of a sandbox situation, with no real necessities driving us to do one thing or another. Comparatively a lot of freedom.

A Simpler Language

The farm had been purchased from a longtime local farmer who owned several places in the immediate area, but who, like everyone else in the region, had come upon hard times and had put his prize place on the market. He still lived and worked in the area with his family, and in his folksy, uneducated way and with his very limited understanding of what we were up to, gave us plenty of support and help. Through him, we met other neighbors and townspeople. We were accepted readily enough, even though our worldly ways and cross-country traveling and mysterious stories of the larger community that we were a part of must have seemed very weird and puzzling. But we were attempting to blend in as best we could, which involved learning to be interested in the things rural Kansans were interested in, trading favors when possible, and learning to speak a simpler kind of language. We learned to tend (and bully) the farm animals, to drive tractors and flatbed trucks, to run chainsaws and baling machines, to repair barbed wire fences. We became familiar with the local landscape and some of the local history.

Much of the area had been slated to be flooded by an Army Corps of Engineers dam, and several nearby villages had been vacated and demolished; but the dam had been defective and was never filled completely, so some of the land was spared. Still, the local economy was severely damaged, both by the dislocation and by the general downturn in farm income. The county road that bisected our place came across a new bridge the Corps of Engineers had built over a small creek near our house, marking what would have been the edge of the lake if the dam had been filled. Many farms had been abandoned or had changed hands recently; some people were amassing more property and others were making do with less. It was a strange and surprising time for a flock of newcomers to arrive in the area.

I especially appreciated the chance to learn more about speaking American and acting like a down-home kind of guy. The years in Boston and New York had gone a long way toward cultivating an anti-intellectual attitude in me, but had not been very successful in replacing my former appreciation for the intellect and for precise language with something else more functional. Learning to imitate and converse with our neighbors in Kansas gave me an opportunity to do that, and surprising as it may seem, this served me well at the time and ever since. I found out that most ideas can be broken down into simple, everyday thoughts and expressed as such, and that most relationships of ideas or mechanical processes, no matter how complex, can be translated into everyday images and familiar ideas. This makes them much easier to communicate, especially if there is humor in the mix. (Later I also learned that even deep and subtle feelings can be named simply and discussed matter-of-factly, but that lesson didn't come easily or quickly for me, even at the farm.)

I appreciated working with Wayne and the others on the huge variety of maintenance and fix-up tasks we confronted, and also enjoyed a period of several months working for one of the local carpenter-builders, as his helper and sidekick. And I enjoyed the couple of women at the farm, who tended the garden and the children, and were enthusiastically learning the old skills and cultivating relations with the neighbors. But before long, the idyllic nature of this respite was put under pressure reminiscent of the burdens that all the urban communities were constantly under. Periodically we would receive a new "Melzak" tape or other communication to keep us feeling connected to the larger community we were a part of, and that was nice for us. But sometimes there would also come a directive to do something or other that would seem to come out of the blue and just make our lives harder. Mel needs his own bedroom and bathroom at the farm; find a way to build what's needed and make space for him. Figure out some way to provide more bunk space for people to come visit. Build an outhouse and use it, instead of the indoor plumbing. Take out the telephone; learn to live more like they did in the old days. Fix one of our women up with a local bachelor farmer; maybe he'll do us more favors that way.

These kinds of directives had been hard enough to take in the city. In the country, where practicality is king, they seemed completely irrational and out of context. The result was similar to what it was in the city when people overloaded; periodically someone would up and leave, usually during or just after one of the occasional visits we received from Mel and his traveling entourage. The couple who had been the first to move out from Boston to help populate the place, shortly after it was purchased, took hard the first visit from Mel and company that occurred after my arrival. Instead of welcoming the visitors and their many suggestions for how life could be improved, Neil and Judy just drew inward, resenting what they perceived as criticism. I remember George Peper complaining that Neil was lurking around like a surly farmhand instead of acting like the gracious host he was expected to be. On that visit, Sofie was being deposited at the farm to become mistress of the place, and it was a good thing, because a few days after the traveling crew left, Neil and Judy were gone too, taking Judy's young son and everything they could pack in their car. Wayne also walked away from the farm, either during that visit or the next one. Somehow the comments and suggestions from the traveling crew made him feel inadequate to the task and in some way disloyal to Mel; I felt loyal to Wayne and offered to accompany him in an expression of solidarity, but he wouldn't have me. He soon returned to the community via Hollywood.

Wayne's "replacement" as man-in-charge at the farm was a young, overconfident newcomer to the community from Boston known as Mike Aries. Mike Aries was one of those people Mel and friends loved because they wouldn't stop at anything, certainly would never let abstract thoughts or moral compunctions keep them from acting. Before long, Mike and Sofie were having an affair; I was enlisted to perform a "marriage" ceremony for them. Mike did his best to direct activities at the farm, to be the "man" around the place, but he was little more than a boy and was overly impressed by property and power. We instinctively disliked each other and even competed for the name we shared. I lost, of course. Sofie asked me what other name I would like to use; I combined "Mike" with my middle name, Jay, and came up with "Jake," which became my name for the duration of my time at the farm.

A couple of newcomers joined the community in Kansas. A freelance journalist based in Kansas City, Dick Russell, read about us somewhere and made it his business to connect. He came visiting as frequently as he could, eventually met Mel, was quickly encouraged to visit the other communities, and generally become one of the insiders. Dick also brought along a sometime lover of his, Carol Burger, whom Sofie dubbed Carolee, who took to the place immediately and soon moved in with her two school-age sons. She quickly became involved with David Wilson (not the same David Wilson who worked on the earliest *Avatar*), whom I considered a friend from my earliest days around the *Avatar* office, and who had recently been transferred out from the Boston work crew. When their brief affair was over, David moved into a side room in the barn, leaving Carolee free to receive flirtatious attentions from me, just in time for Christmas. We exchanged romantic gifts (I made her a hand-drawn horoscope, superimposed over a copy of a painting that resembled the local landscape in winter) and a day or two later spent the night together. It was the first time in over three years I had slept with someone, since I had broken up with Carol, and I could hardly believe it was happening.

The very next day, a car arrived on its way from Boston to Hollywood. Two of the men were moving out there and were bringing three of the little girls from Fort Hill to live with us. Sofie had to figure out the new accommodations, and announced to Carolee and me that we were moving in together. What a surprise! A couple of weeks later, we were given the job of caring for the growing number of children at the farm. To do the job, we were moved to a small house a few miles away, another one owned by the same local farmer who had sold us our farm. The arrangement was hell on a new and fragile relationship. Fortunately, it was only temporary, while David and Mike and I struggled to build a new bunkhouse on the hillside above our main farmhouse that would serve as a children's house when no guests were present.

This disorienting arrangement was how we were living when Mel and his traveling crew came visiting again in January, with snow and ice on the ground. We all collected at the main house to have a welcoming breakfast, but Sofie was nervous that she didn't have enough maple syrup to serve with Mel's pancakes. For his part, David was nervous about seeing Mel and company at all, and volunteered to drive into town to get more syrup. He took the Toyota Land Cruiser that was our most reliable vehicle. But David was our least reliable driver; he didn't even have a license. He finally returned a couple of hours later, delivered by a neighbor. He had skidded on the icy road and rolled the Land Cruiser, which landed on its roof in a ditch. All for a bottle of maple syrup in a snowstorm. David was okay, but the Land Cruiser was quite severely damaged and was not insured, because we had been so cash-poor trying to keep up with all the other demands on our time and money. Mel's response, delivered at the breakfast table where there was in fact no shortage of syrup or anything else, was to chastise us for not placing priority on finding the money for insurance. It was another moment when I wish I had had the clarity to say the obvious: "If you hadn't placed such unreasonable demands on us, if Sofie wasn't so afraid of not pleasing you, if David wasn't so afraid of facing you, none of this would have happened, and now all you can say is that we should have insured ourselves against the loss." I didn't say a word, but my respect and appreciation for Mel's "gifts" of leadership and guidance fell still further. A few days after Mel's visit ended, while the same snow was still on the ground, we woke up one morning to find that David had run away during the night.

It was the beginning of the end for me. Mike and I labored on to finish the new bunk-house, working with lumber milled by a neighbor from a beech tree we had felled. We were also finishing a new bathroom for Mel's use, tucked under the eaves of the farmhouse, with a secret storage closet hidden behind the wood-paneled walls. (We had fantasies of developing a "cash crop" out of the volunteer marijuana that grew everywhere in that area, the aftereffects of widespread cultivation of hemp during World War II.) Carolee and I gamely tried to act like appropriate caretakers for the flock of children in our care, but we both felt like we were in over our heads and had no time at all to explore our own relationship with each other. Sofie was being her imperious self, which by now I recognized as the personality she assumed when she felt inadequate to the role she had taken on. My best friend throughout this period was Dick Russell, who was splitting his time between Kansas City and the farm, and who somehow seemed able to reconcile the distance between using his mind as a working tool and otherwise operating by instinct and conviction, as Mel and company always urged us to do. I was envious of his working life as a freelance writer, and depended on him for some perspective on events at the farm.

Another visit from Mel and the road crew occurred around the time of spring equinox. The bunkhouse and Mel's new bathroom were finished just in time to be put to use. The bunkhouse was a success, and the bathroom would have been, too, if I hadn't made an error in the plumbing that prevented the drains from working properly. Uh oh. Again, it was no excuse that I had been working under so much pressure; I should have asked all the local tradespeople what I needed to know to get it done right. As usual, the visit was the occasion to move someone new to the farm. This time it was Jeremy, the Englishman who had been with us in New York, where we staged a wedding for him in order to keep him in the country legally; now he was to have what Mel called his "American period." Jeremy and I, who had been friends for years in both Boston and New York, didn't get along at all this time. He was very committed to being an agent of positive change at the farm, and he and Mike and Sofie were gearing up to take whatever steps were necessary to make that happen.

History Lesson

As soon as the traveling crew left, and Carolee and I reoccupied the bunkhouse with all the kids, Jeremy started questioning whether Carolee's two sons really belonged at the farm. Somehow they didn't fit in with the others; maybe they should go back to the city and live with their father. No one asked me what I thought, and I know Carolee was upset at the question being asked at all, but within a few hours, literally, the boys were gone from the farm, collected by their father's new wife, who drove up to get them as soon as she heard they were no longer welcome with us. I didn't understand this at all, and Carolee could hardly talk about it. Neither of us protested as the boys drove away; when they were gone, Carolee hid out in the bunkhouse. Then, as though nothing had happened, Jeremy made a weird request to me: Could I give a little talk on American history after dinner that night to those of us who remained at the farm? It's easy now to see that this was a set-up, but at the time I just tried to do what I was asked.

Almost as soon as I began speaking, Jeremy interrupted me: Why didn't I say something "real," why was I just talking about all this abstract stuff? "But, Jeremy, you asked me to talk about this." That's not the point; why was I such a wimp? (or whatever word was used at the time to convey that idea; "pissant," pronounced "piss-ant," was a popular one). When was I finally going to get out of my head and start feeling? As always when confronted by this kind of attack, I didn't know what to say or do, and froze. Sofie stepped in, with a large kitchen knife in hand, and suggested that maybe it would be sufficient to elicit some reaction from me. I could hardly believe this was happening. What was she willing to do with that knife? I didn't get to find out, because Jeremy came up with a new idea: What was my most precious possession? I answered that probably my copy of the *I Ching* was it. He told me to go up to the bunkhouse and get it. I did so, assuming we were going to refer to the oracle to help us out of this difficult moment, as all of us had used it many times before.

Jeremy had something else in mind. He started tearing pages out of the book. When I moved to stop him, Mike held my arms down to the table. This was not rational, of course, even in their terms. If they were trying to elicit a reaction, why stop me when I react? It made no sense. But Jeremy proceeded to destroy the book, and then he and Mike invited me down to the basement for some more discussion. Carolee ran into the living room crying, and that was the last time I saw her. In the basement, Jeremy and Mike aggressively started asking me again what it would take for me to get out of my head. They started hitting me, and asked me what did I like and dislike. For some reason, I could only think of complaining about having to wear eyeglasses all the time, that I found them really frustrating. Jeremy suggested I just get rid of them, and I did, throwing them on the floor and breaking them. But this was not enough to prove my conversion. They hit me some more, giving me a black eye and otherwise hurting me around the face. Then Jeremy made me look into a mirror and ordered me to "Look at what all your thinking has gotten you." My thinking? As though his fist had had nothing to do with it. He and Mike ordered me to go out to the outhouse and spend the night there, contemplating what had just happened.

I sat in the outhouse, conveniently located facing the creek near the small bridge where the county road crossed onto our property. After a short time, a voice in my head—a clear, still voice speaking up for the first time in what seemed like ages—started saying, "These people want to kill me. These people want to kill me, and I'd better get out of here." As I listened to this voice, it made more and more sense to me. Here I was, at the edge of the property; all I'd have to do is slip down toward the creek bed, and it would be an easy matter to get away without being seen. But I had just broken my glasses, my wallet with ID and money were up in the bunkhouse, and I was wearing completely inappropriate clothing, including my painful, oversized cowboy boots. But it was now or never. I quietly left the outhouse and walked up the creek bed, looking back only enough to see that I wasn't being followed. I walked the several miles out to the small house where Carolee and I had lived briefly. I knew how to get into the basement storage room there, where there was a sleeping bag that belonged to Dick Russell and an old leather jacket that belonged to Dick Libra, the "real" Richard Herbruck. I took them both and continued walking until I found a barn close to where the county road met the state highway, and spent the night there. I was amazed I had gotten this far without being intercepted. Was making me run away what they had in mind all along? In any case, I was gone now. The morning would be March 24, 1973, Mel Lyman's 35th birthday, and the first day of the rest of my life.

CHAPTER 16

What Next?

In the morning, I began walking south along the state highway, which would eventually take me to the interstate that ran across the state from Kansas City in the east to the Colorado border in the west. I wasn't at all sure where I was headed or what I wanted. In fact, I wasn't even sure who I wanted to be. I knew "Jake the plumber" was a thing of the past, and there was nothing on me to identify who I was or how I had gotten where I was, with my face all beat up again. I found a broken-down outbuilding on a farm alongside the road and sat down inside it to contemplate my future, if I even wanted a future. Maybe I would just sit there and die. I still wasn't sure that at any moment someone from the farm wouldn't find me and drag me home, but they did not. If I was on my own, did I want to become Michael again, or become someone new? Did I want to reconnect with people from my past, or start over? Did I want to live at all? I tried to sort it out, but couldn't.

Again, the voice inside gave me guidance: Of course I wanted to be myself again; losing track of that had been the problem. But how? Somehow, I decided it would be acceptable to start out by dropping in on Dick Russell in Kansas City. I went back to the road and was immediately offered a ride by a kind gentleman, a minister from one of the nearby towns who offered me a few dollars and a small pocket Bible that was his treasured possession. I had no use for a Bible, but thought his gesture extraordinarily kind. I refused to tell him where I had come from or why I was in the shape I was in, other than to say some friends and I had come to a serious disagreement. Maybe he figured it out; I don't know whether he knew about our farm or not. (Months later, when I was settled in California, I returned his Bible to him by mail, with an anonymous thank-you note and no return address.) A second kind driver gave me a few more dollars and took me all the way to the interstate. I was astounded, and very grateful. My feet hurt.

Before I knew it, I was in Kansas City, wandering around trying to get myself oriented, still unsure whether dropping in on Dick was a good idea. I went to a thrift shop to get some reasonable clothes and a small suitcase to travel with. When I finally saw Dick, he was gracious and reasonably understanding. We acted just like normal friends for a couple of days, sharing stories of the people we had in common, helping me figure out what to do next, going to his favorite bars and hangouts. I tried to find temporary work, and when I couldn't, I sold a pint of blood to make a few dollars. Dick offered to give me a few dollars also to use on the road, but confessed he was getting worried harboring me as a runaway from the community. He asked me to leave, and gave me two mementos from the community to travel with, which I still have—a copy of Mel's book, and one of the smallest of John Kostick's "tetraxi" stars. He took me out to the interstate, and I was on my own again.

It was a Friday afternoon. I easily got rides out of town and halfway across the state, but later that evening I got busted for hitchhiking on the highway near Salina, Kansas. Since I had no identification on me, and my story was kind of difficult to comprehend, the arresting police found it necessary to hold me in jail for the weekend, until I could prove to an arraigning judge on Monday that I was who I said I was. Somehow, it got worked out and I was on the road again on Monday, I think by my giving the phone number of the farm to corroborate my story and promising to send verification of my identity and payment of a fine when I got settled somewhere.

I was imagining traveling south through New Mexico, by way of Denver, and then on to California, but by the time I got to Denver, a blizzard had enveloped all of Colorado and New Mexico. I spent the night in an empty semitrailer with some other hitchhikers and a helpful truck driver, and in the morning started hitching north toward Wyoming and out of the blizzard. In Cheyenne, I met some old hoboes who encouraged me to ride a freight train out of town and told me how, but the train they put me on turned out to be a shuttle that only went back and forth between Cheyenne and a coal mine in the middle of the state. When I figured out what was happening, I shamefacedly presented myself to the engineers, and they agreed to take me back to Cheyenne. I hitchhiked out of Cheyenne, but halfway across Wyoming my highway luck ran out, and I decided to try a freight train again. This time I did it right; before long (and before my fingers froze completely), I was in Provo, Utah, north of Salt Lake City, where the train line took off around the north side of the Great Salt Lake and on westward.

It hadn't been my plan, but suddenly it made sense to hitchhike into Salt Lake City, where Sofie had two brothers and a sister, all of them relocated recently from San Francisco. I had met one of the brothers, Patrick, in Boston; now he was living an upstanding life with his Mormon convert wife and managing a hairstyling salon. I knew I could find him if I tried, and even though it seemed a bit weird, I couldn't think of any better way out of the cold just then.

I did find Patrick at his salon on the south side of town, and he was cordial but uneasy about putting me up in his middle-class family home. After the first night, he took me over to meet his brother James and sister Ruby, both of whom I had heard of but never met, who were living in a house much closer to downtown, where they both worked in a methadone clinic. They made me a bed on the back porch of their house, and I promised to find work as quickly as I could so I could buy my way into a place of my own. I was uncomfortable accepting these favors from the siblings of one of the people who had thrown me out of the farm, and at the same time I welcomed the sense of familiarity, and felt in need of some help if I was to get on my feet again. Within a couple of days, I found a job as a laborer and ditch digger, preparing to pour the foundations of a small apartment complex in the suburbs north of Salt Lake. My employer was a young, rather rude second-generation building contractor with family ties to the Mormon Church. We had an uneasy connection, and he thought I was too strange for words, but he admired my work and quickly offered to keep me on as a carpenter if I wanted to stay. I agreed, and planned to use my first paycheck to rent a place of my own.

I wrote to Dick Russell, telling him of the amusing turn of events by which I had been kicked out of the farm by Sofie and was now hanging out with her siblings. I suggested I might want to connect with the community's house in San Francisco when I eventually got to California, and asked if he could help retrieve my wallet and ID to make my journey easier. He wrote back an angry letter, with news of more personnel changes at the farm and a strong rebuke to me:

> It seems to me you're still using people as crutches to maintain your sense of a "tie to Mel," when what you keep talking about doing is finding out if you can maintain that tie ON YOUR OWN. . . . Goddamn it, DO what you're saying you want to—get out there in the world and bum around and make some money so you can start feeling useful, but quit expecting someone else to fill the connection you have to find YOURSELF! . . . If you really want to be the kind of man you told me you wanted to be, it's up to you to do it! It would seem ill-advised for you to go to the San Francisco Community until you are certain you are ready to contribute more than a physical body. You belong to the world and to yourself now, not to me or to Sofi's [sic] relatives or to San Francisco, and it is up to you to jump over that barrier and work your way back—if you want it badly enough! . . . I will see what I can do about your wallet. You should write soon and tell me your plans.

Dick's letter was quite a blow to me; I had thought I was behaving the way nearly anyone would when confronted with as much dislocation and separation as I was. Dick's reaction seemed based in his own fear of endorsing and supporting me in behavior the community might dislike. I saw myself humbly seeking out the help I thought I could find among the people I knew in a strange place, and was busily putting myself together as quickly as I could. When my first paycheck was imminent, I found a room in a rooming house near the University of Utah, and proudly brought that news home to James and Ruby. I then learned something very revealing about their characters that made some truths about Fort Hill clear to me as well.

It seems that on the day I brought the news home, I made a blunder: I sat in on a conversation between Ruby and one of her methadone clients, thinking this was just a friendly visit and that I was welcome. Ruby said nothing to me, but asked James in an aside to announce that this was an intolerable intrusion and I would have to leave. So James took me out on a shopping errand, where I proudly told him that I had already rented a room and would be leaving in a day or two. His reply was as though I had said nothing. "Sofie called us from the farm, you know, and we knew you were coming." (Surely this was a fabrication; I didn't know myself I was coming until the weather and my hitchhiking luck made me change course.) "But Ruby says you're really getting in the way, and you'll have to leave." (But, James, I just told you I was leaving. Why didn't Ruby just ask me to give her and her client some privacy?)

The similarity to the tactics used at Fort Hill was a shock and an eye-opener for me. This was evidently the morality of the street as practiced in San Francisco's cross-cultural immigrant neighborhoods, where Sofie's family had lived for years, and where Mel Lyman, too, had come of age. I was not only an inept player according to these rules, I was also the kind of person—short, soft-spoken, educated, distinctly un-macho—who was automatically perceived as an outsider and treated with suspicion. So that's what had been happening at Fort Hill during all that painful time, I concluded. The game was stacked against me.

Rebuilding

I moved into my rooming house and continued working my construction job. How was I going to put my life together again? My second paycheck was dedicated to new shoes and eyeglasses so I could again see what was happening around me. I asked my mother in New York to make arrangements to get a copy of my New York driver's license so I could use it to obtain a new one in Utah. It would all be a slow climb, but a possible one. But what would fill my mind, and my life? I felt unbelievably bereft.

A couple of weeks after I settled in at the rooming house, my birthday came along, and I wanted to give myself a gift of some kind. I gave myself permission to shoplift a felt-tip pen, with which to begin keeping a journal. I was busted in the attempt and felt completely stupid about it. The first entry in the brief journal I started keeping began, "Today I turned 28. At the age of 28 I am living the life of someone who has just finished school and left home for the first time." I discuss my departure from the farm, my confusion about it, and the help I got from Sofie's family in deciding to stay on in Salt Lake, and the irony of letting myself get busted for shoplifting: "Lessons and opportunities and such things here in 'the world' tend to come in such a veiled manner, it all depends on what you make of them. It feels like I'm here for a while at least and must try like hell to be straight. [Remember when 'straight' meant 'un-hip'?] I'm so unused to this kind of thing. Thank God for the months I spent with the simple folk in Kansas. . . . Maybe I can become such a one some time." The similarities, and the differences, between what was happening to me and the early phase of Mel's wandering life, as recorded in *Mirror at the End of the Road*, were compelling reasons to attempt to record my thoughts and feelings.

My journal entry ten days later is full of news: I got my driver's license transferred and received my third paycheck, and immediately bought an old car for $75. I have friends in the rooming house; we hang out together and harass the Mormon missionaries who come visiting us. And work for my young employer is a struggle: "[H]e irks me so much, and I piss him off so much of the time, he still treats me like a dumb shit no matter what I do. And I don't do good work for him. I'm in a fog most of the time there, he brings out the worst in me, and at least once or twice a day we just glare at each other, murder in both our eyes. It's a real bad situation." Shades of Fort Hill. Two days later, I describe a significant dream, the first of many over the years in which I have various kinds of encounters with people from Fort Hill:

> I was with Carolee, and she came to me with the news that Faith wanted to see me up on her mountain, a ceremonious occasion. It felt like a pilgrimage or a communion meeting of some sort as we made our way to where Faith was. There were many gathered on a steep hill, and she stood in a white gown like a queen, with two similarly blond, long-haired attendants in ivory gowns. One was [a friend from high school], the other

I can't remember, perhaps [someone from the community]. Carol Ann [Schneider] was there, too, behind Faith like a lady-in-waiting. I greeted Faith and teased them for being "white goddesses," but she went on talking to the others gathered there without answering me at all. After a while I asked Carolee if she knew why I'd been summoned since Faith didn't seem to intend to speak to me, and she just said it wasn't a mistake, if she was ignoring me then that must be what she intended. Then it was time to go, and we walked down the hill, separate from all the others, and got on a trolley car. The driver was my high school chemistry teacher [who in my memory resembled Carolee in appearance], who seemed to know more than she was letting on, but she was very courteous. While we were riding, I told Carolee that I was *trying* to be a man and do what I had to—and I was very specific about what that meant to me, like being an example, directing my loved ones toward the right way, et cetera—and I knew I was blowing it and didn't know why. Carolee listened and was both sympathetic and impassive, the way she can be, and then it was time to get off the trolley. We thanked Miss Krahm and said goodbye, and I woke up.

The next entry a few days later discusses my return to the study of astrology. I had reconstructed my own chart from memory, had found an occult bookstore from which to begin acquiring reference books and taking classes, had found the astrology section of the university library, and had begun reexamining myself in terms of the information I was finding. I describe "quite a struggle" I'd been having internally:

Ever since the dream I had Sunday about Faith and Fort Hill, I've been feeling the Community slipping away in myself, and that is a painful change to observe, though it seems a necessary one. It is all becoming very distant, and more and more I am seeing the basic disagreements between myself and the regimen of continual sacrifice and externally imposed justice. I just can't fit in with all that, never could, it didn't fit the pattern (or lack of it) by which I have to live in order to be me. The lack of conscious understanding of who I am which I always felt in the community (and which I could never penetrate there) makes sense when I see who I am by my chart, but I feel a need and have a responsibility to live in such a way that the potential of this mysterious person becomes manifest. I cannot consciously live a lie.

Sadly, this is the last entry in my brief journal; but a couple of weeks later, I wrote a long letter to a close friend from grade school and high school who had remained in touch with my life through all the traumas of college and the years in Boston. A letter from him had been forwarded to me by my mother; I responded with a description of my departure from the farm and a discussion of what I thought it all meant:

Much of what I was hoping to find and attach myself to in the Community—purpose, eternal purpose, I mean, and a place in the evolution of mankind, family, security and the productivity and creativity which they can inspire—somehow never came to me while I was there, even though I did and do believe they were there. As far as I can see, I can only blame the inadequate evolution of my soul for that fact, because I sure busted ass trying to make the grade. Others were not so charitable. They blamed my pride, egotism, stubbornness, insensitivity, stupidity, et cetera—doubtless true charges but obviously things of the moment, albeit long moments, and subject to change if we could only have come to terms with our differences. There were times when I was very close to people there and we loved each other and worked together truly, but when circumstances changed and demanded different things from us, I could not always readily adjust, and in the end I guess I just wasn't worth the effort it would have taken to bring me along.

Does that make sense to you? You have to realize that the Community has a very high and in many ways an egoless and depersonalized sense of mission and destiny for itself. In many ways the people who carry out the details of that destiny are not up to its demands, and so the means of bringing about "justice" (that is, karma) are often crude and superficially heartless or senseless, but in general the dedication to the demands of "spirit," as manifested in the creation of complete and resilient individuals, is such that what happens is somehow right despite the methods used. What I'm saying is I trust what happened to me even though it seemed a butcher-job at the time and was very difficult to go through and left a residue of bitterness, as unresolved tension and frustration always do, which I've had to live with and purge gradually and replace with a higher level of patience and understanding. I dream about people and situations in the Community very, very often, from the little kids all the way to Mel, surprising dreams, good ones, bad ones, ones in which I feel very good and useful to them, ones in which I'm a fool and a pompous ass. I miss them all, but I am far away from them. I don't know if I'll ever go back or not. I'm waiting for signals and working on my own development. . . .

Perhaps, if I prove to have an aptitude for it and the determination which is required, astrology will become a serious study for me and will become my method of teaching which I have sought for so long. I have the feeling for teaching or communion or whatever it is that you described so well in your letter, but as you once knew and can now see again, I have had only intermittent success in passing anything of value on to others through it. Also, someday I expect I will have to have a career, and very little appeals to me unless it serves the purpose of showing people themselves. . . . At present, I am a carpenter again, and that and related trades are my most useful means of surviving in the material world—universally useful, in fact; I never have to want for work for very long—but I don't want to spend my whole life with a hammer or a paintbrush or a wrench in my dirty hands, so I am wishing that this delicate business of evolving a higher purpose in life would get on with itself.

More Dancing Lessons from God

In my letter I discuss the probability of making my way to California to visit my sister and her family at their new home in Redwood City, near San Francisco, at a time when my mother and possibly my brother and his family would also be visiting, and then perhaps returning to New York with my mother to help her ready her house for sale so she could retire to Florida. I didn't know exactly how or when all this would happen. (In fact, it was another three years before the trip to New York occurred.) As it turned out, I stayed in Salt Lake City slightly more than another month; when my car broke down just before I was due to drive it to California,

I decided instead to abandon it and take a bus to San Francisco. I left Salt Lake City on July 24, four months to the day after walking away from the farm in Kansas.

I had enlisted my mother's collaboration in keeping my plans secret from my sister, so I could surprise her by showing up unexpectedly at her door, but since I was traveling by bus and had to be collected at the terminal, it didn't happen that way. Still, it was a joyous reunion. We had been very close at times in the past, but I had only seen her and her husband and three young sons once during all my time in the community, when they had visited overnight at the farm the previous summer during a cross-country trip, and that experience was uncomfortable for everyone. They were happy to have me on their turf now and to be able to help me move on in my life. In fact, they had already arranged work for me, doing construction and decorating for the people from whom they had recently bought their house, an elderly couple who previously ran a construction business and still owned and managed a nursing home and an apartment building. There was also the possibility of purchasing used construction equipment and vehicles from the former owners, and of collaborating with my brother-in-law in putting a house on an empty lot next door that he and my sister had already bought.

I was dumbfounded. I had expected to visit briefly in Redwood City, get reacquainted with my family, find out if we had anything in common, and then move on to San Francisco to reconnect with the counterculture that I had left behind years ago and assumed was still going strong there, and where I hoped to raise the question of whether I wanted to continue living as a straight man (meaning in the sense of sexual identity) or return to exploring life as a gay man. The last thing I expected was to find a congenial home in the suburbs of the San Francisco Peninsula. But there I was.

For five months, I lived in an extra room in my sister's house while I got to know the local area, and while I became used to living on my own again in the regular world. In many ways I was relieved to simply move into an established household and do the things that were presented to me, which in this case meant working by day for the elderly couple and various other friends of my sister's family who offered me work, and socializing with my sister's and her husband's large circle of friends by night and on days off. I also bought an old dump truck in hopes of establishing myself in the hauling business; while that outcome did not occur, the dump truck did lead me out of my sister's circle of acquaintances and into some friendships of my own, when it blew its engine soon after I started using it for hauling.

From the elderly couple's grandson, I learned about a consumer-owned cooperative auto repair shop in nearby Palo Alto where I might be able to rebuild an engine myself with guidance from the shop personnel. I had no history at all of doing major automotive repairs—quite the opposite; my history with vehicles was filled with misadventures, poor judgments, and the pursuit of bad advice. I had never even seen an engine rebuild in progress—but this seemed like the next step at the moment. My self-image was so corrupted that I had no idea what was appropriate to do from one minute to the next, and I seemed to have a distinct inclination under the circumstances toward masculine-image adventures and involvements, toward seeing myself as capable of any feat of physical work and heroic challenge. Rebuild a truck engine? Sure, no problem!

CHAPTER 17

There's a Place in the Sun

Redwood City and Palo Alto are, in a sense, the twin capitals of a small suburban metropolis known as the Mid-Peninsula, midway down the San Francisco Peninsula from San Francisco to San Jose, both much larger metropolises in themselves and with very different characters from each other. The Mid-Peninsula contains a little of each—some of the urbanity and worldliness of San Francisco, some of the provincial quality of San Jose, an old agricultural capital grown into a modern industrial center—as well as a distinct personality of its own, a blend of traditional and modern styles, several small cities jammed close together, each of which runs from the wetlands of San Francisco Bay through low-lying residential and commercial neighborhoods and up into the foothills of the adjoining Santa Cruz Mountains, with their history of redwood logging and rebellious individualism. Poor and rich, intellectual and working class, Anglo, black, Mexican, and occasional Asian communities intermingle in each of the cities. Stanford University, a world-class center of scientific and cultural research, sits square in the middle of all this, the legacy of robber-baron industrialist and one-time senator Leland Stanford. An enormous endowment of land and money dominates the area with shopping centers, industrial parks, research facilities, spin-off electronics industries, and traffic problems. As host community to Stanford, Palo Alto has always been somewhat overshadowed and underfunded by its famous guest, but during the 1960s and into the 1970s, the growth of the "Silicon Valley" electronics industry and the general prosperity of the area had been good to Palo Alto; a progressive city government had developed a wide range of city-funded services, and big portions of the foothills had been annexed into the city to provide for the possibility of continuing growth.

Palo Alto during those days was also home to an innovative alternative-culture community, curiously scattered throughout the traditional downtown area and the surrounding neighborhoods with their more suburban character, with numerous outposts in the adjoining towns and the nearby rural, hilly areas. The Briarpatch Cooperative Auto Shop was just one of the unusual expressions of that community. The *Whole Earth Catalog* was being published in the adjoining town of Menlo Park, where a retail outlet, the Whole Earth Truck Store, was also located (an early source of environmentally sensitive new technology), along with several related consulting and publishing ventures. Several consumer-operated food-buying cooperatives operated in the area, as did a string of community-based health services. The Briarpatch Network of alternative businesses linked these various enterprises together, and helped to promote a new philosophy of ecologically sound entrepreneurship.

The Stanford campus had been a significant center of antiwar organizing; its onetime student body president David Harris became nationally famous when he burned his draft card, and later when he married folksinger Joan Baez and moved with her to a home among a group of rural communes in the Santa Cruz Mountain foothills above Palo Alto. Harris's imprisonment for draft evasion, and Baez's continuous performing and speaking in support of his cause brought national attention to the counterculture community of which they were a part. The leftist think tank Baez helped found and to a large degree supported, the Institute for the Study of Non-Violence, was located in an old house in downtown Palo Alto. The idea of "peace conversion" was born there when the local peace movement began asking the question: how can we redirect the "defense"-based economy toward something more useful? A couple of research and lobbying organizations formed around this issue, and a new monthly, community-based newspaper, the *Grapevine*, began publishing in June 1973. The *Grapevine* spoke for all the alternative communities of the Mid-Peninsula, with a bias toward leftist politics, small-scale economics, and do-it-yourself socialism. It contained lots of coverage of Third World anticolonial struggles. In format, it was a modest, even somewhat conservative tabloid.

I began learning of all these developments when I developed a friendship with Bill Duncan, the manager of the cooperative auto shop, who was deeply involved in the community. Bill was very helpful to me in getting my truck-repair project under way—though not so helpful as to help me avoid a disaster the first time I started the new engine, which burned out almost immediately and had to be rebuilt again, to my great frustration and considerable expense. (I eventually sold the truck at a loss.) He offered me remodeling work around the shop to help offset my bill, listened to my stories of the commune that went bad, and told me stories of communal life as he had experienced it. He even put out the idea of the two of us forming a cooperative home-repair business modeled after the auto shop, in which craftspeople and property owners would share responsibilities and benefits. We gave up the notion when we learned that licensing and insurance requirements were all but insurmountable.

When I expressed interest in moving out of my sister's house and closer to the Palo Alto community, Bill arranged for me to rent one of several small apartments upstairs from the Whole Earth Truck Store in downtown Menlo Park. I moved in during Christmas week of 1973. Something told me it was a good time to make other changes in my life, so on the day I moved out of my sister's house, I also stopped smoking cigarettes, after about four years, and stopped eating meat, less than a year after I stopped butchering animals at the farm. Amazingly, I had no difficulty at all with these changes; I've never resumed smoking (cigarettes, that is), remained a committed vegetarian for more than fifteen years, and still shun red meat.

Moving into a place of my own forced me to examine my very negative and self-deprecating self-image. Everything in this apartment is mine, I would say to myself, and I have a right to have it. This kitchen is here just for me; all this furniture is mine and I deserve to use it. Following one of Mel Lyman's basic principles, I made sure I deserved my possessions by taking very good care of them, starting with a complete redecorating of the apartment. I collected items that reflected my innate sense of recycling and reusing, of living low on the economic ladder. I learned to shop at flea markets and thrift stores. I gave myself a few significant gifts that affirmed my right to pleasure myself at least a little—such as a waterbed to sleep on, and contact lenses to replace my still-hated eyeglasses.

I was meeting lots of new people, and presented myself to all of them as a knowledgeable amateur astrologer; almost the first thing I would do was ask for people's birth information and calculate their charts, then interpret these as best I could. My offering of astrology was much deeper and more meaningful than the perfunctory "What's your sign?" that had become the standing joke of superficial pop culture, but it served almost the same purpose: if I spoke about astrology with a new friend, we wouldn't have to cast about, wondering what we had in common and what we were really thinking and feeling. As I settled in and relaxed, I gradually began seeing myself in a more positive light, and even had a brief affair with a woman I met while working for a time at the nursing home owned by the elderly couple.

I was responding to notices I would see around town for freelance tradespeople, looking for possible collaborators in the remodeling cooperative Bill Duncan and I were imagining. One of the people I met in this way, Henry Jackson, proved to be a congenial collaborator in a carpentry project that was offered to me by some friends of my sister; we proceeded to become work partners and remained so for the next several years. He was a recent graduate of the rather progressive architecture program at UC-Berkeley; working with him stimulated my longstanding interest in design and unusual uses of both old and new materials. Our workdays were a running conversation about architecture, construction methods, popular culture, and current events. For about a year, we got to invest our creative energies in a huge remodeling and room-addition project designed around a client's collection of stained glass and other antique treasures.

During the same time, we also planned major renovations on my sister's rather plain house, hiring friends to do the work when we were unavailable. When we did spend some time starting what was intended to be the major interior remodel, we discovered evidence of incompetent construction and hidden fire damage in the house, and a long period of research began in which I helped my sister and her husband bring legal charges against the former owners. Their house sat torn open for more than two years while the legal battle waited for resolution. Henry and I filled our time working for a growing network of contacts among the real estate community in Palo Alto.

Is This Déjà Vu, or Do You Just Look Familiar?

My life was starting to take form. An important connection that I made during this period helped me enormously in putting the Fort Hill Community experience in perspective. During the time I was still living in my sister's house, but beginning to explore for community in Palo Alto, I answered a notice I saw in an occult bookstore for astrology classes. The instructor, William Lonsdale, immediately recognized me as having the same birthday he had (though I was two years older), and this made him curious whether our life experiences had resembled each other. I stayed late after my first class to share stories, and I was amazed to discover not only that William had grown up in circumstances fairly similar to mine and had pursued a long path of exploring various aspects of the counterculture, but also that our paths had actually crossed quite directly.

He became a professional astrologer after being turned on to the subject by a person doing horoscope readings for money on a street corner in Boston. That street-corner astrologer was Joseph Dellamore, one of the more independent-minded members of the Fort Hill crew, who used to simply ignore the peer pressure to work on the building projects and go off instead to do astrology. William's first horoscope reading was actually calculated from my set of astrology books, which I had lent to Joseph when it was obvious he was going to have more use for them than I had. Joseph invited William back to Fort Hill for a visit, and William was intrigued but rather turned off by the sight of all of us working away like beavers on Mel's studio. He decided Fort Hill was not for him, but went on to live in communal groups in New York and Vermont, where he had his own share of authoritarian experiences. He was now making the study of such groups a major focus of his life, second only to astrology, in which he had become quite expert and innovative. We had plenty to talk about.

One of the most transformative moments for me in growing away from the traumas of the Fort Hill experience was the day William and I reconstructed the charts of Mel Lyman and several other key players in the community and then reinterpreted them according to his understanding of astrology, which differed considerably from the interpretations that were used among the community's members. Mel emerged not so much as an avatar and cultural leader, but more as a needy person with a very low sense of self-worth, who needed to manipulate others into supporting his self-aggrandizing fantasies. The people around him appeared similarly deficient in self-image, and seemed all to be of a personality type that would prefer to let someone else make decisions for them rather than live according to their own guidance. My chart looked not so much like that of a person unable to get himself together as it did that of a person with an undeniable independence of spirit, whose inner strength inevitably clashed with someone who could only be served by undermining that independence. What an eye-opener that was for me!

It felt like William and I had stumbled onto something terribly important that only we understood, almost conspiratorially. He told me about making the acquaintance some time earlier of Paul Williams, the former editor of *Crawdaddy* magazine and future writer of several well-received books of essays on the emerging counterculture, who had been friends with Mel for years and had lived briefly at Fort Hill (and whose sudden departure from the Hill had been the subject of the lead passage of David Felton's coverage of the community in *Rolling Stone*). Paul had had to go through a debriefing and reprogramming of himself after his experiences, not very different from what I was going through, and William had met him toward the end of that phase.

They had discussed the paradox that Fort Hill appeared to both itself and to observers to represent a new direction in collective living, a new development in culture unlike anything that had gone before, when in fact the essential energies on which the community ran were really very traditional, based deeply in patriarchal values and authoritarian power structures—not the newest of the new, but merely the latest expression of the old ways. This idea, too, seemed a revelation to me, and helped to clarify some of my ongoing confusion. It enabled me to feel better about my inability to fit in there, since I had no particular use for the values of the traditional society, and also to see more clearly why Fort Hill seemed to have so little appreciation for the various expressions of the newly emerging culture that were in fact springing up everywhere in those days. The revelation gave me new enthusiasm for exploring just how that counterculture had developed during the years while I had my back turned.

William had a theory that each oppressive charismatic community focused on and took advantage of one particular aspect of the personalities of its participants, and that aspect was the last part to heal and find its way back to normal after a person returned to regular life. In the case of Fort Hill, he hypothesized, it was the will that was undermined and thrown off course, and he guessed that my will would be the last part of myself I would be able to reclaim. This theory was difficult to hear and to understand at the time, but looking back on the many years it took me to recognize the difference between my own desires and impulses and those that came to me from outside myself, I guess his idea makes good sense.

William and his wife Diana turned me on to two expressions of the new culture that represented breakthroughs for me, one each for my body and my soul. My body loved Earth Shoes, the negative-heel shoes that were just becoming popular, and which for me represented the other end of the spectrum from the cowboy boots I had worn in Kansas and during my pilgrimage west. My body breathed a sigh of relief when it learned it didn't have to live with that kind of tension anymore. And the weekend I spent at the Living Love Center in Berkeley, the teaching space at that time of Ken Keyes (who would go on to form several other teaching centers around the country and to write *Handbook to Higher Consciousness* and *The Hundredth Monkey*, among other books), let me know that even after what I had been through, I could have transformative personal experiences and achieve easy intimacy if I wanted to.

My friendship with William, and our ongoing discussion about Fort Hill continued for a number of months, until he and Diana decided it was time to move back East; I did them the favor of building a customized camper on their pickup truck in which to travel and live. William paid me back by doing an extensive reading of my "progressions," the closest means to predicting the future used by humanistic astrologers. From the reading, William told me that I would only come into my own as a fully grown person sometime in my middle thirties (I was then turning twenty-nine). This long-term perspective enabled me to see my difficulties up to then as simply a phase in my growth.

I made another significant friend during that time, Jonathan Rosenbloom, one of my neighbors in the apartments above the Truck Store. He and I would prepare meals together from time to time, and would discuss a variety of intellectual and countercultural topics. Through him I became familiar with *The Seth Material*, Jane Roberts's then recently published account of her developing relationship with a disembodied spirit who dictated—through Jane's voice when she was in a self-induced trance—astounding philosophical lessons about the meaning of life and the malleability of human experience, which Jane's artist husband would write down in longhand and then edit into readable manuscripts. I was fascinated, and remained devoted to Jane and Seth over the next several years as each book of the extensive and best-selling series appeared. (Jane Roberts had the same birthday as William Lonsdale and me, and this gave me a subtle but real sense of connection to her.)

Many of the key ideas in the Seth books were challenging and difficult to assimilate, but they were very stimulating. They portrayed a world with many dimensions of experience and a wide and diverse realm of interactions between living people and other kinds of spirits, all occurring in simultaneous time. The idea from Seth that I found most useful in terms of recovering from my Fort Hill experience was the notion that communications that appear to happen in dreams are in fact happening in an "alternate reality" that only touches what we recognize as ordinary reality in momentary tangents. This idea helped me consider my continuing frequent dreams about the Fort Hill people in a new light; maybe I was actually working out the various incompletes and traumas from my time with them, but in ways that only penetrated my consciousness in dream form. I liked thinking that I was really communicating with Mel and the others, and not just obsessing on my memories.

I also found myself in my waking life rolling memories of Fort Hill over and over in my mind, often when I was working on repetitive tasks that required little mental attention. I would relive one experience after another, trying to make sense of all that had happened, and would compose long, often angry speeches in my mind with which to tell off this person or that, trying to give myself, internally at least, the sense that at last justice and balance had been spoken for. Gradually, over a period of years, I put the various experiences in perspective and saw that I had not been crazy or less than a whole person during all those difficulties, but that I had allowed myself to be overwhelmed by a bunch of strong personalities, most of whom had never given me the chance to express myself in my own terms, and had not recognized me when I did so spontaneously. I felt wonderful to be reclaiming myself by bits and pieces.

News from Home

One day during the early period in Palo Alto, while doing carpentry work for one of the *Whole Earth Catalog* operators, I got my first new information about the actual people of Fort Hill. On a break from my work, I sat down to browse through a stack of recent *Rolling Stone* magazines that caught my eye. Included among the feature articles and news updates were stories about the blossoming solo career of Maria Muldaur, former singer with Jim Kweskin's Jug Band. I felt a certain connection to Maria, even though I had only seen her once at Jim's house on Fort Hill and had never met her personally. The *Rolling Stone* dated October 11, 1973, had an article I wanted to read on the arrest for alleged cocaine dealing of Abbie Hoffman. But adjoining that article was a headline that captured my attention: "Ricky Nelson to Jimmy Dean." The article began, "Behind bars Mark Frechette is a curiously satisfied man. 'It was a good bank robbery,' he said. 'Maybe it *wasn't* a successful one, but it was *real*, ya know?'"

It seems Mark and two others from the community—Terry Bernhard, Mel's and Jim's piano-playing friend, who was the father of the two little girls given up for adoption because of their birth defects; and Chris Thein, or "Hercules," who had been recruited by Owen during his cross-country proselytizing trip and whom I had never met—had decided on the spur of the moment to rob a bank, in a personal act of revolution, or something like that. Mark and Herc had just returned from a summer working in the community's compound on Martha's Vineyard, and perhaps the pressure of the city was too much for them. Terry decided at the last minute to join them, and they had walked an easy half mile to the nearest bank, hadn't even taken a car to get away in, carrying unloaded guns. The bank they chose happened to be the one where all the community's money was deposited, but they didn't know that. A totally silly act, in other words. In the course of committing their act, they answered a question I had been considering for a long time: Who would be the first to die for, or because of, Mel? Herc was shot and killed by police who responded to the alarm call. Mark and Terry were arrested.

In the article in *Rolling Stone*, the usual suspects from the Hill make several characteristically overconfident and ridiculous comments, willing to use anything at all to further their image of themselves. For example, Jessie is quoted as saying, "We're not political here. We don't have any ideas up here. But we're very aware. We're bound to the soul of the country. We *are* the soul of the country. . . . this was the most honest thing those three boys could do." Mark is quoted as saying, "I did what I did to stay awake. This society runs amok asleep. I was running amok but I was awake."

A few months later, Mark and Terry pleaded guilty and were sentenced to prison terms of six to fifteen years. But the story had an even unhappier outcome than that. Even though they were apparently well liked in the state prison and kept their senses of humor there—an article in the *New York Times* of March 23, 1975, describes Mark directing and Terry starring in a theater production, for inmates, staff, and visiting dignitaries, of *The White House Transcripts*, about the antics of Richard Nixon that led to his downfall—Mark apparently became more and more depressed in prison. The November 6, 1975, issue of *Rolling Stone* contained the final chapter of his story, "The Sorry Life and Death of Mark Frechette." Early one morning in late September, Mark, who had lost a lot of weight and strength, was found alone in the recreation room of the prison, lying dead with a 150-pound barbell (that he was apparently trying to bench press) across his neck. Despite the unusual circumstances, it was deemed neither suicide nor murder, but merely the fitting end to an unhappy and star-crossed life.

Settle Down

I stayed in my apartment above the Truck Store for eight months, the longest time in my life of living alone, and then decided it was time to move into a collective household. I found a room at the back of a large house with a big yard and a bunch of housemates. The couple who owned the home were followers of Leonard Orr and Sondra Ray, the people who were at that time developing the new practice of Rebirthing, a New Age–style method of therapy and personal transformation based on a particular kind of "circular" controlled breathing. Shortly after I moved in, Leonard Orr came to the house to conduct their marriage ceremony, but I was not drawn into trying rebirthing (just yet; many years later I did). Another housemate was studying with Ida Rolf to become a practitioner of Rolfing, deep-tissue reconstructive massage therapy. He introduced me to some chiropractor friends, who gave me some food supplements to begin healing and strengthening my body from within. (A few years later, I went through a series of Rolfing sessions with the same friend, when he was studying a less-painful variation of Rolfing known as Aston Patterning.)

While I was living with those folks, I was contacted by David Freedman, a friend from East Lansing who had worked on *The Paper* both during my time and after I left. David found me by way of my mother and invited me to visit him in Los Angeles. He had gotten caught up in radical antiwar politics of the sort I had left East Lansing partly to avoid, and had felt it necessary to go underground and live in hiding for several years. When he emerged, he met up with American followers of the Indian Sikh leader Yogi Bhajan, and he was now wearing white robes and a turban, living in their community in L.A. with a new name, Darshan

Singh, and a new wife, but he was in many ways the same gentle, goofy-humored person I knew before. We had a pleasant visit for a few days, during which time I got up before dawn and meditated with my hosts and their community mates. I seemed to be getting a gradual introduction to all of the new spiritual and transformational disciplines that were going around in those days. Darshan indulged me in seeking out the Fort Hill houses in Hollywood to see them with my own eyes. I don't know what I expected to do; I certainly didn't have the nerve to knock on the door and say hello, but I wanted to know where they were and what they looked like.

Jonathan and I remained friends after I moved, and in January he suggested we rent a place together and start a household of our own. We found a ranch house in South Palo Alto on the day we started looking, and before long we were conducting interviews for two other housemates and choosing paint colors and furniture. During this time I got another bulletin from the real world of Fort Hill. *Time* magazine for February 3, 1975, contained an obituary for Thomas Hart Benton, who had died of heart disease at the age of eighty-five at his home in Kansas City. *Time* had little good to say about the lasting significance of Benton's work, but it paid him respect as an old-fashioned American individualist who had dabbled in modern art and had then resoundingly returned to traditional, even primitive forms for the bulk of his career.

Reading this account sent me into long reminiscences about his daughter Jessie, and all the people around her with whom I had interacted for so long. I had never met Benton, but had certainly felt his influence on Mel and all of us; his paintings and prints were everywhere in the communities. Somehow, remembering all this gave me the urge to write a letter to my old partner Carol Schneider, now known as Carol Franck after partnering with Kurt Franck, mathematician-turned-photographer-turned-carpenter for the community, by whom she had been pregnant during the season when I ran away from the farm. I didn't want to reveal to her exactly where I was, but I figured out I could send my letter by way of William Lonsdale in New York and encourage her to respond by way of my mother's address if she wanted to.

In my letter I describe my current life in general terms and speak, a little defensively, of my continuing process of making sense of my experiences at Fort Hill and of rediscovering myself separate from all that. "Mainly," I write, "I realize now that we are *all* working and striving to expand ourselves in the best way we know, but my faith in the value of self-determination is (and always was) greater than that which was manifested by Fort Hill. It is clear from the way the world is moving that many, many people are acting out essentially the same intuitions about how the next phase in history and evolution is to shape itself, and the most we can do for each other is recognize our common needs and goals. Don't you agree?" I don't know if she agreed or not, as I received no response.

But my life was moving forward, with or without Carol's and Fort Hill's blessings. One of the people who moved into our new house was a young woman named Carol Settle, a student ballerina, an enthusiastic feminist, and a former follower of the teenage Guru Maharaj Ji. She and I had plenty to talk about, and were rather attracted to each other as well. After a few months of simply being friendly housemates, we decided we felt safe enough to act on our attraction, and started spending more private time together. (You can bet I was struck by the coincidence of her name; it seemed practically every time I became involved with a woman, her name was Carol.)

The day we had our first definitive date together—to a nude beach on the ocean side of the peninsula—we came home to find Jonathan sitting angrily amid an enormous, outraged note he had written to us complaining about our behavior, on yards and yards of computer paper (he was a programmer) that he had taped all over the walls and ceilings of the public rooms of the house. We could hardly believe our eyes, but clearly we were dealing with a high order of jealousy. Nevertheless, we began spending our nights together. The first night, Carol asked me what my "ideal woman" looked like, and I told her I wasn't sure my ideal woman wasn't a man. She took that news bravely and we plunged forward just the same. I figured her horoscope—she had sun in Aries and moon in Taurus to match my sun in Taurus and moon in Aries, and, like me, three other planets in Aries to keep the fires going—and sent a copy of her chart to my astrologer friend William Lonsdale, who wrote back, "She's more like you than you are. Good luck."

I was still working construction, but was starting to feel restless and resentful of all the time I was spending helping affluent people improve their oversized suburban homes. One night in November, I wrote a complaint to the universe about my circumstances. I had just found a copy of *Jim Kweskin's America* in a remainder bin in a record store and had heard the music for the first time in years. It left me feeling nostalgic and restive:

It's a dark and dismal Saturday night. A night when it's impossible to remember the daylight. Has it ever been brighter than this? My imagination is at low tide, my ambition doesn't exist at all. All around me are things I "want" or "have" to do, . . . and what I want to do is be in New York City. Scrap the business, scrap the house and the lease and the relationship there within, and head straight for the center of debauchery and culture. Palo Alto is so fucking boring, but I can't help but notice I'm not in the van driving to San Francisco right now. I seem pretty frozen, in fact. When I'm not playing Mr. Together, I don't really have very much going for me. Mr. Together is a builder by trade. He can do anything beautifully. The $100-a-night call girl of the building trades, he sells his time to homeowners in big chunks. "During the month of November 1975, the purpose of my life shall be to make of your barren attic a beautiful extra room with bath. I shall occupy myself with nothing else, and when the room is complete, I will leave you, and you need never think of me again." Sometimes I get tired of doing that. I want to claim myself back to myself, but I'm so out of the habit. What else do I do besides build things? I read magazines, occasionally books, and have grand theories and ineffable feelings about them. I move like a heavy mechanical object, though; all the fineness is still inside me and few if any can see it or feel it. Years ago Mel Lyman told me to go to work, to work and work and sooner or later I would find myself wanting to say and do finer, more delicate things, and I would find the way. He promised to teach me, but of course he never did. Now I am a long time away from him, and I am still looking for the fine gestures, the inexpressibly subtle and delicate word or facial expression.

Relations with Jonathan continued deteriorating, and during the fall he moved out. Carol and I wanted to move, too. In the course of looking for a new place, we interviewed with a couple named Robert and Meg Beeler, who taught in one of the experimental private schools in Palo Alto, and who were involved in all sorts of interesting community affairs.

They told us about the new men's group Robert and a few friends were starting, patterned after the women's "consciousness-raising" groups that characterized the seminal phase of the women's movement, and inspired by a recent talk at Stanford by Warren Farrell, one of the writers exploring the new subject of men's attempts to free themselves from traditional role models. We were fascinated and immediately recognized this as an opportunity for me to do some growing.

CHAPTER 18

A New Movement,
A New Paper

arol and I did not move in with our new friends, mainly because the space didn't seem adequate, but I was invited to begin meeting with the men's group, and did so promptly. On the day of the first meeting I was scheduled to attend, some particularly horrible event occurred (I don't remember whether it was another insult from Jonathan in the house or some difficulty getting paid for my work, or some combination of affronts). I told my story and related my frustration and need for support to this small group of men, most of whom I was meeting for the first time; they found my candor to be a breakthrough for their group, which they celebrated by taking me outside and hoisting me above their heads as an expression of solidarity and support. The group was off and running.

We remained together for more than two years from that point, meeting weekly and sharing every aspect of our rapidly changing lives with each other. It was a tremendously important focus for me during that time, an anchor of support, a standard of understanding against which to measure all kinds of other changes going on in my life, and a cauldron in which to explore my feelings and my willingness to allow others to see parts of myself I had always hidden. Several group members were in various stages of rethinking their sexual orientation, and over time that gave me permission to look at that subject, too, with no pressure to make a definitive decision about it.

Carol and I found a charming little two-bedroom house near downtown Palo Alto on January 1, 1976. It faced the creek that separated Palo Alto from Menlo Park, and had a low brick wall around the front yard and a small backyard with fruit trees. We were thrilled, and made the house just as homey as we could. The extra bedroom served as an office for both of us. We relished taking our place in the community as an involved young couple.

My men's group joined with other like-minded men to initiate a Palo Alto Men's Center. We rented the basement of the Institute for the Study of Non-Violence as our meeting space. Various of us from the Men's Center took turns producing a Men's Page for the *Grapevine*, partly as a device to raise interest in the activities of the center, and partly to encourage people to question their own adherence to traditional roles. As other special-interest groups had done before us, we would send delegates to the monthly meetings, where editorial decisions were made by collective consensus, and to the weekend-long paste-up sessions.

My turn came up to work on the page when I wrote a description of our opening event at the Men's Center, which was heralded with a full-page article in the local daily, the *Palo Alto Times*, and was attended by 150 people. I began my article with a description of the opening night and a discussion of how the men's movement that seemed to be coming together owed a lot to both the women's movement and the history of countercultural exploration many of us shared. Playfully, I offered several different ways of describing this development, then wrote:

> These little statements are getting closer to how I'm feeling, but they still don't say it the way I would like to:
>
> I'm glad I'm learning to show my feelings. I'm glad I'm making so many new friends, and that it feels like home to me here. I haven't been home in so long. It's good to share again this building of something that belongs to all of us. I feel myself unfolding inside, getting ready for a rush of New and Alive. I haven't felt this way in years.
>
> It brings tears to my eyes to realize this; my eyes are so unused to tears, especially happy, fulfilled tears. It seems I can begin to show myself at last, and it's good not to be alone.
>
> Hello, brothers! Glad to see you!

It's easy for me to see Mel Lyman's influence in the writing style of this piece, but that would not have been apparent to anyone else. It's also easy to relate to the great relief I was feeling and expressing, that at last I was feeling enough courage to "go public" again after the traumas I had been through that had forced me into myself for so long. But the joyous new era did not last long.

Dear Landlord

A political difference was already surfacing within the Non-Violence Institute that soon caused Joan Baez and certain others to question whether they wanted to keep the building and the institute operating in their current form. In the May issue of the *Grapevine*, just two months after I had announced the Men's Center's opening, I wrote an article entitled "'Dear Landlord': Eviction at 667 Lytton," in which I described the summary closing of the institute the previous month and the impending eviction of the Men's Center and several other community organizations. I was taking all this quite personally; in addition to participating in the Men's Center's attempts to lobby the institute board to treat us kindly as they went through their changes, I also wrote a personal letter to Baez detailing my political and social history and the numerous points at which she and her music had touched my life, including the story of her singing Jim Kweskin and Mel Lyman off the stage at Newport, and the current phase in which her political struggle seemed on the verge of putting my new movement out on the street. I hand-carried this letter to her home in the nearby town of Woodside, but received only an acknowledgment from a secretary. Baez was out of town and never answered my letter. And the effort was in vain.

In the next issue of the *Grapevine*, I wrote an article headlined "Non-Violence Institute

Self-Destructs." It seems the various factions within the institute's board and its operating collective, not to mention its various tenants and related projects, were quite unable to agree on how to modernize and face the seventies, and the board decided instead to sell off the assets and reorganize under a new name in a new town, Santa Cruz, fifty miles away.

The move put a premature end to the Men's Center, but our men's group continued, and seeds of a new movement had been planted. (One of the flowers, about two years later, was the first California Men's Gathering [CMG], a weekend-long campout event at which men from around the state got together to commiserate on their experiences as men. I didn't attend that gathering or the follow-up events over the next several years, but the circle completed itself for me when I attended the Seventh CMG in 1984 and subsequent events, and became an organizer of the Ninth CMG in 1986. Many of my friends are still involved in the CMGs, which are going strong, now in their fourteenth year.)

By the time the Non-Violence Institute and the Men's Center "self-destructed," I was a confirmed member of the *Grapevine* staff, and so was Carol. We had found a purpose and a way to participate in the community we were feeling so pleased to be part of. But trouble was brewing in the operation. Distribution was free and all labor was volunteer; printing costs were paid by advertising revenues generated mainly from local, left-oriented retail businesses and independent tradespeople. For some months, the paper had contained plaintive little notices asking readers to subscribe, or to make financial donations to help the paper continue and grow. But not much was coming of these announcements. In the first several of the monthly collective meetings that Carol and I attended, we quickly perceived that lack of finances was the biggest problem for the *Grapevine*, so we offered to take over the job of selling and coordinating advertising. We persuaded the collective to pay us a commission on the ads we sold—the first time anyone had been paid for work on the paper.

The issue for July–August 1976 lists us in our new role and contains a large ad announcing our plans for a new classified column. We established higher display-ad rates and began a more aggressive campaign to sell them. It became Carol's job to kick the campaign off, because I spent the Bicentennial month of July in New York, finally making good on my promise from several years earlier to help my mother get her house there ready to sell.

While I was east, I visited William and Diana Lonsdale and their young daughter in Burlington, Vermont. That completely pleasurable experience proved to me that my new life in California had indeed been producing lasting results of intimacy and growth. I also got in touch with the family of my old East Lansing friend Dale Walker, in nearby Montpelier. I learned that Dale had been living in Prince Edward Island, Canada, with a new wife, but was now in a fundamentalist Bible school somewhere in New England. I gave his mother my address, and a couple of months later received a long letter from him telling of his and his wife's experiences of being "born again" in Jesus and now dedicating their life to spreading his word. I wrote a brief response, giving half-hearted approval to the changes Dale was going through and drawing parallels to the various conversions and reconversions I had lived through. I wish I had sent it to him.

My trip to New York also signaled the end of my working partnership with Henry Jackson. Our recent efforts together had produced more frustration than success, and we were starting to blame each other for having different styles. I was wanting to become more businesslike, partly because of our clients' expectations, but I also wanted to open time in my schedule to work on the *Grapevine*; Henry was wanting to do more with his architectural skills. We parted in as friendly a fashion as we could and remained friends.

I returned in August to a new solo phase of my construction career, to the new partnership with Carol selling *Grapevine* ads, and to a last-ditch attempt under way to save the Non-Violence Institute's building for community-organizing purposes, in the form of a human-potential teaching organization that rented space nearby and was looking for financing to buy the building. I wrote about this for the September *Grapevine*, but nothing came of it. I also wrote an article about the city's attempt, under pressure from outraged citizens, to put limits on the burgeoning massage and adult-bookstore trade in town, focusing on how the proposed ordinance then under discussion would also threaten the two legitimate therapeutic-massage businesses in town, both of which were allies and advertisers of ours. (Eventually a revised ordinance was passed that made exceptions for such businesses.)

Meanwhile, Carol returned to school in order to get free of the cycle of low-paying jobs and spells of unemployment that she had been in since before I met her. She began studying psychology at Stanford that fall, funded by her parents.

Our ad-sales campaign for the *Grapevine* seemed to be paying off; the paper grew in size to twenty pages most issues. But we were frustrated by what we saw as the lack of focus and common goals among the staff, who seemed to just stumble along while the paper somehow tumbled out at a certain time each month. We wanted more, and offered a proposal to create a paid position of coordinator, who could focalize the efforts of the staff and represent the *Grapevine* publicly in the community. During October, I put our thoughts in a long letter to the staff, obviously drawing heavily on my experiences with both *The Paper* and *Avatar*:

> To me, the main reason for doing a newspaper like the *Grapevine* is to carry on a dialogue on the state of things with a large number of people in the community—all those citizens whose needs and feelings are not articulated by the prevailing media. If the paper becomes distant or detached from its readers, if it fails to make itself available to them or neglects to encourage their participation, if it speaks over their heads or concentrates on matters not of interest to them, then it might as well not publish at all.
>
> On the other hand, a community-access newspaper which does perform its function well acts as an exciting and lively forum of ideas, styles, political developments, cultural and social trends. It is democracy and participation operating on the most basic level—the free expression of who we are and how we get along together. When this is happening, the newspaper staff itself becomes a community resource—a clearinghouse of ideas and technical expertise, part of a continually self-renewing process defined by the people who are using it. A good, open newspaper can be a powerful revolutionary device.

My letter lobbies for a much more aggressive stance for the *Grapevine*, challenging the monopoly of the established local media, focusing the dissatisfactions of the community into a strong alternative voice, getting over our fears and inhibitions about making and spending larger amounts of money manifesting a grander vision. I also asked for more honest dialogue among the staff members in order to fuel the other changes. None of this was very well received, and we continued stumbling forward.

For the October issue, I wrote about a debate between the two candidates for Congress in the local district. Liberal Republican Pete McCloskey, who some years earlier had been the first member of his party to speak out against the Vietnam War but who had been moving to the right in recent years, was defending his seat against a famous antiwar challenger, David Harris, the former Mr. Baez and now a well-known freelance writer. "In Harris," I wrote, "as in a small number of other politicians now gaining credibility, the point of view that was the radicalism of the 1960s has become a refreshing hope for a political and ideological housecleaning in the 1970s." Would that it had been so. Despite the best efforts of most of us on the staff to help him mount a strong campaign, Harris lost to McCloskey, of course, and the only consolation prize that year was Jimmy Carter's election as president.

I took time out during election week to write another letter into the wind, aimed in the general direction of Fort Hill. I had been seeing occasional pieces of investigative reporting in the progressive media written by a Dick Russell, who I assumed was the same person I had known in Kansas. Seeing him achieve some success as a writer, and not knowing whether or not he was still with the community, I felt again the affinity for him that had been the basis of our friendship in Kansas, and I wrote to him in care of the magazine that published the latest of his articles I had run across:

> Are you, as I am assuming, the same Dick Russell I knew out in the boonies in Kansas four years ago? Memories of Gary Griffis and grain fields and living under the work ethic gone wild and being probably the only voter for George McGovern in all of Marshall County. Everything comes full circle. . . . The journalist in me . . . has been coming back to life recently. I'm very involved in a monthly community newspaper here, and have just given my heart to David Harris' attempt to get to Congress. It's a long way from here to original investigation into the machinations of history, but we all do what we have to do. I consider it a great victory in myself that I've grown back out toward the world again. I've spent all this time putting back together a personal life, a career, a point of view, and all the other things that contribute to being a whole person—like a sense of one's physical self and intrinsic value, a sense of humor, a family and friends from whom one gets support; finally, now, there seems to be enough security and enough energy left over to use some on the frivolities of political involvement, commitment to things of principle and things that draw highly evolved and articulated expressions out of oneself. I feel like a person in the world again, no longer a prisoner of my painful history, no longer bound to use all my resources just surviving. . . . This letter is part of the process—a gradual unburdening of all those painful, frustrating, degrading memories—so that I can be here in my world. . . .

I then give a lengthy description of the inner mental turmoil I was still going through almost daily, reliving memories of Fort Hill, sorting out the injustices done to me from the useful and pleasant memories, finding myself inadvertently reliving phases of Mel's life disguised as my own:

> I keep recreating things from the past, from my past and Mel's past, Melvin and Michael all mixed together, slowly spiraling upward through the same bugaboos and pitfalls over and over again, toward—I don't know. The instinct tells me I haven't ever been quite

myself yet. I haven't found freedom yet—the real freedom, from one's own past, pride and prejudice. I believe I can, and the vision still leads me onward, but I do have to shake off all this old stuff to feel the way I want to.

I don't know for certain that I sent this letter; the copy I have is a handwritten draft, and ends abruptly. I think I did. Not that it matters; I certainly received no response. What I wrote shows that my internal process was proceeding apace, gradually freeing myself from the psychic hold Fort Hill had on me.

Dear Landlord, Part II

I spent the next few weeks after the election getting to know the people who lived in a large rural commune in the Palo Alto foothills known as "The Land." A close friend of one of my carpenter buddies lived there, and through him I began hearing of the difficulties the commune was facing from the threat of eviction due to a complicated ownership dispute. The Land had been part of Palo Alto mythology for a number of years; I first heard of it when I was working on my dump-truck engine at the Briarpatch garage several years earlier. Now, I decided it was time to get to know these folks and their struggles. I was invited to one of their Sunday-morning public breakfasts, found myself enthralled and quite relaxed in their company, and gradually became a familiar member of the circle of regular visitors. I spent a number of evenings and whole weekend days drawing various residents out on the subject of how their community came to be, on the details of the legal entanglement they were caught in, and on what their intentions were if they could find a way to resist eviction and stay on.

I borrowed photographs and drawings from several of them and put together a lengthy front-page piece for the December *Grapevine*, in which I presented their view of the dilemma and their wishes for a happy resolution. The headline, "Digging In at the Land," was set in bold white type, superimposed over a dramatic half-page silhouette picture of Land residents confronting a bulldozer sent onto the property at dawn in an ill-fated attempt to destroy their homes. The article jumped to the centerfold and beyond of a twenty-four-page issue, our biggest ever, where I included a brief-as-possible summary of the five separate, overlapping legal actions that were then pending, concerning the title, occupancy, and use of the property. All in all, it was the longest and most detailed single article to date in the *Grapevine*, and it was intended as the start of a series, which would go on to tell the history of how the community developed, as well as a continuing account of their current problems.

The longtime owners, Alyce and Emmett Burns, an elderly Republican couple (she an agricultural heiress, he a disbarred lawyer), had lobbied to annex the dramatic 750-acre hilltop property into the City of Palo Alto years before as a precursor to a development plan that included a cemetery and a cattle ranch as well as housing, but had defaulted on the large assessment for utilities improvements that went with the annexation. They eventually agreed instead to sell to Donald Eldridge, a millionaire businessman of Democratic, progressive leanings, in a complicated deal in which title would transfer gradually as he paid off the $2 million cost in installments. He took full title to about 150 acres right away, and provisional title to the rest pending completion of the payments.

Eldridge gave permission for peace activists to use the several informal buildings in the more developed "frontlands" for workshops and a small residential commune, at no cost to them. This move had quickly become the entrée for a much larger group of social experimenters to move into the "backlands" and form a community there, living first in tents and tepees, and later in several dozen shacks and cabins they built with recycled materials and increasingly sophisticated building skills. Hundreds of people had lived there over the years, and thousands had visited. The current population was about fifty. Eldridge had affirmed his tacit support for their presence at times over the years, particularly since he thought their being there both enhanced the chances of environmental preservation and discouraged the possibility of more serious vandalism, but he had otherwise kept a very low profile. The city had attempted halfheartedly over a period of time to enforce its building codes in order to outlaw the houses and evict the residents; an article by two of the residents in the *Grapevine* a year earlier had solicited community support.

The agreement for sale of the property had broken down after the city changed its zoning for the foothills, which increased the minimum parcel size for homes and thus in effect diminished the value of properties. This action precipitated a dispute between Eldridge and the Burnses, as Eldridge withheld further payments until he could be sure of the value of what he was buying; he sued the city for relief, following the lead of other landowners similarly affected. The Burnses, in turn, refused to grant Eldridge title even to the acreage he had already paid for, and ultimately foreclosed against him for title to four-fifths of the total acreage. A court gave them the right to purchase this portion of land back at a foreclosure auction, thus causing Eldridge a loss of over a million dollars. The foreclosure decision was on appeal in state courts.

The foreclosure left the community of residents without its angel, and the Burnses began attempting eviction. Their bungled attempts to serve notices of eviction, and their perceived propensity toward violence when they didn't get their way, precipitated the current crisis. A collective of civil rights lawyers was providing the residents with excellent legal help at minimum cost, and the eviction struggle was proceeding slowly and methodically through the courts. Meanwhile, the city was teaming up with the Burnses and the courts to crack down again on the building-code violations; the residents were responding with a campaign to persuade the city to liberalize its building code to allow for such "owner-built" housing in rural areas, as several other cities and rural counties in Northern California had already done, with the encouragement of the administration of Governor Jerry Brown. And, in the wings, a local regional-park district was expressing interest in purchasing the entire property to add to its open-space holdings, if it could ever be obtained with a clear title and without a bunch of rowdy residents.

My article was the first time this entire complex struggle had ever been explained in one place, along with a description of the residents' visions and hopes. They were grateful for the support, and I was grateful for their friendship. I saw in my connection with them a chance to make myself part of a functioning community that offered some of the benefits, and few if any of the authoritarian drawbacks, of the community I had left behind at Fort Hill. It was clear I was compensating, and seeking a way to balance out my earlier experiences. Here was a group of long-haired, relaxed men and strong, self-confident women easily accepting me into their ranks and welcoming my input. The Land offered a chance to be in a communal setting where free expression, spontaneity, and relaxation were the norm. I chose to overlook internal dissensions and difficulties as I developed my alliance with them, and I especially failed to see the degree to which the relaxed exteriors of most of the men masked rather traditional values and role-model limitations. I attended Saturday-night dances in the "Long Hall," the large meeting space that was the community center of the "frontlands," and there I finally learned to cut loose and let my body dance to rock-and-roll music, an ability that had evaded me for years. I was also interested in the fact that many of the men, and some of the women, of The Land made their livings doing carpentry and other construction work; I started seeing visions of collective enterprises.

The January *Grapevine* contained a relatively brief update on current events, telling of the latest legal entanglements between the attempts to evict the residents, and the residents' response of asking the courts to hold off until the ownership dispute had moved further along. There had also been some alliance-building done with members of the Palo Alto city council, in hopes of thus dampening the enthusiasm of the city staff to pursue the enforcement of building- and health-code violations.

The February *Grapevine* included my anticipated long article on the history of The Land, starting from a brief reference to its sacredness for the now-extinct local Indian tribes, through its development as a Republican political-organizing retreat from the 1920s through the 1940s, through the period of purchase and attempted development by the Burnses, their sale to Eldridge, the disagreement with the city as its intentions for the foothills gradually shifted from encouraging development to encouraging open space and conservation, the early use of the property for antiwar organizing, and the shift that gradually took place over several years to a more generalized countercultural community, complete with faction splits, influence on the larger antiwar movement at several key junctures (Daniel Ellsberg spent time there, for example, just days before he began copying and releasing to the public the Pentagon Papers), and critical roles in encouraging and hosting several of the socialist-minded enterprises that served the larger Mid-Peninsula community.

In recent years, all this had given way to the anarchic community that now filled the entire property, committed to as free-form a lifestyle as feasible. My concluding sentence said: "Most of the residents seem to agree that two things about The Land are special—the chance to live in close contact with a relatively unspoiled environment, and the tacit understanding that each person's life is his or her own business, which no one else can control or interfere with." Needless to say, this attitude made for a fun life, but in the current circumstances made it difficult to stay focused and together through the complex demands of the legal struggle.

I was increasingly seen as an ally of the community members most involved in this struggle, not simply a neutral observer and reporter, and was also beginning to pursue the option of employing several of the members on some larger construction projects I was planning—including at my sister's house, where money was now coming available to continue the work we had put on hold two years earlier when we found it necessary to sue the original builders.

The March *Grapevine* again included an article on recent developments in the eviction drama. During February, the judge who was hearing the numerous preliminary motions from both sides decided to take a look for himself, to verify or deny the Burnses' claim that serving each resident with an individual proper eviction notice was impossible because of the way they lived. The judge and his assistants, and the Burnses and their lawyers, and a group of residents and observers such as myself spent several hours walking through the backlands, getting acquainted, and checking out what it was about the residents' life at The Land that made it special and worth defending and preserving. The only practical result of the tour was the opportunity it gave the Burnses' representatives to continue serving individual eviction notices.

Burning Out on Success

After the March issue, the conflicts Carol and I were feeling with most of the *Grapevine* staff came to a head. An important Palo Alto city council election was coming up on May 10, and planning was under way to give special coverage to that election and the issues it raised. At the planning meeting at the end of March, a schedule was developed; we would give preliminary coverage as the lead of the April issue, then publish extra copies of the May issue, including a special election supplement, and distribute those copies door-to-door in selected neighborhoods in town. This was an ambitious plan for the *Grapevine*, and Carol and I saw in the relatively half-hearted acceptance of it by some of the staff, a fatal problem that we no longer saw it within our power to resolve. After a year of increasing efforts on our part—selling and laying out ads, researching and writing articles, laying out pages, wrestling with staff resistance, and coordinating distribution—we were burning out. I wrote a joint letter of resignation, announcing that we would be leaving the staff after the May election issue, blaming our decision not on our work load but on

> the prevailing short-sightedness and mistrust that is able to look at our contributions to the *Grapevine* and the personal sacrifices which have accompanied those contributions and . . . accuse us repeatedly of ego-tripping and trying to "take over" the paper. The increased efficiency and concern for budget-balancing that we've struggled to create has backfired two months in a row in edit. board decisions to keep the size of the paper smaller than the available copy justified, in both cases for want of a few dollars worth of ads or the willingness to take a small risk. (A year ago, entire issues would be published with no idea of where the money was coming from to pay for them; we feel that by improving the cash flow we've created a monster, a fiscal and moral conservatism of the left that denies any of the spontaneity and faith in the process that is so essential in this kind of work.)

Making good on the promise to participate in the election coverage, I wrote three major articles for the April issue. A front-page piece, "Palo Alto Chooses a Future," discussed the unusual character of this election. Five of nine seats on the council were up for grabs, and the two slate organizations that had dominated city politics for some years, a "residential-ist" slate and a "commercialist" slate, had both decided to sit out the election and not run formal slates of candidates. This move opened the way for some seventeen active candidates, including only one incumbent, to campaign as independents, which would have seemed to allow for more freewheeling debate on the options facing the city. But we perceived what amounted almost to a conspiracy of silence on the part of the candidates and saw it as the *Grapevine*'s role to elucidate the choices facing voters. There were important issues of foothills and baylands development or conservation, questions of mass transit versus more suburban sprawl, relations with Stanford, maintenance of city services in an impending era of budget constraints, et cetera, et cetera. With another staff member, I interviewed all the candidates and published summaries of their views on some of these issues, as well as their likely positions on a left-to-right spectrum, to help voters make sense of the choices.

My third article, "Imperial Palo Alto," discussed the city's new comprehensive plan, enforcement of which was one of the background issues in the election. Palo Alto had for years been an employment magnet for the entire Santa Clara Valley, attracting a large work force from elsewhere in the county and the surrounding area, and the generous tax base and special services this funded, while the surrounding bedroom communities suffered in comparison. The comprehensive plan, prepared under the administration of a relatively development-oriented council, mainly accepted this situation without confronting its assumptions. We were challenging the candidates to break their political and moral silence on the questions this dilemma raised.

In May, as promised, we continued our analysis and gave our recommendations. An article by one of the long-time *Grapevine* staffers, one of Carol's and my conservative opponents in the ongoing planning discussions, explored the possibility that moneyed interests in the city—including the leadership of the Hewlett-Packard Corporation, the electronics outfit that had spun out of Stanford years earlier and begun the entire Silicon Valley revolution—were secretly supporting a slate of "commercialist" candidates in the election. I wrote an article on how the local monopoly newspaper, the *Palo Alto Times*, influenced elections in town by publishing prejudiced news coverage and refusing to publish letters critical of its policies, as well as by publishing editorial endorsements decided by two editors who didn't even live in Palo Alto, and by the publisher, who did. These endorsements were considered to be worth two or three thousand votes, which in a low-turnout election could well represent the margin of victory.

In response, we offered an endorsed slate of progressive, independent-minded candidates, and encouraged our readers to review our coverage of all the candidates' policies in order to make an informed choice. Additional election coverage by a variety of staff members, including myself, discussed Palo Alto's relations with its neighboring communities, its role in planning for approach roads for a new bridge about to be built across San Francisco Bay, the deteriorating turnouts in recent city council elections and the consequences this implied for city housing policies, the city's legal involvement in the various lawsuits and zoning questions concerning the foothills, the traffic problems increasingly facing the entire Mid-Peninsula and Santa Clara Valley areas, child care policies and implications for the commuting work force, and solid-waste disposal in the city.

Somehow I also managed to produce yet another article on The Land, this time reporting on the complex negotiations now actively under way to sell the entire property to the regional park district if the ownership and eviction disputes ever got settled. Both the Burnses and Eldridge, the two disputing owners, had signed agreements with the park district promising to give the district first dibs on the land if the other disputes could be cleared up. In the process, an internal struggle within the district's staff had precipitated the resignation of its longtime land negotiator, thus giving more political influence to its general manager, whom we found generally distasteful.

This heroic effort was indeed my and Carol's last for the *Grapevine*, so I did not get to write the follow-up articles over the next several months, as the dramas of The Land intensified and finally came to a dramatic conclusion. The June issue offered congratulations to the winners of the city council election: four of our five endorsed candidates won, signaling a significant turn to the left and away from a developmental majority; the fifth winning candidate, who turned out to be the swing vote for the next couple of years, was the youngest person running—a favorite son of Hewlett-Packard, which simultaneous to supporting his campaign hired him into its public-relations department. But on balance, it seemed the *Grapevine* had had a salutary effect on the process. Carol and I were proud of our role in all that, and anxious for a rest.

A Letter from the Lord

Our efforts with the *Grapevine* produced an additional surprising side effect during this period. One day, a stranger knocked on our door and introduced himself to Carol as David Lerner, an acquaintance of mine from Fort Hill, who lived in Palo Alto now and had been reading my articles in the *Grapevine* for nearly a year. He finally felt ready to make contact with me, presuming I was the person he thought I was. She strongly encouraged him to come back another time so we could visit. David had never been a close friend of mine. He had moved to Fort Hill during the period of intensive work on the building projects, when I was unhappy and lonely and always working. He was at the time an eighteen-year-old from New York who had become familiar with the community through our sales efforts there. He was perceived to be a disagreeable and difficult community member, and in fact had been the first person to spend time in the infamous "vault," but the net effect of this was that he developed a strong bond with Mel and with some of the others, which continued even though he now lived on his own and was an aspiring writer. He visited regularly at the community houses in Hollywood and San Francisco.

When he and I finally saw each other in early May, it happened to be on a day when he received a new letter from Mel that contained some sad and surprising news. A close protégé of Mel's in the community, David Lanier, known as David Libra, had recently become depressed and had blown his own brains out, ostensibly because of a broken heart from a love relationship. "Libes" had been a mainstay in Mel's close-in network for years, and it's easy to imagine how his suicide would have shocked the community. He had been the person whose picture standing guard with a rifle in Mel's garden had been published in the *American Avatar* community issue, and he had been the person who with Mel's encouragement had guided Eric and me on our acid trips on the fateful night before we began demolishing House Number 4, and who had told me then that I had a murderer lurking inside me. But I suspected there were other issues at work besides love-life difficulties. I had always believed he had a bisexual component that was active before he joined the community and that had been suppressed there; he had arrived shortly before I did in early 1968 in the company of an Australian writer, now openly gay, whom he had met in California and traveled cross-country with. His brief, unhappy relationship with Alison Peper had produced a lost little girl child, who was moved to the farm for foster parenting after their relationship ended. I could imagine a sensitive person terminally overloading on the usual everyday demands of the community.

I decided to write Mel a letter about this hypothesis, relating it to my experiences with him. My letter amounted to a declaration of independence, the most honest words I had ever written to him (see sidebar 6). Despite this thoroughgoing criticism of Mel and his community, however, I concluded with praise for his original music and his music anthology tapes, and asked whether copies were available. To my great surprise, I received a response from Mel barely a week later, sent from Martha's Vineyard. It's the only letter I ever received from him, and one of the most personal communications of any kind he had shared with me. It was full of shocking news, puzzles, and confessions, including some statements that appeared to be exaggerations and untruths (see sidebar 7).

SIDEBAR 6

FROM AUTHOR'S LETTER TO MEL LYMAN, MAY 22, 1977

To me, though, what is sadder than the loss of a few people is the wasting of the many who are here—the continual overloading and bloodletting and exploitation that was the daily diet of everyone in your community. Like you, I believe in difficult lessons, and would not protect people from the things they need to go through. But at Fort Hill, at least when I was there, that idea ran amok; the most outrageously painful and chaotic turns of fate became commonplace, while even the simplest concession to one's natural rhythms and instincts became suspect and dangerous. There was always someone willing to tear someone else's life apart in hopes of inspiring the changes that seemed necessary, but it was nearly impossible to speak to anyone about the experience of not living one's own life, or to find room within the prevailing conditions to begin living according to one's own impulses. . . .

It looks to me now as though [my] long time at Fort Hill was a real setback, a lot of time spent ingraining old habits and patterns when I could just as easily have been developing new and healthier ones. I've seen much of value in the world that I lost touch with when I was with you. There are many people in the world who seem to know the truth, and seem to be here for the good of humanity. Everyone compromises some things in expressing such a purpose, but the compromises that prevailed in your community seem so extensive to me that I wonder whether anyone was helped to do their best.

My basic belief is that we all possess the wisdom to understand life and death and spirit, and to learn to live creatively, if we are not hampered in doing so. The job, then, is to remove the limitations that keep us from becoming what we are—not to create extra limitations and demands.

Fort Hill could have been an experiment in space, with everyone helping each other to discover the source of their own creativity and spontaneity. That's what I thought it was when I moved there in 1968, when I was very weak and needy. Instead it became a straitjacket of prejudices and social pressures and neverending responsibilities that drove everyone crazy; and the more you tried to expand the scope, the worse it became. You made yourself responsible for all of us, Mel, and made us all responsive to your every word. Why didn't you use your influence in the community to clear away the bullshit that separated us from each other and kept us from producing really good stuff, instead of always piling on more demands and distances and making the job harder and harder? Is it that one must compete with one's teacher for a chance to grasp at the truth? I would have preferred a teacher who simply made the truth accessible, along with the space to appreciate it—or, perhaps even better, no teacher at all, just a chance to see life on my own.

MEL LYMAN'S LETTER TO AUTHOR, MAY 28, 1977

My son,

Your criticism was well taken. And how fascinating that you and brother David are in such close quarters. "He" certainly has a way of keeping kindred souls in proximity. I have become quite a "private" person in these ensuing years now upon us and therefore know little of what has been transpiring out there in the greater world. I see that you are well on your way to some manifestation of glory and fame, in contrast to my state of meditation.

I, too, have had to undergo the stress of overload, and some time back made the regrettable but unavoidable decision to withdraw from further contact and retire into the grace of my own mind to continue my efforts to root out the truth. No, there's no denying it, I'm not the man I used to be. Not that I'm giving up, mind you; only a brief respite to eventually prepare for even greater battle. I have received quite a numerous number of setbacks in my pursuits and have found, like many others in my station, that the quest is multifaceted. Consistency is a hobgoblin.

I am, basically, quite relieved that you finally saw fit to initiate contact with yours truly. How often I have questioned your fate and pondered upon your eventual outcome. Back in those days I never really knew which way the winds of fate would blow. I had my hopes, naturally, and my visions, (of which I never spoke) also. No, it was no mere whim I was following; though it may have seemed to some (yourself probably included), that my ways were strange, to say the least. And I can't now say, in all honesty, that I have learned anything or really changed radically, but I must admit that I have witnessed some unforeseen surprises and therefore can say that experience itself has been added unto me and, in a way, that may be said to be some kind of change. The people who followed me, willingly or the opposite, had, of course, to find their own way too, eventually and you might remember that, though I may have been labeled as some kind of guru or spiritual teacher, in my own secret recesses I never felt this way. Much like Charlie Manson, the interpretation [sic] of my normal actions was in the hands of others. If I gave the unfortunate impression that I wished others to imitate my solitary acts it was involuntary. I only issued orders upon request. In my own way I was seeking, and still am, all alone. That hasn't changed, though the world has. The world (whatever that is) is fast approaching a reckoning, and my only hope is that I may be allowed to make myself ready for it. The overloading cannot continue indefinitely and examples must be set. I hope you are writing about this, for I remember your early AVATAR letters and recall you always had a way with the written word. Speaking of the early days, you remember Candy, the child you brought up to me. Well, she is still with us though I'm afraid she has grown a little withdrawn. She ought to get out on her own, like you did, but of course I will never tell her this. One must, as you say, find their own natural rhythms and instincts within the prevailing conditions and follow these impulses according to how one is individually programmed before one can really ever begin to develop their own spontaneity and creative abilities to express the holy "Self." No, it's good you got out when you did, before the continual stress and pressures built up to the inevitable overload that brought so many down. But, we bury our dead and look for a brighter day.

Jeremy, the one who held you up to the mirror to witness your squashed face, has gone off the deep end. Quite mad, as the English say. I believe he's in jail someplace for child-molesting. Now I hope you don't attribute these unfortunate events to my influence, soley (or is that "solely") but we all must shoulder our share of the blame; even you, as I'm sure you know. Sofie has gone back to her people of Mexican heritage and last I heard was drinking rather heavily. In a word, the Community is Kaput! But I'm sure you foresaw that it would turn out that way. After all, force and brutality cannot continue unimpinged forever as a normal mode of expressing life. But I do, at some future date, have plans of erecting a true space station where individuals who have only the good of humanity at heart may orbit freely. To this end I pledge myself, and only in this way do I find the courage to go on, stilted as that may sound. Not to be a teacher, not a guru, not even as a shining example but only as a free human being expressing my thanks to God and breathing the good, clean air with similar beings. If I have made mistakes, then that is a private matter and, as the *I Ching* says, there is "no blame," and if, yet, in treading my own private trail, I have, in some indistinct way or other, happened to be of some use to my fellow man, then, that is probably the most we can ever dare to hope for, for we tread alone AND together. . . .

I almost forgot. About the music, I have given it up. Only when the compounded joy of ALL humanity is their [*sic*] to be born forth in song will I feel free to add my voice to the melee. My message awaits that consumation [*sic*].

Mel's quick response, with its confusing combination of humility, confession, and arrogance, took me completely by surprise. I didn't know how to react, or whether to respond; I went to David Lerner for help, but he wasn't able to offer me much. He still saw the community in a much more favorable and unequivocal light than I did. It seemed unlikely we would remain close friends, and in fact we did not, although we did continue visiting infrequently for some months.

As was so often the case when I reflected on Fort Hill, the mix of conflicting feelings gradually gave way to one overriding emotion: deep anger, to which everything else was an afterthought. Eventually, I wrote this anger down in a draft of a return letter to Mel, which I'm quite sure I never completed or sent, though later events made me wish I had. The draft is undated, but it was evidently written late in 1977 or early in 1978, shortly before the tenth anniversary of my arrival at Fort Hill, and the fifth anniversary of my departure.

In it, I go on for a number of pages, detailing specific complaints about life in the community and how it undermined individual creativity and spontaneity; how it encouraged hierarchical power struggles; how it reflected traditional values and enforced traditional gender role models; how it abused our willingly given contributions of time, money, and energy, and created a structure in which it was impossible to claim any of those gifts back; how it was all based on an assumption of personal loyalty to Mel even when that loyalty was not present (as in my case); how the rules were enforced by violence and public humiliation; how much of this system was brought about by the creation of false expectations (such as my hope of moving to Fort Hill to work on a functioning newspaper, which was already falling apart before I arrived), and was perpetuated by the steadily increasing control of our thoughts and our access to cultural information from the world at large. I conclude with a scathing criticism of Mel's statement that he is no longer producing music, because the world is not yet ready for it. I then criticize Mel's and the community's apparent inability to achieve commercial success with any of its efforts at media or creating public influence for itself (see sidebar 8).

SIDEBAR 8

AUTHOR'S UNMAILED, UNDATED LETTER TO MEL LYMAN, LATER 1977 OR EARLY 1978

Dear Mel,

I'm writing in response to your letter of May 28, 1977, the one that begins, "My son, your criticism was well taken . . ." and goes on to explain away a lot of your current difficulties.

Let's begin by getting something straight: I'm not your son, and never have been; you're not my father, and never have been. We are *something* to each other, but it's not father and son. . . .

I'd like to say early on that most of what you say in your letter is a shuck, and I don't believe a word of it. I don't know what purpose it serves for you to continue to fool yourself with that sort of pompous talk, if indeed you do fool yourself with it, or to continue to attempt to fool people like me with it. You're about as innocent of wrongdoing as Richard Nixon was, and about as naïve.

Another thing that really bugs me is your statement that you have "pondered" my "eventual outcome"—as though I were a TV movie whose last segment you accidentally missed. My "eventual outcome" hasn't been written yet; I'm still living and changing my life, just as you are yours. What you probably meant was you have pondered the question of how I've done in the world outside your community after being *in* your community for so long. And well might you ponder. It provides telling insight into a person's character to see how they behave in the aftermath of massive trauma. You must do a lot of that sort of pondering; a great many people have passed through your community over the years, and I'm sure most have been rather intensely influenced by it.

The attitude that people's lives are curious dramas to be studied from afar—*and no more*—is right at the crux of what's wrong with your act, and the act of certain strong others, like your friend Charlie Manson. People like you know how to respond to the imperatives of history and spirit, at least sometimes, and you can mobilize the disorganized energies of yearning souls, but can you see the pain and confusion you cause in the people around you when you allow yourself to be blown up bigger than life?

I know you disclaim responsibility for what has happened to the people who've followed you because, after all, each of us is responsible for his or her own fate, but you must realize that is a cop-out. For one thing, if you had really "become compassion," as you admonished the readers of *Avatar* to do, you would have learned to use your personal power to urge people toward their best unfolding, rather than just watching us as though we were laboratory specimens, and using us for your own purposes. For another thing, it just isn't true that you "only issued orders upon request."

I can recall many, many incidents in which you directly ordered people to behave in ways not of their choosing, or directly forbade actions people had chosen, or demanded certain types of obeisance, or forced people into compromising positions, or interpreted people's motives in ways that violated their own intentions. And people close to you behaved in exactly the same way, often in attempts to emulate you or to do your bidding. I'm tempted to catalog some of the incidents I remember here just to get them off my chest, but if I did so my letter would threaten to become a book. Suffice it to say my head is filled with memories of weirdness and injustice perpetrated by you and yours. And while all these things were going on, you were hiding behind the same lie that your followers expected this of you, that the noblesse oblige of the spiritually privileged required this callous behavior.

Why so many of us were ready to believe you, and others "of your station," is one of the mysteries of this age, but there is no doubt you were lying to us then and you're lying now when you say you had no choice whether to give the orders.

. . . I must say, it is a severe disappointment, though perfectly consistent with everything else, that you say you've given up music until "the compounded joy of ALL humanity" creates enough space for your voice to sing out again. What was wrong with being a musician, anyway, or a creative artist in any other field? What hole in your sense of self required more than that? You seem to have felt that the world owed you a living, and you've gone about insuring that you have a very nice living indeed, but why does that need to be couched inside a belief that the world at large is not even worth raising your voice in song? How do you ever expect it to become ready, and why *should* the world become more ready than it is before you sing again? Do you believe you were placed here to pass judgment on us all, rather than to participate in the process with everyone else?

I know that once you believed you were here mainly for the process of life, and you wrote eloquently about the how and why of it all. That writing drew me to you, and when I reread your words now they *still* fire my imagination and stir deep feelings in me, even though they are written with the simplistic innocence we all shared then. Who do you think you've become that using your gifts is no longer the most important thing? When you say "my message awaits" the moment when "ALL humanity" sings together, who do you think *you* are while you wait?

. . . Always a dream of grandeur, but the inability to let events unfold at their own pace. And always, your followers continued working at demeaning jobs and hoping for something better. It made me wonder, to say the least, how sincere you were about amassing any influence, and just how truly God was on your side.

Meanwhile, out here in the rough-and-tumble of the world, music and literature, cinema and broadcasting, politics and religion and social thought have all continued progressing and changing, no thanks to you. Do you think this is what God intends for His loyal servant, as you seem still to think you are?

I think you've largely missed it and wasted it, Mel, and your letter, if it represents a real belief of yours, indicates that nothing much is moving where you are. It all makes me wonder why you don't just give it up, tell everybody to take their share and go home, or do whatever they want, and get yourself back on the road or someplace where some fresh wind can blow through the old bod. Maybe take a couple of your favorite wives and kids and helpers and go back to the woods and start over. Remember how you used to threaten to do just that, every year or so? We ingrates just weren't worthy of your presence, and it was too hard to create with all these panderers around, and so forth? You never managed to make the break then; evidently you were as addicted to being followed as we were to following. I'm not sure where you are now in relation to all that, but in your letter you sure sound stuck. And, man, you sure could make music before.

O BlaDi, O BlaDa, Life Goes On Now

During the months while all these intense feelings about Mel and Fort Hill were brewing in me, a number of other issues were also coming to a head. I spent the spring and summer employing a number of people from The Land, and some other friends as well, including Carol, as a crew to complete the long-awaited remodel on my sister's house, spending the money obtained in an out-of-court settlement of our suit against the former owners. When the money ran out, my sister and brother-in-law agreed to pay me some of what was due in the form of a shared title to the empty lot next to their house. My work associates and I saw this as a chance to develop a model solar house, in a financial environment in which the long cycle of real estate inflation in the area finally seemed to be slowing down, but the tax benefits of solar development were increasing. It looked like our last best chance to get in on the game, after a number of disappointing overtures over the preceding years. I prepared to apply for my building contractor's license so I would be legally able to build and sell a speculation house.

My mother finally sold her house in New York and moved to Redwood City to be near my sister and me, rather than to Florida, as she had previously planned. Carol was close to finishing her work at Stanford, getting ready to graduate with a degree in psychology, which she promptly decided to apply to a career in real estate.

We watched from a distance, sadly, as the *Grapevine* proceeded to wither away. In size and format, it reverted to the form it had had before we got involved; the appeals for financial and volunteer support began appearing again, but evidently to little avail. It went on like this for nearly another year, and in June 1978, an issue was published that announced there would be a publication break for the summer while the remaining staff reviewed its plans and options. The paper never reappeared.

This was all the sadder for us because the drama of The Land's eviction struggle and the transition to a new era for the people and the property richly deserved to be covered, but we no longer felt we had an outlet for this. The Burnses eventually succeeded in serving the residents with an adequate and legal set of eviction papers, and the case came to trial in county court. It was a sideshow that went on for weeks and drained everyone involved of a great deal of personal energy that all became focused, tragically, on the three-year-old daughter of two of the residents most involved in the eviction fight. They left her one day in the care of another resident, one of my close work associates who was also one of little Sierra's closest friends. He took her to the beach for the day and photographed her wistfully staring out to the ocean and the sky, then took her back to Struggle Mountain, the associated commune nearby The Land that had once been Joan Baez's and David Harris's home. While he had his back turned briefly, Sierra fell into the doughboy swimming pool; by the time she was discovered, she had suffered brain damage and nearly drowned. She was taken to the intensive-care unit of Stanford Hospital and remained there in a coma for several weeks while the eviction fight continued.

The Land's residents and supporters found ourselves conducting simultaneous vigils at both the hospital and the courthouse. We lost both fights. Sierra's body eventually gave out without ever regaining consciousness, and the eviction fight was lost. The Burnses proceeded to complete their sale of most of the acreage to the Midpeninsula Regional Open Space District, and collaborated with city officials to conduct the eviction and nearly simultaneous demolition of all the buildings of both the "frontlands" and the "backlands," which occurred with great fanfare during October 1977. Donald Eldridge also completed his deal with the Open Space District, although I'm unable to remember how that transaction related to his continuing appeal in the state courts for some satisfaction on all the money he had invested.

When the demolitions occurred immediately following the eviction, they were carried out with what we perceived to be great contempt for the still relatively pristine nature of the land. A large hole was dug next to each building, and the debris unceremoniously bulldozed in and buried, causing what seemed completely unnecessary long-term damage to the environment. The spring box and gravity distribution water system that had been built many decades before, and had been lovingly revived and maintained and extended by the residents, was completely destroyed, leaving the land without any usable water source as it entered its new life as an open space resource for the people of the area. The entire property was fenced and kept off-limits to the public for a number of months while the Open Space District cleared up the mess it had made and developed walking trails, marker signs, parking lots, and the like. Former residents and friends of The Land, including myself, did obtain special permission to return to the property the next Easter Sunday to have one more experience of what had become a traditional celebration on a particular hilltop, but it was a small and bittersweet victory.

I found myself that summer, while working with a friend from The Land, becoming uncontrollably infatuated with him. He was kind enough to let me talk this out with him and, I presume, to at least consider allowing some action on my infatuation, but that proved impossible. It did put me on notice that the old issue of my sexual identity was unresolved, and I raised the issue both in my men's group and with Carol, for eventual resolution. In other ways also, my relationship with Carol was becoming more tense. She was making more and more demands on my time and attention, and I was more and more unable to be available to her emotionally in the way that she wanted. A tone of psychological and occasional physical violence was creeping into the relationship that disturbed us both a great deal. I felt quite out of control with it.

During the fall, I completed my application for my contractor's license, which involved documenting years of work experience, collecting testimonials from customers and coworkers, proving my financial stability, and sending all this off with proof of a performance-bond insurance policy and a passport-type picture of myself.

About the time I accomplished all this, I happened to run across a new album by Jim Kweskin, *Jim Kweskin Lives Again*, a live concert album on a minor record label from the Midwest. It gave no indication of whether he was still with the community, and so, assuming that he was not, I sent off a brief fan letter to him, congratulating him on what I perceived to be his new independence and return to the music biz. I enclosed my extra copy of the passport picture taken for my license application, as a simple way of demonstrating that I too was living again. He sent back a brief note, using the return address of the record company, and mailed from Atlanta, Georgia, where he was evidently touring: "Dear Michael, Life is a ball. It's hard, but the harder it is the better I like it. If you are open to it, you shall receive it. With all sincerety [sic] Jim." He enclosed a fan-type picture of himself sitting naked on a lawn with his guitar covering the private parts, quite a departure for the formerly very traditional Jim Kweskin. Still no clear evidence of whether or not he was with the community.

By the time this arrived, the date for my license exam had also arrived, and I spent the day in San Francisco being tested. When the exam ended early, I decided, okay, today is the day, and I went to knock on the door of the remaining Fort Hill house in San Francisco, near Buena Vista Park in the Upper Haight-Ashbury district, with a spectacular view of downtown from the living rooms. I was greeted by three women of the house: Kay Rose, who had once owned House Number 3 on Fort Hill, and who then, after divorcing her husband, had returned to the community by way of the farm, where she was a resident during the time I was there, with her young daughter in tow; Peggy McGill, a young Taurus woman with whom I had had a brief infatuation when we both were living in New York; and Nell Turner, whom I had never met before but who was the younger sister of Bess Turner, one of my close friends from the early days of working on *Avatar* in the South End. Bess was the mother of a young girl who had been born around that time, who was forcibly separated from Bess during the days of sexual behavior modification on the Hill, and was later sent to live with us at the farm while Bess was in New York being a stockbroker. Meeting Nell was a peculiar kind of déjà vu for me.

All three of the women were cordial but cryptic, giving me little information about what was going on with the community, but letting me know the San Francisco house was about to be given up and its personnel transferred to Hollywood. They also told me they had heard about the note and picture I had sent to Jim, and found that amusing. So the gossip network was evidently in full operation, and Jim was evidently hooked into it. When I spoke about my current life and tried to put my relationship with Carol in a perspective that included my earlier relationships with the Carol and Candy they knew, I remember Kay just saying in an aside to Nell, paraphrasing my words, "He says he keeps having to go through the same things over and over." It must have been a reference to lessons they were experiencing, but they did not explain. One of Mel's favorite aphorisms in earlier years had been that "recapitulation is the only real learning." After a while the conversation wound down, and the women were nervous about starting dinner, so I left, thanking them for their cordiality. So that was my one and only visit to Fort Hill turf in all the years since leaving in 1973. Not too satisfying.

Come Out, Come Out, Wherever You Are

That spring, I got pushed farther into exploring the question of my sexual identity. One of my men's group friends, Gordon Murray, was invited to co-facilitate a course at Stanford on the philosophy and growing body of literature of the new men's movement, through a new program at the university to encourage community participation; the course was open to both Stanford students and community members. I signed up for the course and immediately became infatuated with the other co-facilitator, a senior in the same psychology program Carol was in, who encouraged my friendship but was pretty freaked out by my amorous intentions. By the time the course ended, it was all but impossible for either of us to retain our equanimity.

I decided I had to do something about this dilemma. I wrote a letter to Don Clark, a well-known therapist and writer in the field, whose book *Loving Someone Gay* had been very helpful to me in defining the questions I was facing, and who had been Gordon's therapist while he was exploring similar issues. I asked Clark if he was available to do some work with me; he wrote back that he was not taking new clients, but recommended another local therapist, whom I had met a couple of years earlier when he "married" one of my associates in the Men's Center. I started individual therapy with him, and soon was invited to join his weekly gay men's "coming out" group, which quickly became one of the most important aspects of my ever-changing life. I did not appreciate the professional distance the therapist insisted on keeping, but the other men in the group became important new friends for me, and I had affairs with a couple of them.

Carol was as supportive as she could be of this new interest in my life. For the 1978 Gay Freedom Day parade in San Francisco, I spent the weekend with my friend Gordon and some friends of his, a breakthrough for me, while Carol and her women's group from Stanford marched in the parade under a banner, "Straights for Gay Rights."

Carol graduated from Stanford. She and I signed up together for courses in real estate law and business management at the downtown Palo Alto branch of the local junior college. Soon she obtained her real estate sales license and found a job with a local office. She made new friends there and even had a brief affair with a coworker, which was a generally unsatisfying experience, but it did affirm for her that there were other possibilities open to her.

I was exploring the gay night-life scene around Palo Alto and San Jose, such as they were, and quickly concluded that to find what I was looking for, I would probably have to get in the habit of commuting to the much larger and more diverse gay scene in San Francisco. I began doing this in all my available time, with a lot of encouragement but some palpable disappointment on Carol's part. It was increasingly clear that our relationship was not likely to hold together, but it was equally clear that I was very happy finally letting the truth out in the air about my longings and fantasies.

Not too long into this phase, I realized that I had to separate from Carol in order to have the freedom to explore freely. As ever, she was both supportive and reluctant to see this change occur, but I began searching for an appropriate new home. I found one just before Halloween, when I interviewed with a single mother named Patricia Rain at a wonderful home in the woodsy part of Redwood City not far from my sister's home. When Patricia, almost immediately upon meeting me, lent me one of her most flamboyant dresses to wear to the upcoming obligatory drag event of my coming-out group (she and I are almost exactly the same size), I knew I had found a home and a friend. I moved on November 1, and we became instant best friends. We remained together through two years in that house, and nearly two more years in another house in Los Altos, and remain close friends today. I introduced her to my carpenter friend with whom I had had my infatuation the year before, and they remain a couple now ten years later.

Carol and I attempted to remain close and supportive friends, but it did not turn out to be easy. She soon became involved in a very surprising relationship with an older man, a person of some spiritual and scientific and worldly accomplishments, who was suffering from terminal cancer and blindness caused by a laboratory accident. He was still very spirited, however, and urged Carol to marry him in his last days. He proved his devotion by helping her through some amazing changes, even inducing physical growth and changes in her through processes only he seemed to understand. He remained alive through nearly a year of a marriage that was quite transformative for Carol, and when it was over, she and I had little to say to each other. Her real estate career was in full swing.

Before long, as I was exploring the gay scene in San Francisco, I came across the early expressions of a network of spiritually seeking and politically active gay men known as "radical fairies." They were coming together around the work and the philosophy of Harry Hay, a longtime political activist who in 1950 had founded the first openly gay organization of the modern era, the Mattachine Society, and Harry's longtime partner, John Burnside, among others. They wanted to offer the gay community an alternative to the assimilationist and rather materialist trend that had become dominant in the community in the decade or so since the Stonewall riots had brought "gay liberation" out of the closet. They were organizing the first of what was to become a long series of "spiritual gatherings for radical fairies," to be held in the Arizona desert in September 1979. I was invited by a friend, but I was too busy with my work to attend. But over the next months, the radical fairies became my home base in the gay scene, and I was making friends and lovers who drew me to San Francisco more and more frequently. I was also exploring actively in the gay scene generally, figuring out what I liked and didn't like. In short, I was developing a new community for myself, this time rather better tailored to my current needs than some of my earlier efforts. One of the central principles of the radical fairies was that everyone is equal, that everyone's viewpoint is valid. All fairy groups made decisions by consensus, and all fairy events were held in circles, imitating the practice of the pagan community, which was one of the major influences on us.

I affirmed my connection with the larger gay community by traveling solo to the first National March for Gay and Lesbian Rights in Washington, D.C., in October 1979, which was for me an exciting opportunity to experience the old familiar protoreligious rush of collective political action in a new context. I volunteered as a parade monitor and ushered the huge crowd from the line of march onto the Washington Monument grounds for the big rally, so I got to see the entire crowd walk past me at a distance of a few feet. I was in heaven.

After the march, I went to New York to visit my brother and other relatives and affirm my coming out to them. I also had a rare visit with some friends from high school, from whom I learned, just before I was scheduled to leave, that my old partner Carol Schneider-Franck was living in the Fort Hill New York house with her two children, and was keeping at least occasional contact with friends and family on Long Island. I was disappointed to learn this too late to act on it, and when I was back home in California, I wrote yet another letter to her, hoping to reestablish friendly relations. This was a nonconfrontational and rather wistful letter, wishing her well and telling her a little of my current life, but once again it elicited no response.

Are You Ready for the Eighties?

During this entire period of a couple of years, I continued my work relationship with a number of the people I had met at The Land, all of whom had by now long since relocated to homes in town and were paying rent each month like the rest of us and needed the cash flow. I hoped and strongly encouraged this to become a collective operation, but all the credentials and bank credits were in my name, and the truth of the relationships was that I was the employer and they were the employees. I disliked the role intensely.

Our hope of building a speculation house in Redwood City next to my sister's house fell through for several reasons; primary among them was that my sister decided to parlay a career she had developed for herself as a lecturer and color consultant into a retail decorating business, and she used the available second-mortgage money from her house, which had been intended to fund our building project, to open a store in the Silicon Valley town of Cupertino. I was left with my contractor's license and a crew of employees, but no major project to work on.

The fallback plan was to pursue ever-larger contracting projects through the real estate network in the Palo Alto area, and also to accept federally funded contracts to rehabilitate housing in the nearby city of Mountain View. I found myself, against my will, forced to compete for jobs, respect, and recognition of my own and my crew's ability to produce the work that was expected of us, despite our unorthodox appearance and behavior. Sometimes I hardly knew how to keep up appearances, and I always resented having to make the effort to do so. I felt constantly torn between my personal impulses and the requirements of my work.

Nearly all the projects we did during this period turned out to be disasters one way or another, frequently running way over budget, frequently getting completed despite antagonistic relations with clients and employees, frequently requiring investment in tools and equipment I could scarcely afford, occasionally requiring difficult negotiations to extract payments from angry clients, and on one occasion actually tumbling unhappily into a mechanic's lien suit, which I lost. I didn't seem able to find adequate legal or accounting help; I was juggling finances with my relatives to keep my credit going; I was falling farther and farther behind in employment taxes and other overhead payments; and my stress level was going through the ceiling. And all this was going on while in the other department of my life, I was actively exploring the gay counterculture and looking for a truer expression of myself free of traditional gender roles. Something had to give.

By April 1980, I finally found the courage to do an accurate accounting of how far behind I was, at the point where the owner of the largest federally funded rehab project we had done was capriciously withholding more than $8,000 in final payments, even though the city and the federal overseers had already approved the work. I found that even when that money came in, I would be more than $20,000 in debt. This meant that if I had sat home and lived on borrowed money for the previous two years, I would have been farther ahead than I was for all my hard work. I was devastated and completely lost the spirit to continue in the same mode, acting as employer and whip-cracker over a reluctant crew that could not perform up to my needs. I laid them all off and faced the unhappy prospect of working overtime for the next couple of years to pay off the debts and get back to zero. But cutting my losses in this way seemed the only sane direction to go.

I decided that I needed to give myself a couple of gifts to assuage my broken spirits. I signed up for classes in improvisational dance and vocal expression; the dance lessons continued for several years and eventually provided me access to a gay men's contact improvisation group in San Francisco, which became another important support group for me. I began therapy sessions in a kind of regression therapy aimed at identifying and clearing up residual birth trauma, and found this very helpful in suggesting reasons I seemed to be so prone to claustrophobic and enervating karmic involvements. I checked out my intuitions about the circumstances of my birth with my mother, and she confirmed that my birth had indeed been very painful for both her and me, that a rough and unsympathetic doctor had been in charge, and that it had taken weeks to find a feeding scheme for me that did not make me ill. This all provided a new sense of the inner work I would have to do to eventually heal myself.

I also felt a need to heal on the external political level. It was the year of Jimmy Carter's downfall and Ronald Reagan's ascendancy, and I worried about the state of the economy and the rising prospects for nuclear war. I was feeling a strong urge to devote as much of myself as I could to the task of keeping the earth alive, somehow, and at the same time was feeling trapped in the task of paying off my debts and resurrecting my career. I fantasized about running away, becoming an itinerant activist and handyman, but couldn't see myself voluntarily giving up the friends and family and sense of home I had developed.

To support an alternative course for the future, I aligned myself with environmentalist Barry Commoner's campaign for the presidency, under the third-party banner of the Citizens Party. I became active with the Palo Alto chapter and quickly found myself speaking for that chapter in a Northern California coordinating committee, from which base—this is hardly a surprise—I also became involved in publishing an occasional tabloid newspaper for the Citizens Party, *The Citizens Voice*. We published perhaps half a dozen issues over the two-year period I remained with the party. After the rout of the 1980 election, we continued organizing various other efforts locally and statewide, hoping to create a lasting third party, but that did not come about, and eventually I found other commitments more important to me than continuing the effort.

During the summer of 1980, I was offered a long-term construction job, as the foreman of a major remodel and second-story addition to a house in Palo Alto owned by a gay property developer. This was a good opportunity for steady income in a friendly environment, and it relieved a bit of the pressure of constantly finding new work. On that job, I developed a friendship and then a lover relationship with a rather shy and somewhat closeted gay laborer. We dated and became increasingly close over a two-year period, living at opposite ends of the town of Los Altos and exploring in the radical fairies scene together.

We missed our second opportunity at a major fairy gathering in the fall of 1980, again because of work, but by the third opportunity, late summer of 1981, we were finally able to attend one, in the mountains of northern New Mexico. The four-day event was marked by heavy rainstorms and some other disappointments, but it was transformative for us nevertheless. As we were getting ready to leave on the last day, I found my new name, literally in the ground at the gathering site, where the shiny, soft stone mica was in abundance. I was looking for a name that would resonate with Michael but have a character of its own. I claimed the name, and spent the next couple of years growing into it; for some years now, I have used the name Mica in nearly every part of my life.

I made a serious effort to enlist the help of my former employees in paying off the remaining debts from our business disasters, but to no avail. As part of that effort, in early 1981, I found myself obsessed with trying to tell them more about myself, about the history that had led me into involvement with them, and what it meant for me in my personal growth to be burdened by the unreasonable debts. I wrote a major chunk of autobiography for their benefit and shared it with them, along with more accounting information about how the business had failed, but it drew no financial or even much emotional support from them. I felt stung and betrayed.

Bobby Bolchalk and I remained a couple and continued working together into 1982, but in that year, I decided to cut way back on my contracting career and instead to join my sister's retail business, which was going out on a financial limb to open a second location. I helped find a building in San Carlos, near Redwood City, and Bobby and I and other friends performed a major remodel on it. When the store opened, I became its manager, receiving only minimal support from the partner with whom my sister had opened the first store. But with a great deal of creative energy and overtime, working for minimal wages, we got the store off the ground.

Bobby and I broke up on short notice when we went to our second radical fairy gathering in San Diego in late 1982 and he met someone who quickly attracted him away from me. This gave me the excuse I needed to finally move to San Francisco, since I was now commuting almost twenty miles each way on the Peninsula, and the drive from San Carlos to San Francisco was only slightly longer. One of my close radical fairy friends and I decided to start a collective household together, and we found a house in the Haight-Ashbury late in 1982. This was a homecoming, a completion of a circle for me, having decided many years earlier that I wanted to live in the Haight and then seen my life unexpectedly take a completely different direction. I am still living in that house eight years later, and it has become an institution in the radical fairy community. A great deal of community-organizing work has taken place in our living rooms.

My sister split her time between the two store locations, but eventually made the San Carlos store her primary base, and she and I became closer than ever as we worked together for the next couple of years. Our mother went through a series of hospitalizations for emphysema during this period, and finally succumbed in the spring of 1983. Our business grew rapidly and looked like it was going to be successful in the long term; a third partner merged her store with us, and the three partners and I attempted to function as a "management team" for the three stores. But we were overextended financially, and our personnel resources were stretched to the limit. By late 1984 there was serious dissension between me and my sister and the third partner on the one hand, and the original managing partner on the other hand. He walked out without notice one day when we were challenging his management style, leaving the rest of us to attempt to rescue the business from bankruptcy. We were unable to do so, and placed it in a Chapter 11 reorganization mode, which involved closing the San Carlos store and phasing out my job by early 1985, while also relocating and reducing the size of the other two stores we had at the time. This strategy was not enough to save the business from ultimate failure, and this failure was accompanied by the development of neurological symptoms in my sister. What at first looked like a nervous breakdown turned out to be a fatal brain tumor, which was diagnosed too late to be operable. She died in late 1985.

My response to all these developments was to reassess my own life strategy, since I was clearly at risk for the same kind of stress-induced illness that had killed my sister. I felt I had little choice but to return to freelance construction to earn my living, but I did so in as informal a fashion as I could, assuring myself that I did not have to get in over my head again as I had so many times before. I declared my intention to keep my life a little bit simpler, for a change, and did my best to live up to that intention. Doing so, however, wasn't easy or natural for me. I was already very committed to projects that were more than willing to fill all my available time.

Over the previous few years, I had become enmeshed in the San Francisco radical fairies network. I attended many gatherings of fairies in various locations up and down the West Coast, getting used to seeing myself in a wide range of roles across the spectrum of gender possibilities. Being with the fairies gave me a welcome chance to choose who to be and how to behave moment to moment, and to change at will. I decided to use my organizing abilities to make this opportunity consistently available to people who wanted it.

After playing a key role in organizing several major gatherings, I became involved in an effort within the fairies network to organize a nonprofit corporation in order to collectively purchase land on which to establish a spiritual sanctuary for ourselves. We decided to seek government recognition as a religion, figuring that what we did together was the equivalent of what standard religions did. We named our sanctuary project Nomenus, making up a word that contained the sounds and implicitly the meanings of half a dozen other names we had considered. In mid-1985, I assumed the role of president of Nomenus; over the next two years, I led the organization through the agonizing process of convincing the Internal Revenue Service to grant us our religious organization status (it finally did), and through the equally agonizing process of searching for land, raising money for the down payment, buying land that was offered to us by a dying friend, and holding a "Homecoming Gathering" attended by nearly three hundred people, most of whom became member-directors of the consensus organization. At the same time, I was also involved for about a year in organizing the California Men's Gatherings, helping to guide that informal consensus network of gay and straight men working together through a difficult reformulation of its purposes and way of operating. The men's contact improvisation dance group that I met and danced with weekly was an important base of support and encouragement in all these efforts.

Early in the decade, I decided to spend my activist time helping to create positive and useful alternatives, rather than simply protesting and worrying about the mess that the world was in. Seeing how well my efforts with the men's movement were going, and how powerfully our efforts to offer men a wider choice of behavior models helped strengthen them to oppose the status quo of the larger society, I felt that at last I had found a meaning to all my previous experiences. Despite the financial and career difficulties I was still feeling, I felt a unity with myself that was new. And an opportunity came along to articulate this unity to some of my former tormentors.

More News from the Front

One of the last gifts my sister gave me before she became ill was to point out to me, on August 5, 1985, an article in the *San Francisco Chronicle* about "The Last Hippies in Boston." "I think it's about those people you used to live with," she said. That was indeed true. The article was a wire-service report, datelined Boston, about the new affluence of the former hippies of Fort Hill that resulted from their construction businesses on both coasts and their substantial inheritance from Tom Benton, and about the new magazine, *U and I,* they were now beginning to publish to tell the world about what they had become, and about how the visions of the old days had transformed with the community's increasing worldliness and long-term relationships with each other. The article gave the current census of the community as seventy-two adults and thirty-nine children, and mentioned their homes in Boston, New York, Los Angeles, Kansas, and Martha's Vineyard. It spoke of the history of Mel Lyman's influence over them, and his dominance of the community's media efforts in the early years. Most surprising, the article reported, "Group members say Lyman died in 1978, but refuse to discuss the cause of death. They deny rumors that Lyman quit the group and is now living in Europe." Two pictures accompanied the article, showing community members happily playing music after dinner one night and admiring their new magazine. All but two of the people pictured were long-familiar faces to me.

Well, well, well. What a strange and unexpected news flash. The community alive and well and reaching out to the public again. Mel reportedly dead, years ago, evidently not long after my exchange of letters with him. It was a lot to take in. I imagined Mel killing himself, or becoming depressed and dying of some mysterious disease. Who could know? In the background of the picture of the music-making that accompanied the article was someone playing harmonica, Mel's instrument, who looked for all the world like Mel himself. I had to look carefully and repeatedly to decide that it wasn't Mel after all but Richie Guerin, who had always been a near-ringer for Mel. Unless it was Mel, after all. I believed they were capable of telling the media anything, regardless of the truth.

It became very important to me to track down a copy of this magazine, but I wondered how I could do it. I spoke to a radical fairy friend who maintains a legal practice in both San Francisco and Boston, and he gave me the name of someone who was likely to be willing to find a copy on a newsstand in Boston. That person was Charley Shively, longtime writer and editor of *Fag Rag* in Boston. We spoke at length by telephone; Charley was fascinated by my story and immediately went out and found me both the magazine and a copy of a poster advertising an appearance at some local clubs in Cambridge by "The U and I Band featuring Jim Kweskin."

The magazine was little more than a slicker update of the old *American Avatar* format. It was in a standard magazine-sized page, with a full-color cover and some color pages inside, front- and back-cover paintings clearly done by Eben Given, recognizably of himself and Candy, in a fictional country setting surrounded by friendly dragons. Much of the writing was on the theme of dragons, evidently a new archetypal symbol of life force for the community. An introductory essay inside the front cover gives the closest thing to a statement of purpose:

> This publication is offered to you with no explanations, no bylines or credentials. It does not set about to sell anything, prove anything, or change anything. It is a series of open and unusual conversations about the things that concern us all. Think of it as a journey we are taking together. Pretend that we are strangers on a train, you and I traveling somewhere that we have never been before. Let's not introduce ourselves, or ask all the usual questions like, "Who are you?" and "What do you do?" It is so much more fun to discover these things along the way. Let's begin with no preconceived ideas about each other, no judgments, no categories. Rather let us take a leap of blind faith from one reality to another, from an external world to a world of inner thoughts, feelings and experiences. This foreign land that we are traveling through is a place where one is not afraid to laugh or cry, to admit failure and defeat, to risk love and aspire to beauty. Let us ask difficult questions and give honest answers, and by no means be objective. Who knows what we will find on this uncharted voyage. Let us begin with a song, and see where it leads us.

Very little about the magazine seemed new to me—only the glimpses I could recognize of news bulletins about people I knew: Candy and Eben in a tumultuous, stormy relationship, tape-recording their intimate conversations to be shared with others (in the style of the electronic linking of the houses that was fantasized but never materialized when I was with them); Dick Russell writing a long paean to their newfound sport of game fishing and a corresponding interest in environmental protection; David Lerner, my Palo Alto friend, corresponding with Jessie about his developing sensitivities as a writer; stories and pictures and letters written by parents about children I've never met. Life in the community obviously goes on, anonymously except to the well-connected.

After receiving and poring over the magazine, and experiencing the inevitable and by now familiar rush of nostalgia and revulsion as my memories of the community were restimulated yet another time, I wrote a thank-you letter to Charley Shively summarizing my view of the new product:

The magazine itself is no surprise at all. It's exactly in line with what they produced in years past; strikingly so, in fact. Amazing, really, that so little has changed, except their financial status. It's the same general tone, the same ideas, the same heroes and villains, the same generalized, disinterested commentary on the current scene, the same arrogance and indrawn narrowness of viewpoint, the same traditional morality presented as though it were new and different, the same adulation of Mel's thoughts and words, even some of the same articles reprinted one more time. Even, to my eye, the same Executive typewriter used to set the copy. Exactly the same, limited repertoire of graphic devices. Overall, kind of incredible, such an anachronism. Can you believe anyone still remembering Bobby Kennedy as the hero who could have made it all work out better, if only . . . ? I really wonder what the impetus was to go public again. It clearly wasn't that they have something new to say. Some of the context suggests that the advent of Reagan, et al., has got them worried enough to look at the larger world again, but I still have a sense they'd prefer to stay in their safe little world of money-making and big-game fishing.

The magazine contained a contact card, encouraging readers to stay in touch so they could be informed of any later issues that would be published, but I couldn't quite bring myself to use it. I did alert my three grown nephews, my sister's sons who were and are all aspiring musicians living in Hollywood nearby the community's big house there, to be on the lookout for this magazine or any subsequent one that might show up in the local stores. As we talked about it, my oldest nephew, who earns his living as a carpenter, and I had a shock of recognition. It turns out that the previous year, he had actually worked on one of the community's construction crews for a while. I had heard about the job he had with an outfit that did primarily fancy remodels for Hollywood stars, but I didn't make the connection at the time. We compared notes on specific people, and there was no doubt he had worked for my onetime friends; he had found them authoritarian and ungenerous, and had quit after a while. But they occasionally saw each other in the local stores, and he would watch out for a new magazine for me.

A Bulletin from the Heartland

A few months later, one of his brothers did indeed come up with a copy for me of *U and I*, no. 2. This issue, even thicker and slicker than the first, was dedicated to life on the Kansas farm. It stimulated deep nostalgia, even homesickness in me, and gave lots of information about current events among the folks, again accessible to me largely because I knew more than the average reader about the context. An unsigned "Prologue" at the front of the magazine, written "six months after leaving California" and "the intense pressures of making and publishing the first magazine in Los Angeles," explained the rationale for this issue:

> . . . . This isolated spot in the center of the country was a much needed contrast. The farm was a place simply to be, and as always a place where new thoughts came to germinate in conjunction with the new spring seed.
> After a few weeks of long walks through the muddy fields, planting the gardens, and getting reacquainted with the rivers, we found ourselves still there, enchanted somehow,

unable to leave as we had planned. We gave ourselves up to the land, absorbed by its changing moods and rhythms, and began to write about it. In the first issue we had promised to talk about the great men of the past, about the '60s and what became of them. But because this magazine is a continuing process like our life, always changing, our earlier intentions will have to wait. Here on the farm, our heroes changed into the people who live around us, the people who make or break heroes in the first place.

A long paragraph pays homage to the land of northeastern Kansas and the rugged people who manage to survive there, and the influence both the land and the people have had on the community's members in the time they have spent there.

We came to this area almost fifteen years ago as strangers to a place that seemed formed by the wind and it captured us. . . . Over the years we have lived through the searing summer heat, ice storms, floods, tornadoes, drought and bugs. With the help of our friends we have learned what to plant and where and when and we have a nice place here after many years of stops and starts. We've given up our horse-drawn ploughs now for an old tractor, built a few more houses, made the silo into a tower for teenagers and generally subdued the mud and weeds around the house. We raise enough grains, vegetables, meat and poultry to feed the farm and send out some for the rest of us on both coasts to have a little of this and that. And in doing this we have learned about the land and its unpredictability, its unyielding demands and the deep humility in it. It is not a place that lets you dream or forget, but concealed in its stark reality is the magic and beauty of a paradise.

The magazine is full of long narrative stories about relations with neighbors and the environment of Kansas, full of photographs and Eben Given drawings of farm life, many of scenes quite recognizable to me, some indicating the results of years of effort and increased prosperity. Articles, again recognizably by Dick Russell, speak of investigative reporting into the continuing environmental degradation of America's heartland, and warn of an impending second Dust Bowl era. A long section at the back discusses relations between men and women, "He and She," with reprints of old poems and new writings on the subject, old photographs of the famous couples and lovers of Fort Hill, and new discussions of current relationships; another piece about Eben's continuing drama with Candy; and a piece about Norma Lynn Lyman, Mel and Sofie's oldest daughter, now a grown-up, and her love affair with a local man named George whom she had brought home to stay. More dragons and mythic characters. A section of letters from readers of the first magazine. An article by Owen de Long on a hypothetical "Blue Party" he is proposing to organize; another exchange of letters between David Lerner and Jessie, in which she challenges him to leave his concepts behind and get on with his life. Does anything ever change?

I couldn't seem to get beyond the nostalgia this all inspired in me and was a bit horrified to find myself thinking so kindly of those people and that place. What is there to do but respond to such strong feelings? I sat down and carefully handwrote a long letter to "Dear United Illuminating Folks," dated February 19, 1986, and sent it to the address in Kansas offered in the magazine, one among four addresses around the country where readers were encouraged to send correspondence. I went on for pages and pages, telling of my lonely journey from Fort Hill to my current life. I spoke of feeling resonance with the purposes expressed in their new magazine, how it softened for me the memories of our long-ago differences.

What had all that suffering been for? I couldn't—and don't—believe that was the only way I was able to learn or grow. There must have been some other explanation, some karmic past-life something-or-other that tied me to you, and has kept me tied to you in a way through these years. Something about mirroring difficult aspects of ourselves to each other, I guess, or about accepting lessons for their content regardless of the packaging they come in. I know that out here in my life, somehow my confusion and aimlessness have transformed over the years into a kind of wisdom and humor, an adaptability and vitality and capability that are quite unusual and exemplary among my peers, if I do say so myself, and I'm proud of my survivorship and of my accomplishments, which are more internal than external, even though I've been working and working all these years, just like all of you have been. My life is very full, and my life begins again empty each day. I feel like I'm ready for anything.

I discuss my sense of nostalgia at seeing new pictures and stories of some of the old friends, and wonder who is and who isn't still with them. I wonder if they wonder about me. I discuss what it has been like for me seeking and occasionally finding in the world at large the kind of security and familiarity they have created for each other in their community/family over the years. And I take a big risk by discussing one of the concerns of my current life:

One of the really big issues for me in my life, and the area where I have come to find some of my most meaningful and public work to date, is the issue of gender, of sex "roles" and gender-related behavior, and the movement that is afoot here in the middle-class world of the 80's to open out the definitions and possibilities. If we really do have just our inner resources to rely on in life, augmented by whatever help we can elicit from the people around us, it becomes important to know what's really in there, who am I anyway?, and what do I have in me? Do I have to behave in the way my father did, or my mother, or can I create a new blend of my own?

I comment on the section of the magazine concerning gender roles, and point out the traditional interpretations of those roles on which the community's viewpoint seems to be based, something that always made me uncomfortable in the past and seemed to exclude me.

One of the real turning points for me in the years after I left you was when I re-connected with the spirit of "feminism" and the evolutionary shift of consciousness of which it is a part. I found that men, too, could learn from exploring the ways in which our behavior and our self-images and even our thoughts are pre-programmed according to outmoded and limiting ideas of what is available to us. This is what comes up for me when I read about your ongoing Battle of the Sexes, and it sheds some light on the dilemma I was in when I was with you. People used to ask me (Randy especially comes to mind), "Don't you want to be a man? . . ." My answer, internally, always was, "Well, yes, but. . . ." I did want to be strong and determined and courageous, and all that kind of thing, but I didn't want to remain locked in inarticulateness and violence and dependency. In those terms, I wanted to be a "man," and I wanted to be something more as well, and my life with you wasn't showing me a way to do that. What about the "manly" qualities inherent in a woman, the "womanly" qualities contained in every man? When the definitions get too rigid, and get applied across the board to each person based only on their physiology, there is too much chance of the complex mix of characteristics each of us possesses getting averaged out and flattened.

I go on to question how rigid the sex roles still are in the community, and remind them that Melvin used to be in some ways a model of androgyny, a strong and yet sensitive and caring man. I point out that some hints in the magazine suggest a loosening of the gender roles: a woman plumber is mentioned; the men are obviously learning to be thoughtful and articulate. I wonder, is there room among them now for individual preferences, for "intermediate types"? I discuss how the men's movement and the gay movement have become the context of my current life, and how the range of my past experiences has become a valuable asset on which I draw constantly as I play a leadership role within those movements. I describe my work with the radical fairies, our battle to achieve recognition by the government as a religion, and our struggle within ourselves to agree on buying land for a retreat center. I describe how all this is going on in the midst of the AIDS epidemic, in circumstances that suggest it could all come tumbling down in a minute, reminiscent of Germany in the thirties, or the Dust Bowl era on the Great Plains.

But in the midst of all this, one by one, we find ourselves having revelations of simple spirit and renewal, find capacities in ourselves that we didn't know were there, learn to reach out to each other and help each other through the transitions. It's quite amazing, really. There's no doubt we are living in "interesting times," as the Chinese used to say—in fact, no doubt we are living in the "last days," as the Bible still says, and, as ever, all we can expect to leave with when it's time for each of us to go, one by one or all together in a big bang, is what we have made of ourselves in our souls through the choices we've made in our lives.

After all this time and all this living, I'm pleased to say I'm still feeling a kinship with all of you and what you are doing, despite the evident differences in the external forms of our lives. And I'm wanting to receive something from you that's the same thing anyone has ever wanted from the family he, or she, has left behind: Acceptance, the knowledge that there is still a relationship across time and space. And I'm feeling, more strongly than ever before, after reading U & I #2, an impulse to offer what has been most difficult for me to feel in the loneliness and occasional bitterness of my memories: Forgiveness, and good wishes for your continued success.

So that was my peace offering to the community, my extension of my new self to their new selves, in 1986. Like so many attempts at communication that preceded it, it elicited no response whatsoever. But it was quite a healing for me in my own process.

By the time it was written, my life had moved forward a few more notches, and continued to do so. I became quite accustomed to the guiding role I was playing with the radical fairies, coordinating the efforts of hundreds of people up and down the West Coast and around the country, organizing gatherings and events, inevitably publishing newsletters to keep us in touch with each other. Having reluctantly returned to earning my living as a builder and contractor, after a while I found myself in a fruitful partnership with a close friend from my improvisational dance group, a contractor as skilled and jaded with it all as myself. It's a good working relationship that continues today. In my personal life, I was exploring the new forms of "safer" sexual expression that were developing in response to the spread of AIDS in the gay community, and had a number of opportunities to help friends produce videos and public events to promote this new form of expression. Increasingly, it seemed the community I had joined was finding ways to meet the basic needs of its members among ourselves.

Mica Kindman, Radical Faerie, San Francisco, circa 1987.
Courtesy Ken Wachsberger archives.

CHAPTER 20

Looking Back, Looking Forward

In some ways, Fort Hill and all the traumas of the past slip farther and farther into a dim unreality of memory; in other ways it is all as real and present as ever. I seem always to be available and alert to reminders of it wherever they may show up—either from my own imagination and memories, or from signals I receive from the world around me. Occasionally I see someone in a store or at a street fair selling wire sculpture stars that resemble those of John Kostick that we used to sell in New York. I always try to find out how it happens that the person selling them knows the designs, but usually it's hard to trace. Recently I met someone in Berkeley who developed some of the same designs himself many years ago by experimenting with mathematical models, the same way John did it. He told me that last year a group of people confronted him on the street in Berkeley, evidently angry and challenging his right to use the designs, but not identifying themselves. Could it have been the Fort Hill crew?

In February 1988, our local listener-supported radio station, KPFA, was planning a day of commemoration of the life and work of Kay Boyle, longtime peace activist and Bay Area resident, who happens, of course, to be the mother of Faith Gude, loyal member of the Fort Hill community, and her brother Ian Franckenstein, one of my friends from back there. The advance notices said that Ian himself would be participating in the programming. I wrote a letter of introduction to Kay and a cover letter to Ian and dropped them by the station, hoping he would receive them before the programming aired and get in touch with me. When this did not happen, I ran over to the station and intercepted him as he was leaving after doing his bit on the air, reintroduced myself (he had not seen my letters), and we began a renewal of our friendship. I have been much refreshed to have a new friendship with someone from that era. Ian lives in Marin County and is primary caretaker for his mother, who is now retired in a nursing home there. He tells me stories of his own recovery from the trauma, of various frustrating attempts to become reacquainted with Faith, of people from the community who he's seen over the years.

In the time since I became reacquainted with Ian, I have found myself in a new drama in my life. I learned in 1988 that I have been infected with the human immunodeficiency virus at least since 1983, based on blood work done then. I believe I was probably infected closer to 1980, when I was under the stress of my construction business bankruptcy and suffered a rash of other sexually transmitted diseases. I was hardly surprised to learn I was HIV-positive; knowing my history, I would have been surprised not to have somehow become caught up in the epidemic. In the last couple of years, I have developed symptoms, and recently "progressed" to a diagnosis of AIDS, with Kaposi's sarcoma lesions here and there on my body, but few other major problems.

I continue to feel like a survivor and an optimist, and identify strongly with the viewpoint that AIDS need not be universally fatal. Having made it through so many setbacks and disappointments, I feel committed to making it through the epidemic as well. I'm involved in a variety of experimental treatment programs and nutritional and holistic efforts, as well as standard medical care, to keep the quality of my life intact, so far successfully. I have cut my contracting work back to half time, and have returned to school half time at a small progressive college, studying to become a health consultant. It seems that at last I'm going to complete a college degree, and maybe even make a career switch.

In the course of all this, I have found an old friend working in the AIDS field close by. My old collaborator on *The Paper*, Larry Tate, is now the manager of the information hotline at Project Inform, one of the most innovative and aggressive community organizations pushing for reform of the drug development process for AIDS and other diseases. After years of being aware of each other in the Bay Area and finding ourselves unable to renew our friendship, Larry and I at last have something in common in our current lives. I also recently got to reintroduce myself to Daria Halprin (now Daria Khalighi) when I took an intensive ritual and dance workshop from her mother and collaborator, choreographer Anna Halprin. "Circle the Earth" is an annual event dedicated to healing AIDS and other life-threatening illnesses. The key line of the performance that culminates the workshop is "My name is (Mica) and I want to live. And I want you to live."

I don't yet feel ready to declare the "eventual outcome" of my life and circumstances, but there is no doubt that all this experience has added up to something. Getting to write about all of it has been a tremendously healing, and confrontational, experience for me. After all, as Mel Lyman used to say, "Recapitulation is the only real learning."

Michael "Mica" Kindman's Last Years

ROSEMARY FOR REMEMBRANCE / STEVEN S. MUCHNICK

A Note about the Radical Fairies, Their Founders, and the Name

The Radical Fairies, or Radical Faeries, or either of them without capital letters (all abbreviated, along with their singular forms, as R.F. in this note) were founded in 1979 by Harry Hay and his longtime companion John Burnside, Don Kilhefner, and Mitch Walker. Harry had been a Communist in the 1930s as documented in Timmons's biography[1] and was also the founder of the Mattachine Society, the first gay men's organization in the United States, in the early 1950s. John and Harry met in 1963 and quickly became inseparable companions, moving to New Mexico a few years later and living in the Sangre de Cristo Mountains among the Tewa Pueblo people. They formed the Circle of Loving Companions that is a model for much of what has happened among the R.F. since. Don Kilhefner has long been involved with the Los Angeles Gay and Lesbian Community Services Center, and Mitch Walker is the author of a relatively early book about gay sexuality and consciousness.[2]

At its founding, the four men called the first national R.F. event, which they wrote was to be called "among other names, 'A SPIRITUAL CONFERENCE FOR RADICAL FAIRIES'"—and for its first year, the group was known by that name. However, by the second national event in 1980, "Conference" was changed to "Gathering," which has stuck, and we were calling ourselves either "Radical Fairies" or "Radical Faeries" or either of those without the capitals and often without the "Radical," depending on who was doing the naming. My experience is that most of us use the "Faerie" form, with or without the "Radical" qualifier, but Mica almost always wrote "radical fairy" and "radical fairies," as he has in his memoir.

Muchnick is well known as a computer science professor, researcher, and author, a Radical Faerie since the group's founding in 1979, and an HIV/AIDS activist. He is the author of *A Manual for Queens Registrar of the Breitenbush Gatherings of the Radical Faerie,* and serves as a member of the National Institutes of Health–sponsored HIV Vaccine Trials Network's Global Community Advisory Board, including its Scientific Working Group, and as chair of its Scientific Literacy Subgroup. He lives in San Francisco with Eric, his lover of twenty-four years and legal spouse since summer 2008.

The R.F. are and always have been an anarchic group. This is not to suggest that we all are (or were) draft-card burners or destroyers, and in fact, our anarchy's political manifestation is much more likely to be lighthearted than serious. We believe, unlike Chairman Mao, that not "all power comes from the barrel of a gun." Rather, we are more likely to do things that seem silly in response to patriarchy but turn out to be powerful because they gently mock the oppressors in something like the 1960s tradition of sticking daisies into the barrels of rifles.

The heart of our anarchy is that we have never had any central authority, and that any dogma we might have varies, often significantly, from one geographical area or R.F. to another. It's often said that if you put three R.F. in a room and ask us to come up with a definition of what an R.F. is, you'll get at least five different answers. Several groups of R.F. have formed formal tax-exempt organizations that exist to serve as stewards for land that serves as R.F. sanctuaries in the country, as educational and spiritual organizations, and/or as organizations that sponsor R.F. gatherings, of which there are now dozens each year across the United States and abroad.

Finally, then, who is an R.F.? *My* answer is simple, though rather nuanced, and in its vagueness, rather unsatisfying for some of us. *Most* of us would say that any gay or bisexual man who says he is an R.F. is one by virtue of saying so. Why might one say so? Usually, that results from either having taken part in a gathering or having become friends with and identifying with R.F.; for most of us an essential component of that identification is a profound feeling of coming home to a psychological place we've only dreamed of before. Some of us would also include women, usually lesbians, who identify with our nature, though I personally don't. Even in that respect, we are anarchic.

Michael/Mica Kindman's Last Years

My recollection of Michael/Mica Kindman's last years is mostly grounded in three oral-history interviews I did with him in the last few weeks of his life; the interviews were done on October 3, 12, and 30, 1991, and he died a mere three weeks after the last one on November 22. Still, he was quite clear-headed and enthusiastic about the project and put a lot of energy into making it happen. And here I must admit—to my great dismay—that the second of the three tapes we made turned out to be mostly blank when I came to transcribe it for the first time fifteen years later. There are about twelve minutes recorded on it of what I know to have been over an hour's interview total; thus there's a large space that I've tried to fill in below from other sources as best I could. The one thing some R.F. might disagree with is some of the dates, which Michael admitted on our first tape he was somewhat vague about and jokingly described as his version of his then-lover's dyslexia.

From the outset, it must be said that Michael's last years cannot be described at all effectively without describing how his personal story wound in and out with the R.F., to which he devoted a tremendous fraction of his time and energy from his introduction in about 1980 until his death. From here on I will use the name Mica for him, even though he didn't discover it for himself for several years nor begin to share it with others for two years beyond then. On the first tape, Mica describes himself as "notorious for being serious."

Mica was one of the members of the second wave of R.F. I met in San Francisco, though I don't recall exactly what year it was (the first were those I had met at the national gatherings in 1979–1981 and some of their friends in the City). He was easily among the most clear-headed, focused, moral, wise, and able thinkers and also one of the most decisive, yet inclusive planners I have ever known. Though I occasionally disagreed with him, he was always a pleasure to be with, even when I thought we could cut through some of the knots in our planning process, and he took the contrary position that we had to go step by step—and I will readily admit he was almost always right. There were many times when I, actually or figuratively, sat at his feet during meetings and absorbed pearls of wisdom from him, often about process, inclusion, and consensus.

Mica (still named Michael) came out as a gay man in 1978 while living in Palo Alto, California. He was still a rather countercultural figure at that point. He abhorred the disco scene that a lot of gay men were heavily involved in at that time and had a revelation that there were other possibilities when he visited a gay bar in San Francisco named the Buena Vista, where he encountered, late one evening, a country and western group doing the last two songs of their set. He also experienced "A Different Kind of Night at the Baths" run by Murray Edelman in 1978–1979 and became aware of Arthur Evans's moonlit fairy dancing circle around the statue of Diana in Sutro Park, both in San Francisco.

He and his closest friend William[3] saw advertising in San Francisco about the 1979 Spiritual Conference for R.F., and about the 1980 Spiritual Gathering of R.F. as well, but didn't go to either. He met a man named Bobby, worked his construction job, and settled down in Los Altos, south of San Francisco near San Jose.

He began making friends among the R.F. in the City, and he and Bobby went to the New Mexico national gathering in summer 1981. There he met John Burnside, experienced the performance troupe known as the Revolting Haggettes, danced in the rain, did contact improvisation, experienced a large circle of R.F. with spontaneously fluid leadership, made many friends, and, perhaps most important, at the end of the gathering took part in a naming circle in which he was so taken by the mica sparkling on the ground that he took the name Mica for himself, though he kept it to himself for another two years as mentioned above. Like so many of us experiencing a gathering for the first time, he felt that he had come home to a place he'd never been before—a profound experience for many of us who have devoted much energy to, and gotten much from, the R.F.

Not long after he returned to the Bay Area, Mica met and befriended a man named David, who did similar work and with whom he found much of the profundity that was so lacking in many of those whom he and others of us have called the "airy fairies."

In 1982, Mica went to the Eagle Creek Gathering east of San Diego, which lasted seven or eight days; he found the length of that gathering to be important because it allowed more time for people to "drop their ugly green feathers" (a phrase used by Harry Hay) and delve more deeply into the experience of being in R.F. space—a concept that might be explained as a psychologically transformed mental place in which it's much easier to be genuinely who you are and to form relationships in what Harry called "subject-SUBJECT consciousness." It was a gathering spread over ten acres with about two hundred participants and a wonderful sense of community for Mica and many of the others who took part. It ended with a powerful Kali fire ritual at the full moon that was an opportunity for the R.F. there to renounce aspects of themselves that they no longer needed or wanted. Bobby went with Mica to that gathering but quickly fell in love with a man named Brian. The two Bs got "married" there and went their way, though they stayed friends with Mica. The time with Bobby was Mica's first significant gay relationship, and its ending, though painful, freed him to form others.

In 1983, Mica went to the Madre Grande Gathering even further east of San Diego than Eagle Creek in the dry mountains edging the desert. He experienced it as wonderful but not long enough: it took a long time for him to really get into being there, and then it was over almost immediately.

Not long thereafter, a group of San Francisco R.F. started planning Blossom of Bone I, the first of two gatherings in Napa County, California. About thirty-five R.F. were involved in planning it; by consensus they decided to let attendees create pretty much what they wanted. Mica was very involved in the physical planning; his most important physical contribution was organizing and taking a major part in building the kitchen. For the first time, this gathering had hot showers in the woods and a covered outdoor gathering space with a large blue tarp strung over it. The gathering lasted between eight and ten days and attracted about three hundred participants. In several ways, it was a big turning point for both him and me, from its very successful collective planning, to its general overall success, to the suggestion put forth by two R.F. named Will and Brad (who were good friends of Harry Hay) that an organization called the Gay Vision Circle—founded in 1980 by a group of San Francisco and Los Angeles R.F. including Harry and John—put its energies into buying land that could serve as an R.F. sanctuary and gathering space.

In 1984, Mica and William formed a collective household named Touchstone at 981 Haight Street in San Francisco. Various R.F. came and went through it and other R.F. households as the years went on, and R.F. households now exist up and down the West Coast of the United States, in other parts of the country, and abroad, just as there are annual or more frequent recurring gatherings in various places in the United States, Canada, Europe, Australia, and Thailand, at the least.

To facilitate the land search and eventual purchase, the Gay Vision Circle decided it was essential to incorporate as a 501(c)(3) tax-exempt church corporation in order to solicit contributions. A meeting was held at Touchstone in early 1985 to conjure a name under which closeted R.F. would be comfortable receiving mail, and that might be more palatable to the IRS. Various names were suggested that seemed to be pointing in a general direction, including Temenos (according to Harry, the place where the queers were banished to outside the city walls in ancient Greece), Not-Men-Us, Anonymous, and numinous ("spirit-infused" from Greek), but there was no immediate consensus. A silent meditation was agreed on that resulted in narrowing down the names to three or four, all of them quite similar. An ensuing group trance resulted in participants eventually shouting out names and narrowing them down further until Nomenus emerged as the nearly unanimous choice. It had the advantages of being original and of relating closely to virtually all the names that had been suggested previously. In the meantime, Will and Brad were "climbing the walls" (to quote Mica) to come up with a name that could be used in the application to the IRS. The first application was filed in February 1986, and a newsletter—named *Nomenews* by Mica, the self-described "underground-press headline writer"—about the land-search project was mailed out to a list of nine hundred to one thousand R.F. in March 1986. A longtime activist named Cass designed a logo of the organization's name over trees for the masthead of that first issue of *Nomenews*, which has been used ever since. That first issue was headed "Dreaming the Dirt" (a takeoff on Starhawk's book *Dreaming the Dark*).[4]

While Nomenus had the typical officers of a small organization (president, secretary, and treasurer), it was and is governed by a consensus process that is maintained by conference calls the last Sunday evening of each month involving R.F. in San Francisco, Seattle, occasionally Portland, and, once land was found and a community begun there, Wolf Creek, Oregon. It also has semiannual Great Circles that bring together large groups of concerned R.F. in what the business world might liken to board meetings, though decisions are made by consensus.

As the amount of money needed to purchase an appropriate parcel of land began to be talked about, Brad got cold feet about the $20,000 figure being bandied about. Mica, from his construction experience, knew it would more likely take $50,000 to $100,000 to realize the group's aspirations, depending on the location, conditions of purchase, and existing facilities.

In spring 1986, the second issue of *Nomenews* was produced by Brad, and though it was sent out by an R.F. named Tom to a database of over a thousand people, only a few copies of it are known to remain. Brad's focus was achieving reassurance and stability in the land search that was beginning, while others, including Mica, envisioned the land as a retreat center and gathering space for as many people as possible, and for gatherings lasting a week or longer. Several groups started searching for land in various areas of California, and at least four sites were identified.

Nomenews no. 3, published in winter 1986/87, described the four principal sites. The newsletter was by far the longest so far, because of the space needed to describe the sites. It was published on green paper and titled "How the Faeries Came Out of the Woods." It also included a lot of pictures from gatherings, and stories of how various R.F. got involved with the group. A small gathering of about twenty participants had taken place in the summer of 1986 at one of the sites, near Clear Lake about 125 miles north of San Francisco, which was virtually eliminated from the land search as a result.

Harry and John were invited to come from Los Angeles to San Francisco for a weekend meeting. Amid dissension about all the sites and their problems (varying from cost to being too close to neighbors), Harry wrote a letter titled "You Chose So Well, My Dear" to George, a man who had purchased a site outside Wolf Creek in southern Oregon, with which Harry had close associations dating back to a fruitful, mostly political meeting there organized by the leftist gay-rights organizer Carl Wittman[5] in 1976. This meeting and Harry's letter swayed the land search toward the Wolf Creek land, despite its being relatively far away—in southern Oregon rather than California—and resulted in Will and Brad abruptly resigning as officers of Nomenus. At that point, Mica became president, a position he held for the next two years.

February 1986 also included a gathering at Breitenbush Hot Springs, Oregon, sponsored by the Northwest R.F. The site is ideal for gatherings: it is run by an intentional community, with a river running by for fresh water and electricity generation, geothermal hot springs that provide heat, an old lodge with several large and small rooms for activities, cabins for accommodations, and a kitchen run by the resident community that produces excellent hot vegetarian meals, requiring us to do little else but pay for and hold our gatherings! That 1986 gathering was easily one of the best in my years as an R.F. I was so taken by its spirit that during the next year, I beaded over two hundred necklaces and took them to the next winter's gathering there, and at Saturday morning's Heart Circle[6] I gave one to each R.F. present.[7] On the other hand, the Portland and Seattle R.F. who had dominated the gatherings that had been running there since 1982 found many of us San Francisco R.F. to be too outrageous, and this almost had serious internal political repercussions for the West Coast R.F. community as a whole.

By spring 1986, a man named Michael who was an R.F. realtor from Marin County was recruited to organize the land purchase. That summer, the first Wolf Creek gathering, titled the "West Coast Symposium," brought together R.F. from Seattle, Portland, rural areas, and San Francisco, including Mica and my lover John and me. The character of that gathering was defined largely by the ongoing drought that left us with nowhere near enough water. A kitchen had to be built quickly in a tumbledown barn on the land, but much of the food rotted anyway because the people preparing meals did not take basic sanitary precautions. Mica played his self-described role as the group's moral teacher to the hilt. He experienced some R.F. as being very turned off by that, while others of us cheered him on.

Another occurrence of 1986 that was profoundly important to a lot of us was the temporary loss of an important talisman (see endnote 6), the Kernunnos Shawl that had been given to the R.F. community at the 1980 national gathering by an R.F. from New Orleans named Dennis Melba'Son. The Shawl was crocheted by Dennis with an image of the Celtic horned god Kernunnos, an erect phallus below him, and vines with leaves spreading across it. It quickly became the most important material object the R.F. community possessed, and traveled from gathering to gathering, being worn in Heart Circles thousands of times.[8] An R.F. named Crit who was going east from California gave the Shawl to his boyfriend Kim, who addressed the package for it with the wrong name and address both ways, going and returning. It ended up in a dead letter office in San Francisco, and Mica was finally able to trace it there and retrieve it seven months later, a mere two weeks before the package would have been discarded by the Postal Service. Mica wrote about that experience for *RFD*, his only article in what has become an important journal devoted largely to the R.F. that started out and still bills itself as "A Country Journal for Gay Men Everywhere."[9] By August 1986, the scales had tipped toward purchasing the land at Wolf Creek, despite its known problems. The deal came with two important conditions: that a man named Assunta[10] who had lived on the land for some years be allowed to stay there, subject to reasonable conditions; and that George, who owned the land but was failing from HIV-related complications, receive an ongoing income while his life continued. At first George said he would sell for $20,000, but others who had been involved in the purchase of the land believed George had no exclusive right to sell it. An R.F. named Jamal conducted the negotiations along with Mica, Ralph, and Tom with George's executor Jonathan; as they did, the price kept rising. By late 1986, Assunta and an R.F. named Len came from Wolf Creek to San Francisco and met with about fifty of us at Touchstone. For some reason, Assunta did not want his remaining on the land to be called renting. However, an agreement was reached to allow Mica and Ralph to spend up to $50,000 to purchase the land. After the meeting, Mica asked Assunta to stay for a few days to work out the terms of his remaining on the land, but he refused—this was the harbinger of some serious ongoing problems with Assunta. In any case, agreement was reached to pay George $5,000 per quarter, and an energetic fundraising campaign was begun to raise the needed $50,000 to finalize the purchase. Within a few months, there was $32,000 in the land-purchase fund, and $18,000 of it was paid out to consummate the purchase.

Mica was acting treasurer of Nomenus at this point, in addition to being president, publishing *Nomenews*, and being active in organizing a more R.F.-friendly space within the then-semiannual California Men's Gatherings. In December 1986 he put out an eight-page *Nomenews* in the course of one weekend, headed "This is it! This is really it! . . . ," about the land purchase. The remaining $18,000 needed to raise the total for the land purchase was in hand by the end of 1987.

The summer of 1987 saw a Homecoming Gathering at Wolf Creek that celebrated the land purchase and mock-christened the space as "Poodlebrook Academy" (the name Poodlebrook was a pun on Wolf Creek.)

In the following years, Mica devoted more and more of his energy to alternative AIDS treatments, and absorbed AIDS activism into his circle of activities with the same high level of commitment he had shown previously in virtually everything else he did. He enrolled in New College of California in San Francisco in 1990 and took part in the Anna Halprin–led ritual dance event *Circle the Earth* in April 1991.

I was deeply involved in planning the memorial for Mica that was held in December 1991 in San Francisco, and as long as I have my wits about me, I shall deeply miss him.

One other person who must be mentioned here is Oskrr Earthsong-Feino, who was the first person to live at Wolf Creek by consensus of the R.F. (His name consists of a misspelling by a little girl, his connection to the earth as holy, and the Esperanto for a fairy being.) Oskrr was a dear friend of mine, as he was of many others, a "Quilter, Lover, Seamstress, Magician, Faerie Elder, Artist, Pagan Clergy She-man, Peace-maker, Trouble-maker, Annoyance, Inspiration, Wise One with the mellifluous accent, Wondrous Being, and Male-Lover of the Goddess," as his obituary in *Nomenews* no. 9 describes him,[11] who died barely five months after Mica. Oskrr was born in 1928 in Buenos Aires, became a Catholic monastic for five years, and then, after meeting the R.F. in the mid-1980s, applied to become a Nomenite monk at Wolf Creek once the space was ours. He helped me assemble the AIDS Memorial Quilt panel for my lover John in 1988. Eight years later, my new lover and now legal spouse Eric and I made panels for Oskrr, Mica, and six others—eight dear, dear friends of ours among the at least 174 I've personally lost to HIV complications. A beautiful four-foot-square star quilt panel Oskrr made hangs over my bed.

Parallels and Coincidences between Mica's Life and Mine

In closing, I would like to note that there are some strong parallels between Mica's life and mine, and even more that almost came to fruition.

Mica and I were both born in 1945 (he in April and I in December) into Jewish families, so he was eighteen when he graduated from high school, while I was seventeen. He grew up on Long Island, while I spent my childhood in Massachusetts and Connecticut and went to high school in Atlanta, Georgia. He got his college education (interrupted to devote himself to the underground press) at Michigan State University, while I did my undergraduate degree at the University of Michigan—even though, as a fellow National Merit Scholarship finalist, I also had been strongly recruited by Michigan State. Thus, we barely missed the chance to meet each other as undergraduates by about fifty miles. We both took part in demonstrations against Lyndon Johnson's escalation of the Vietnam War and were tear-gassed by the local police and sheriff's departments.

Mica and I both came out as gay men in 1978; he was living in the South Bay in Palo Alto, and I was a professor at the University of Kansas in Lawrence. After my lover John and I moved to the East Bay and I became a visiting associate professor at UC Berkeley in August 1979, Mica and I met through the R.F.

Like Mica, I served as an officer of Nomenus, namely, as secretary from August 1989 through September 1991.

I am known as Rosemary for Remembrance among the R.F. from the use of the herb rosemary in renaissance herbals.[12]

Mica went, and I continue to go, to gatherings largely for the community building and personal contacts that happen, but we both found that we also got caught up in the fun aspects, such as talent and drag shows, that many of them include.

Mica and I both became HIV-infected sometime in the 1980s. Mica believed he became infected in about 1985, but wasn't certain. In my case, I know it was no later than the end of 1982, because John and I had been quite promiscuous before that, though we talked about every encounter we had with another man and sometimes shared the men, too. I became convinced by December 1982 that whatever was causing the as-yet unnamed illness was sexually transmitted, and John and I closed our relationship completely after one final fling at the end of that year. John began showing symptoms in 1986 and died in August 1988, while I somehow maintained sufficient health to last until there were drugs that were effective against HIV, and I went through one after another of them until triple-combination therapy or HAART (Highly Active AntiRetroviral Therapy) became available in 1996. My health has been better and better since then, and, as I write this in mid-December 2009, I turned sixty-four recently on December 1, which also happens to be World AIDS Day.

NOTES

1. Stuart Timmons, *The Trouble with Harry Hay* (Boston: Alyson Publications, 1990). Obituaries for Harry and John, respectively, can be found on the Web at http://www.nytimes.com/2002/10/25/obituaries/25HAY.html?pagewanted=1 and at http://www.ebar.com/news/article.php?sec=news&article=3326 (both accessed December 19, 2009).

2. Mitch Walker, *Men Loving Men: A Gay Sex Guide and Consciousness Book* (San Francisco: Gay Sunshine Press, 1977).

3. Many of the people mentioned here are private individuals whose permission to use their names I don't have, so they are referred to by their first names only.

4. Starhawk, *Dreaming the Dark: Magic, Sex, and Politics* (Boston: Beacon Press, 1982). Starhawk is among the most respected women devoted to Earth-based spirituality, and the author of eleven books. Her online biography can be found at http://www.starhawk.org/starhawk/bio.html (accessed December 14, 2009).

5. Carl Wittman, *Refugees from Amerika: A Gay Manifesto* (San Francisco, 1970).

6. Heart Circles are, for many of us R.F., including Mica and me, the essence of a gathering. They typically involve almost all attendees sitting around in a rough circle so they can see each other. They often begin with one member leading a meditation to close the space to the outside and make it safe for whatever we say in it. We then pass a talisman from one speaker to the next. The person with the talisman goes to the center of the Circle and, if conditions are right, speaks from his heart, while the rest listen with theirs. He then passes the talisman to the next R.F. wishing to speak.

7. For several years after that, I was known as "The Bead Faerie."

8. I have been for about ten years the keeper of the Kernunnos Shawl between gatherings and have arranged carefully orchestrated tours for it many of those years. Unfortunately, by now it has been worn so many times that the areas where it goes over the shoulders have disintegrated. It most often ends up being displayed at gatherings now, rather than worn. It has attachments all along the bottom edges that come from gatherings and other life passages of which it's been a part through the years.

9. Anonymous, "Shawl Tells All," *RFD: A Country Journal for Gay Men Everywhere*, no. 46 (Running Water, Bakersville, NC, Spring 1986). A picture of the Shawl worn by its maker Dennis appears on the cover of *RFD* no. 22 (New Orleans, LA, Winter Solstice 1979).

10. Assunta's obituary appears at http://ebar.com/news/article.php?sec=news&article=1318 (accessed December 19, 2009).

11. *Nomenews* no. 9 also includes Mica's obituary and "Nomenus Talks to the I.R.S.," an article that provides an excerpt from the application to the IRS for tax exemption as a church.

12. The most familiar literary reference to "rosemary for remembrance" is in Ophelia's mad scene in Shakespeare's *Hamlet*, act 4, scene 5.

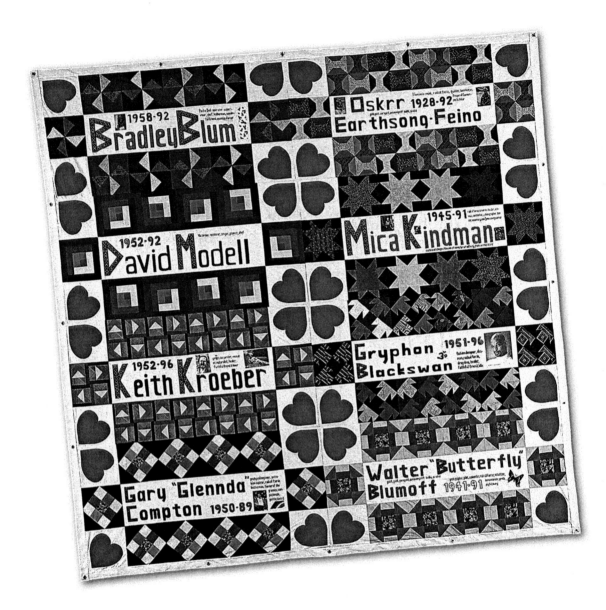

Panel 4217 of the AIDS Memorial Quilt, made by author Steven Muchnick and his spouse, Eric Milliren, to honor the memory of Mica Kindman. Muchnick and Milliren made all panels shown here. According to Muchnick, the panels were made in April and May 1996, "just in time for them to be included in that October's display of the AIDS Memorial Quilt on the National Mall in Washington, D.C. We were there wearing T-shirts with the design of the eight-panel block on them." The couple also made a panel, not shown here, for John Bandy in 1988. Photograph provided courtesy of NAMES Project Foundation.

Index